MUTTS Comics

by PATRICK MCDONNELL

WHO LET the CAT OUT?

**Andrews McMeel
Publishing**

Kansas City

Other Books by Patrick McDonnell

Mutts
Cats and Dogs: Mutts II
More Shtuff: Mutts III
Yesh!: Mutts IV
Our Mutts: Five
A Little Look-See: Mutts VI
What Now: Mutts VII
I Want to Be the Kitty: Mutts VIII
Dog-Eared: Mutts IX

Mutts Sundays
Sunday Mornings
Sunday Afternoons

The Mutts Little Big Book

Mutts is distributed internationally by King Features Syndicate, Inc. For information write King Features Syndicate, Inc., 888 Seventh Avenue, New York, New York 10019.

05 06 07 08 09 BBG 10 9 8 7 6 5 4 3 2 1

ISBN: 0-7407-5006-2

Library of Congress Control Number: 2004114456

Who Let the Cat Out? is printed on recycled paper.

Mutts can now be found on the Internet at
www.muttscomics.com.

ATTENTION: SCHOOLS AND BUSINESSES

Andrews McMeel books are available at quantity discounts with bulk purchase for educational, business, or sales promotional use. For information, please write to: Special Sales Department, Andrews McMeel Publishing, 4520 Main Street, Kansas City, Missouri 64111.

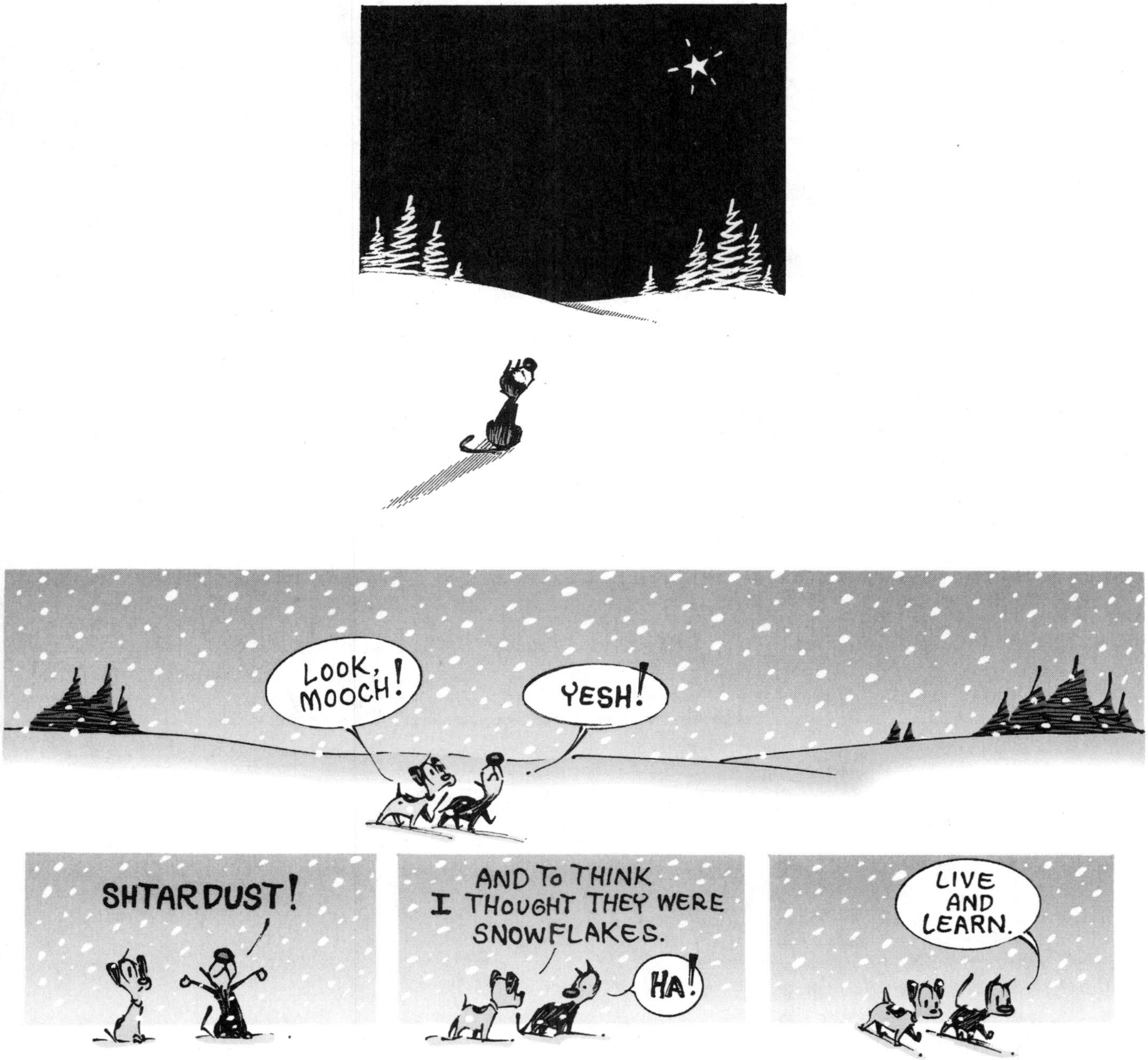
LOOK, MOOCH!
YESH!
SHTARDUST!
AND TO THINK I THOUGHT THEY WERE SNOWFLAKES.
HA!
LIVE AND LEARN.

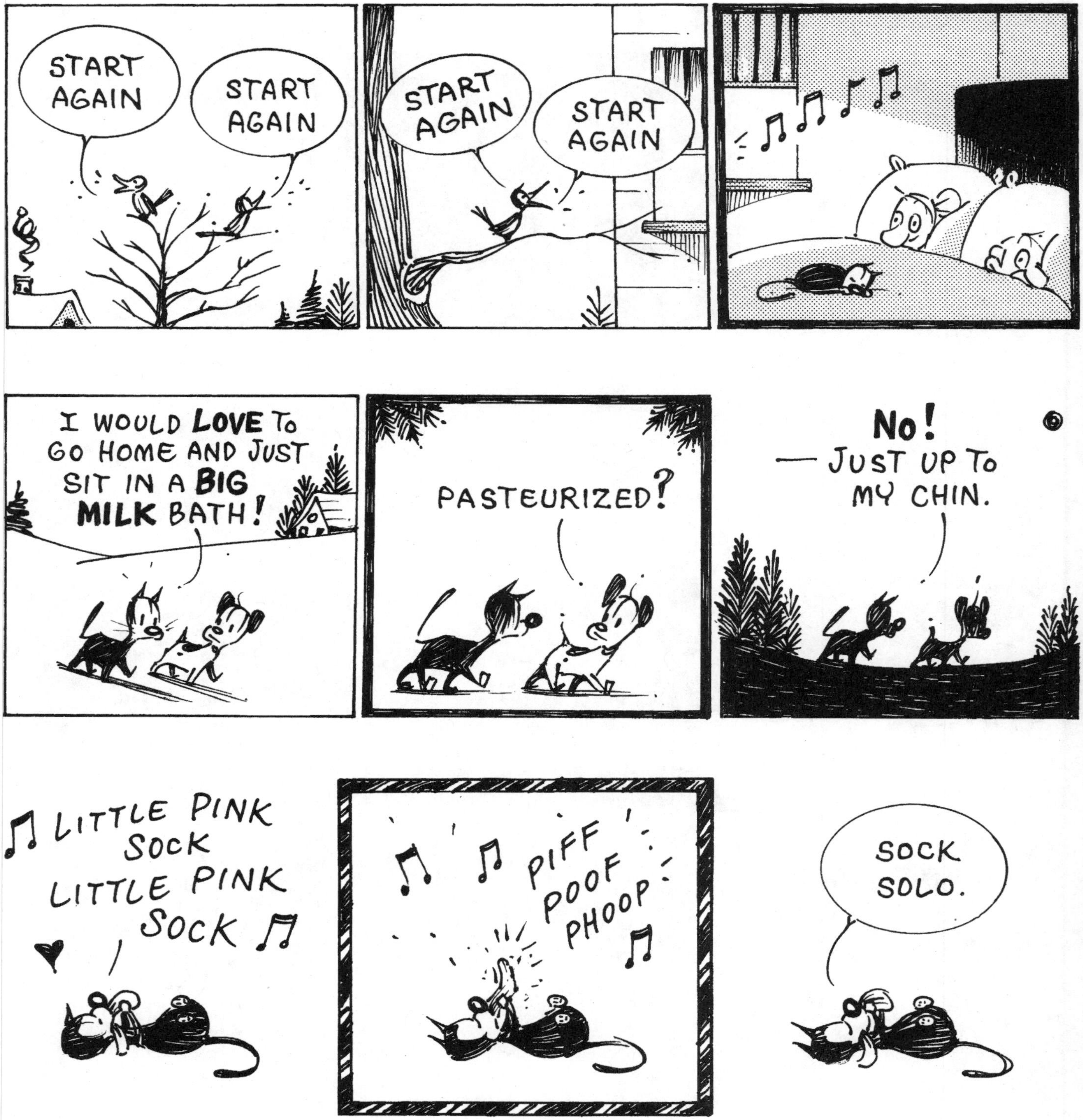
START AGAIN
START AGAIN
START AGAIN
START AGAIN
I WOULD LOVE TO GO HOME AND JUST SIT IN A BIG MILK BATH!
PASTEURIZED?
No! — JUST UP TO MY CHIN.
LITTLE PINK SOCK LITTLE PINK SOCK
PIFF POOF PHOOP
SOCK SOLO.

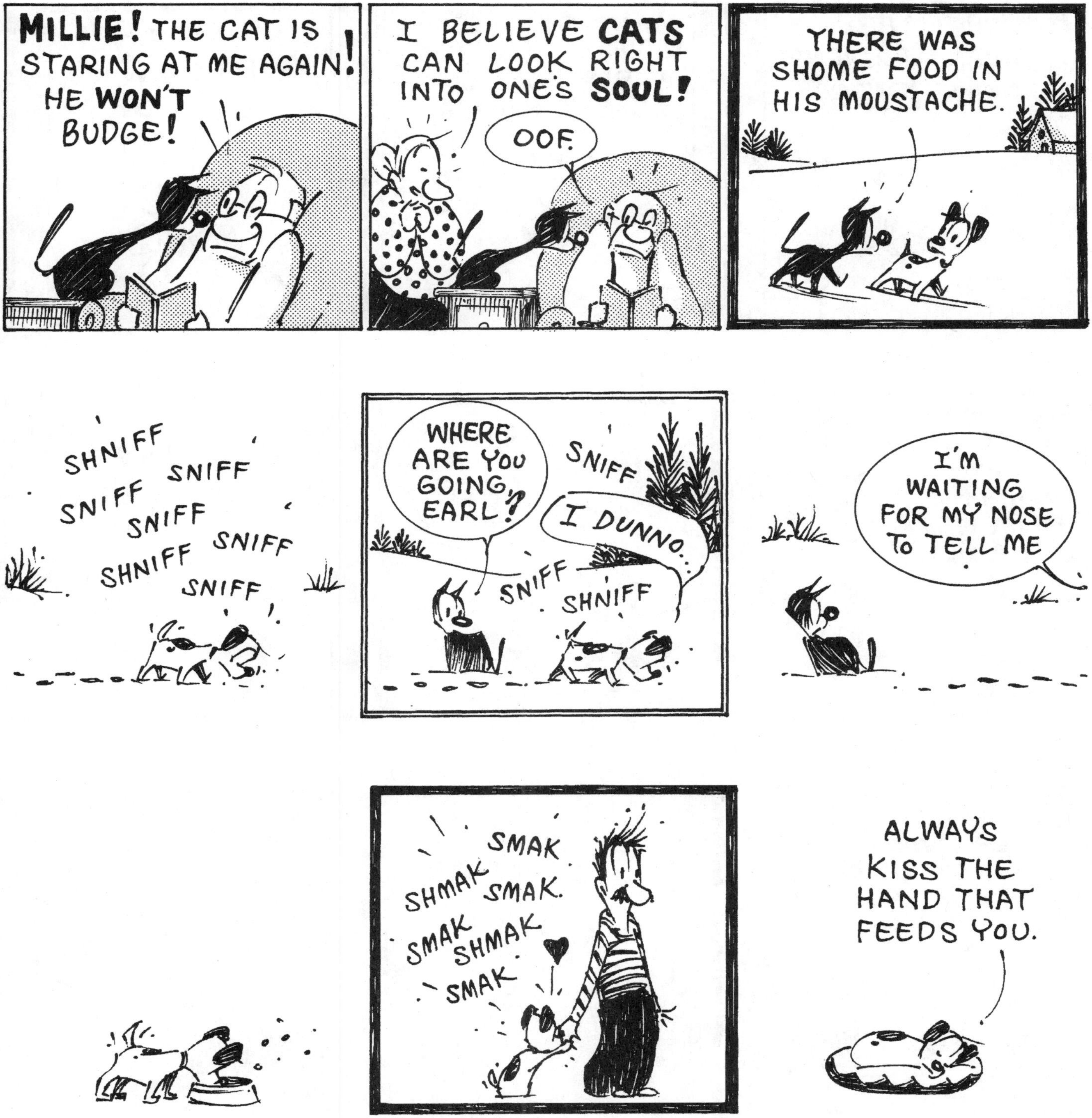
MILLIE! THE CAT IS STARING AT ME AGAIN! HE WON'T BUDGE!
I BELIEVE CATS CAN LOOK RIGHT INTO ONE'S SOUL!
OOF.
THERE WAS SHOME FOOD IN HIS MOUSTACHE.
SHNIFF SNIFF SNIFF SNIFF SHNIFF SNIFF SNIFF
WHERE ARE YOU GOING, EARL?
SNIFF
I DUNNO...
SNIFF SHNIFF
I'M WAITING FOR MY NOSE TO TELL ME
SMAK SHMAK SMAK. SMAK SHMAK SMAK
ALWAYS KISS THE HAND THAT FEEDS YOU.

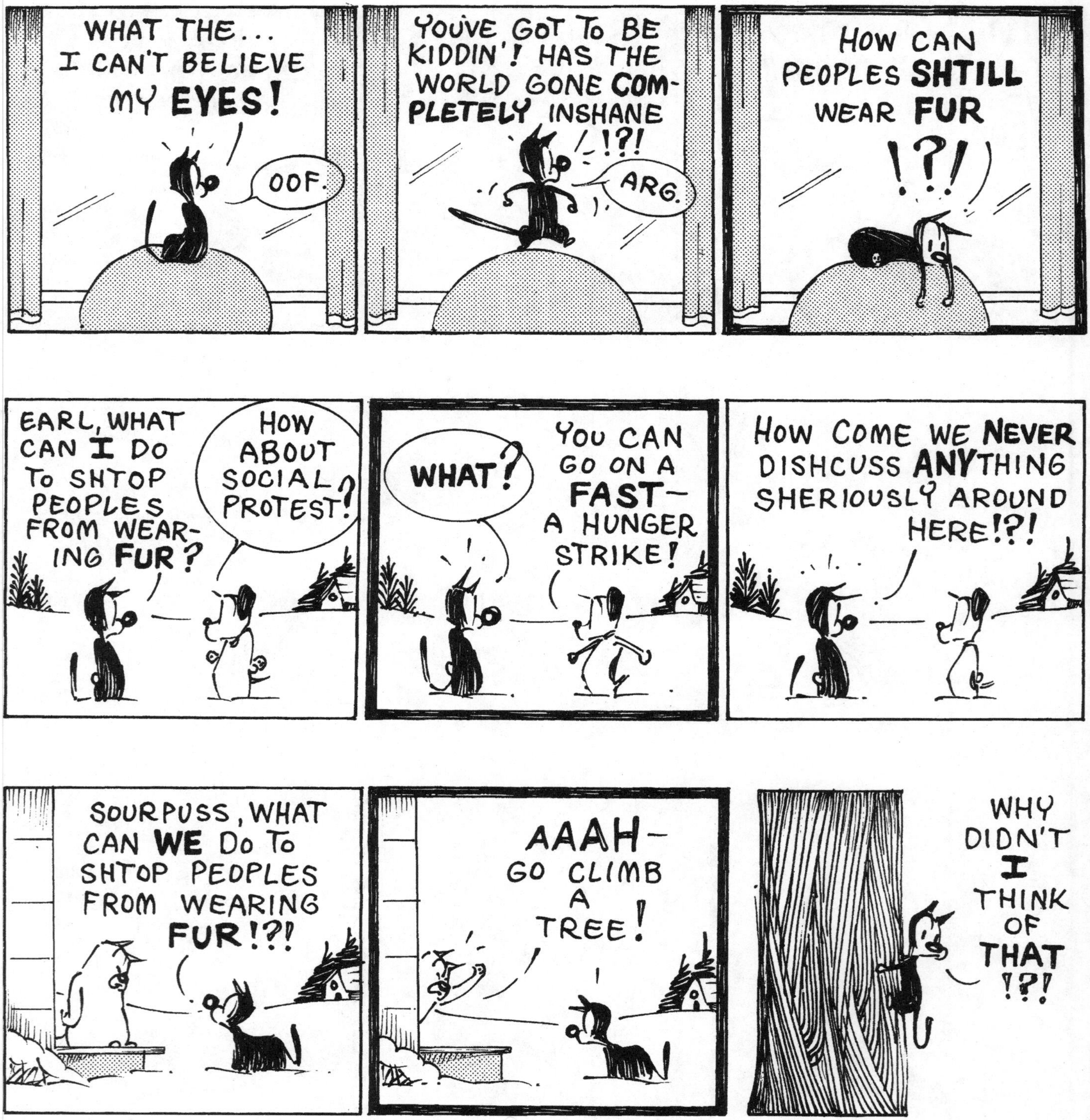
WHAT THE... I CAN'T BELIEVE MY EYES!
OOF.
YOU'VE GOT TO BE KIDDIN'! HAS THE WORLD GONE COMPLETELY INSHANE !?!
ARG.
HOW CAN PEOPLES SHTILL WEAR FUR !?!
EARL, WHAT CAN I DO TO SHTOP PEOPLES FROM WEARING FUR?
HOW ABOUT SOCIAL PROTEST?
WHAT?
YOU CAN GO ON A FAST— A HUNGER STRIKE!
HOW COME WE NEVER DISHCUSS ANYTHING SHERIOUSLY AROUND HERE!?!
SOURPUSS, WHAT CAN WE DO TO SHTOP PEOPLES FROM WEARING FUR!?!
AAAH— GO CLIMB A TREE!
WHY DIDN'T I THINK OF THAT !?!

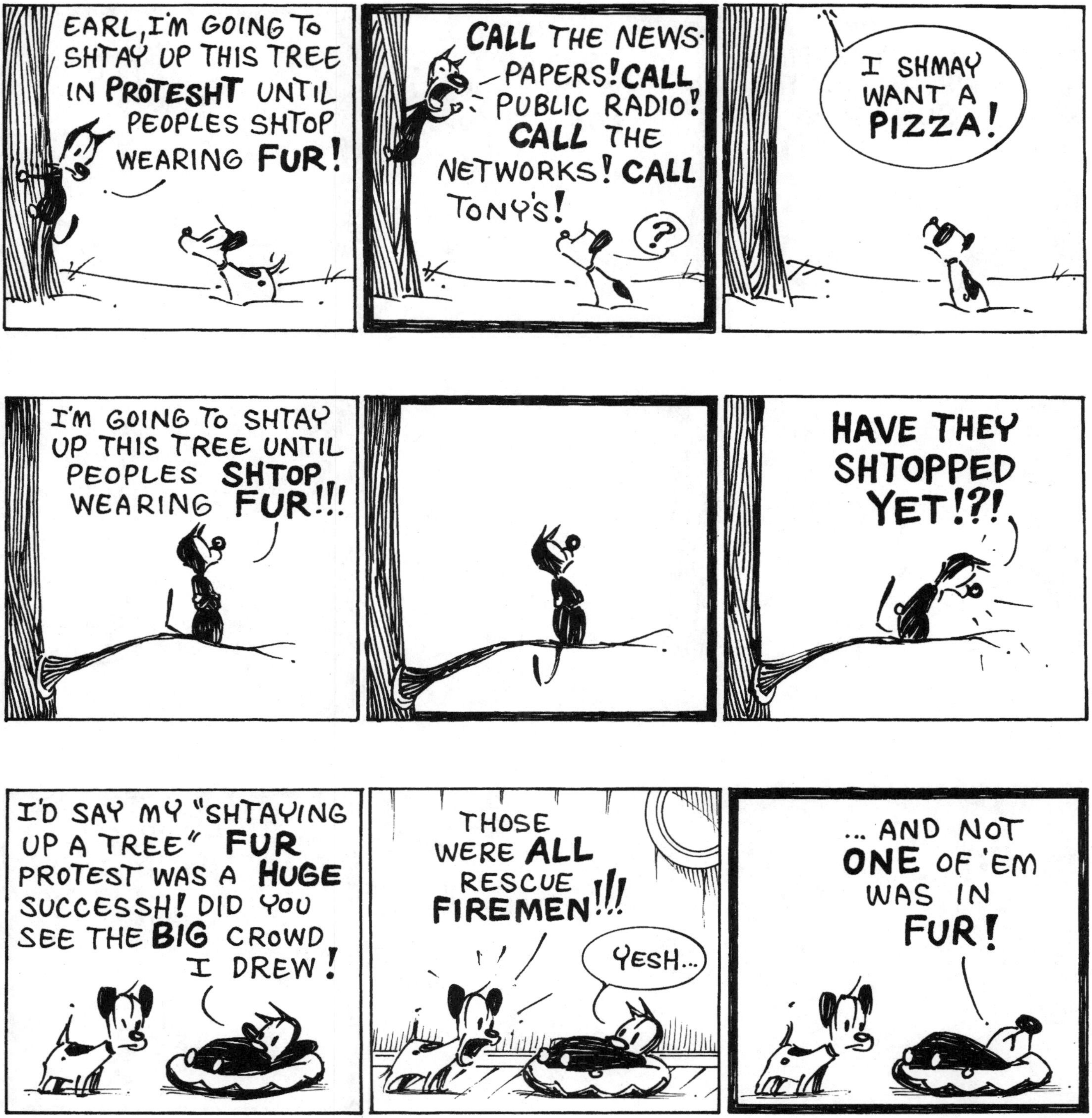
EARL, I'M GOING TO SHTAY UP THIS TREE IN PROTESHT UNTIL PEOPLES SHTOP WEARING FUR!
CALL THE NEWSPAPERS! CALL PUBLIC RADIO! CALL THE NETWORKS! CALL TONY'S!
?
I SHMAY WANT A PIZZA!
I'M GOING TO SHTAY UP THIS TREE UNTIL PEOPLES SHTOP WEARING FUR!!!
HAVE THEY SHTOPPED YET!?!
I'D SAY MY "SHTAYING UP A TREE" FUR PROTEST WAS A HUGE SUCCESSH! DID YOU SEE THE BIG CROWD I DREW!
THOSE WERE ALL RESCUE FIREMEN!!!
YESH...
... AND NOT ONE OF 'EM WAS IN FUR!

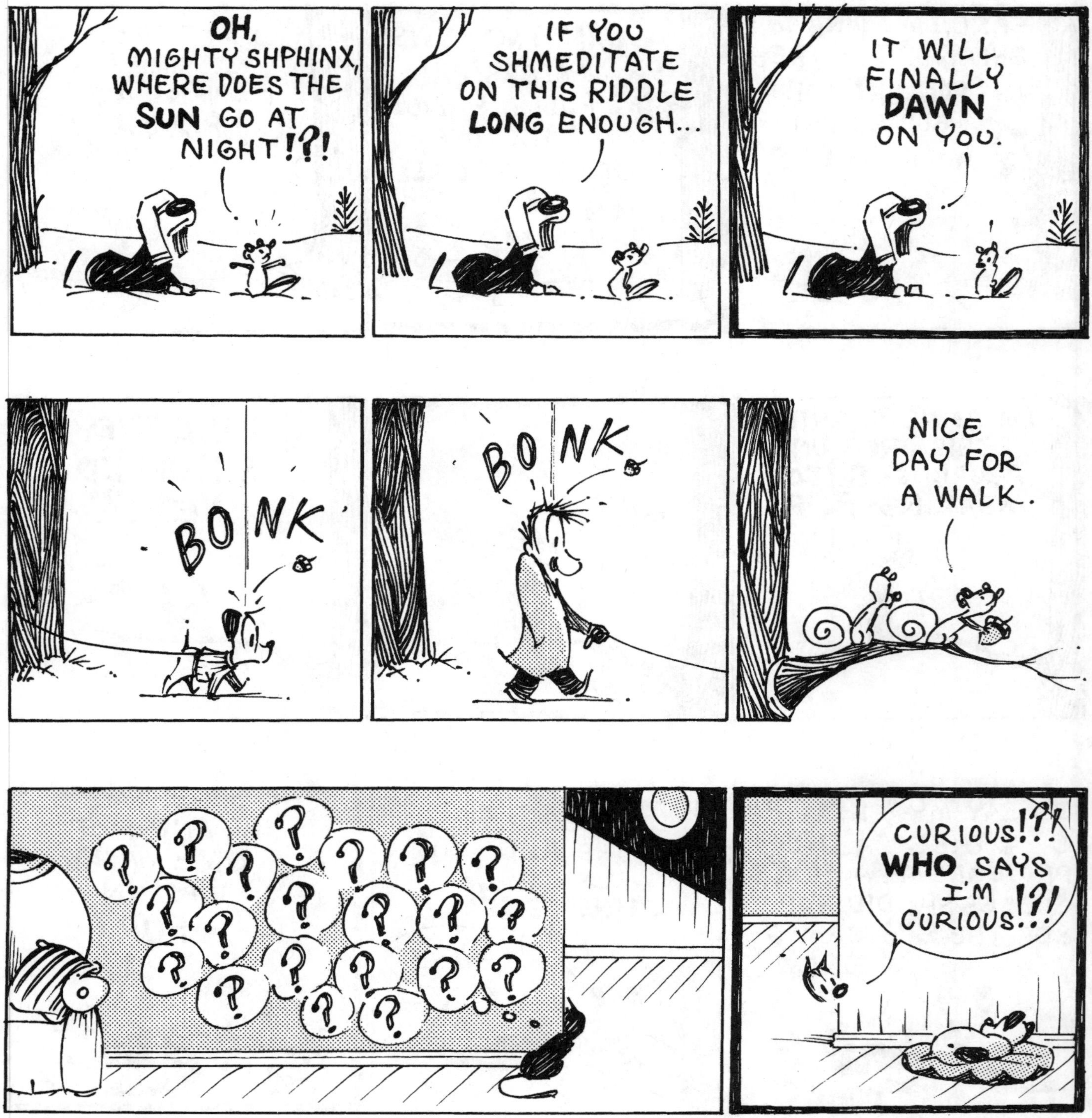
OH, MIGHTY SHPHINX, WHERE DOES THE SUN GO AT NIGHT!?!
IF YOU SHMEDITATE ON THIS RIDDLE LONG ENOUGH...
IT WILL FINALLY DAWN ON YOU.
BONK
BONK
NICE DAY FOR A WALK.
CURIOUS!?! WHO SAYS I'M CURIOUS!?!

MUTTS
McDONNELL

I WAS THINKING OF ALL MY PROBLEMS.
I WAS THINKING OF ALL THE PAIN OF THE PAST AND...
I WAS THINKING OF ALL THE UNCERTAINTY OF THE FUTURE.
AND I WAS THINKING POOR, POOR ME — MY SAD LIFE.
AND THEN I WAS THINKING HOW LITTLE TIME THERE IS...
AND I'M REALLY THINKING IT'S ALL JUST...HOPELESS. ...WHAT CAN I DO?
SHTOP THINKING.

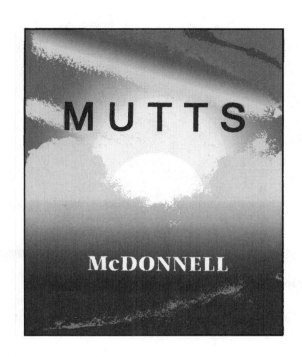

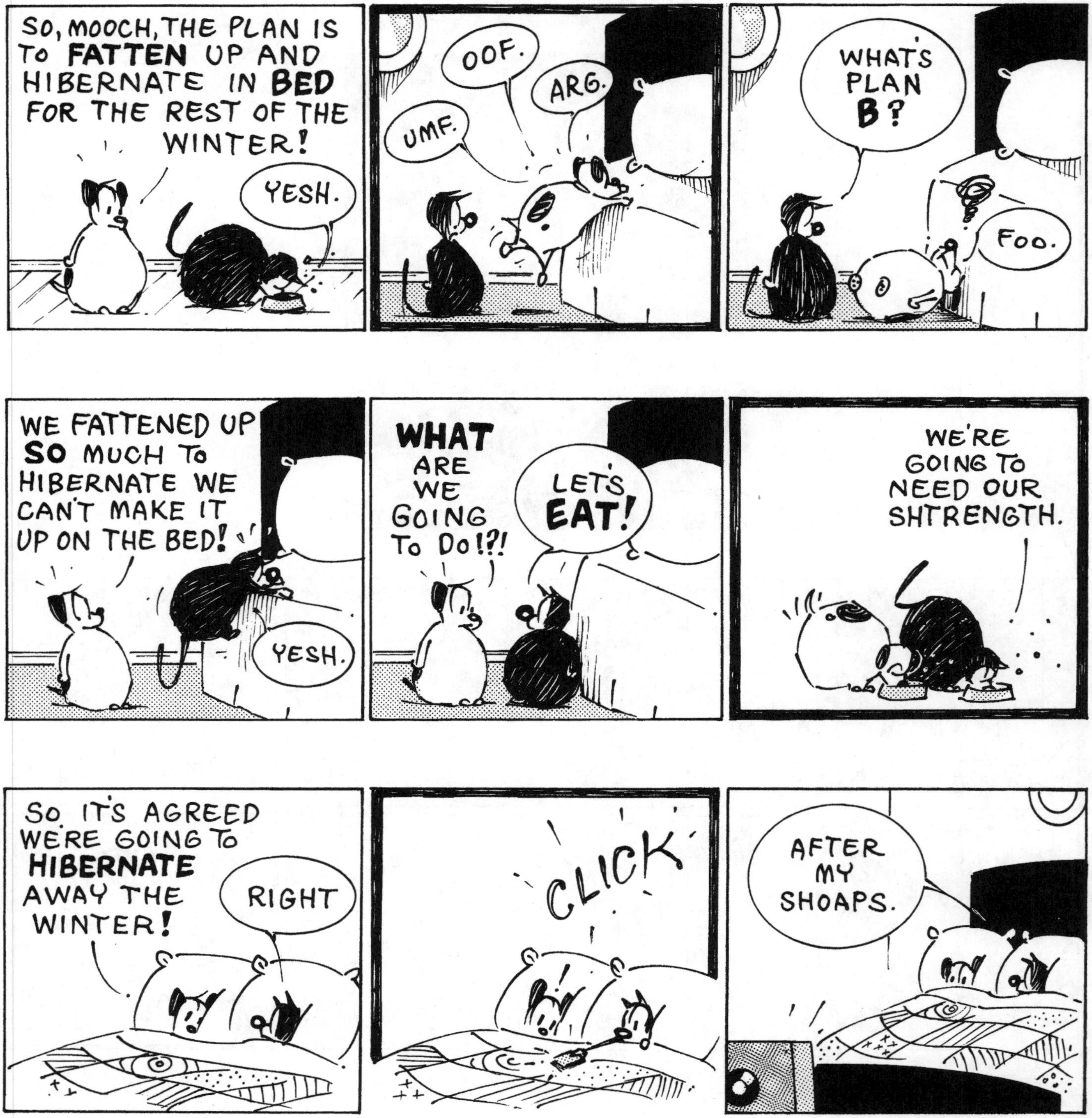

SO, MOOCH, THE PLAN IS TO FATTEN UP AND HIBERNATE IN BED FOR THE REST OF THE WINTER!
YESH.
UMF.
OOF.
ARG.
WHAT'S PLAN B?
FOO.
WE FATTENED UP SO MUCH TO HIBERNATE WE CAN'T MAKE IT UP ON THE BED!
YESH.
WHAT ARE WE GOING TO DO!?!
LET'S EAT!
WE'RE GOING TO NEED OUR SHTRENGTH.
SO IT'S AGREED WE'RE GOING TO HIBERNATE AWAY THE WINTER!
RIGHT
CLICK
AFTER MY SHOAPS.

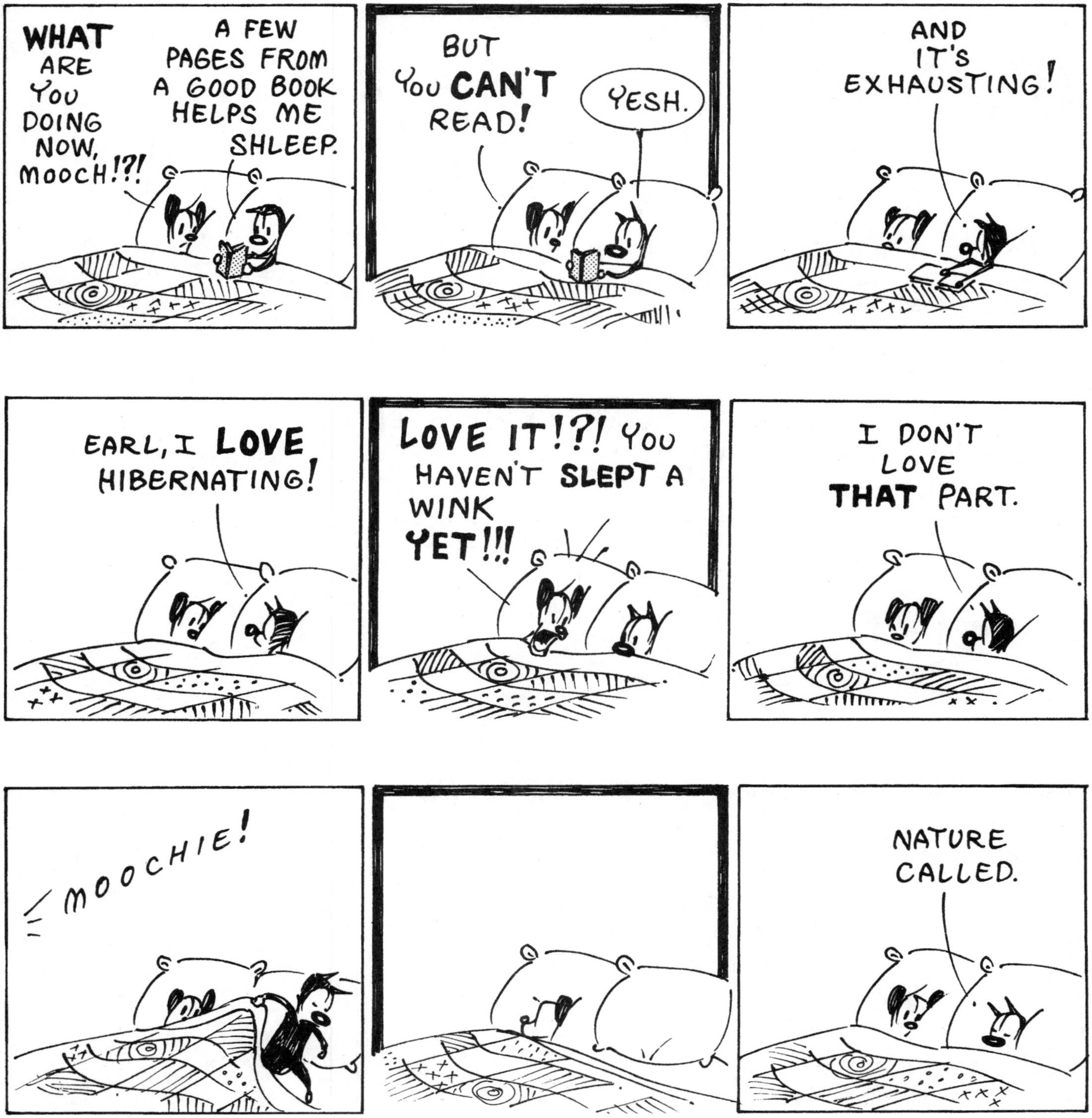
WHAT ARE YOU DOING NOW, MOOCH!?!
A FEW PAGES FROM A GOOD BOOK HELPS ME SHLEEP.
BUT YOU CAN'T READ!
YESH.
AND IT'S EXHAUSTING!
EARL, I LOVE HIBERNATING!
LOVE IT!?! YOU HAVEN'T SLEPT A WINK YET!!!
I DON'T LOVE THAT PART.
MOOCHIE!
NATURE CALLED.

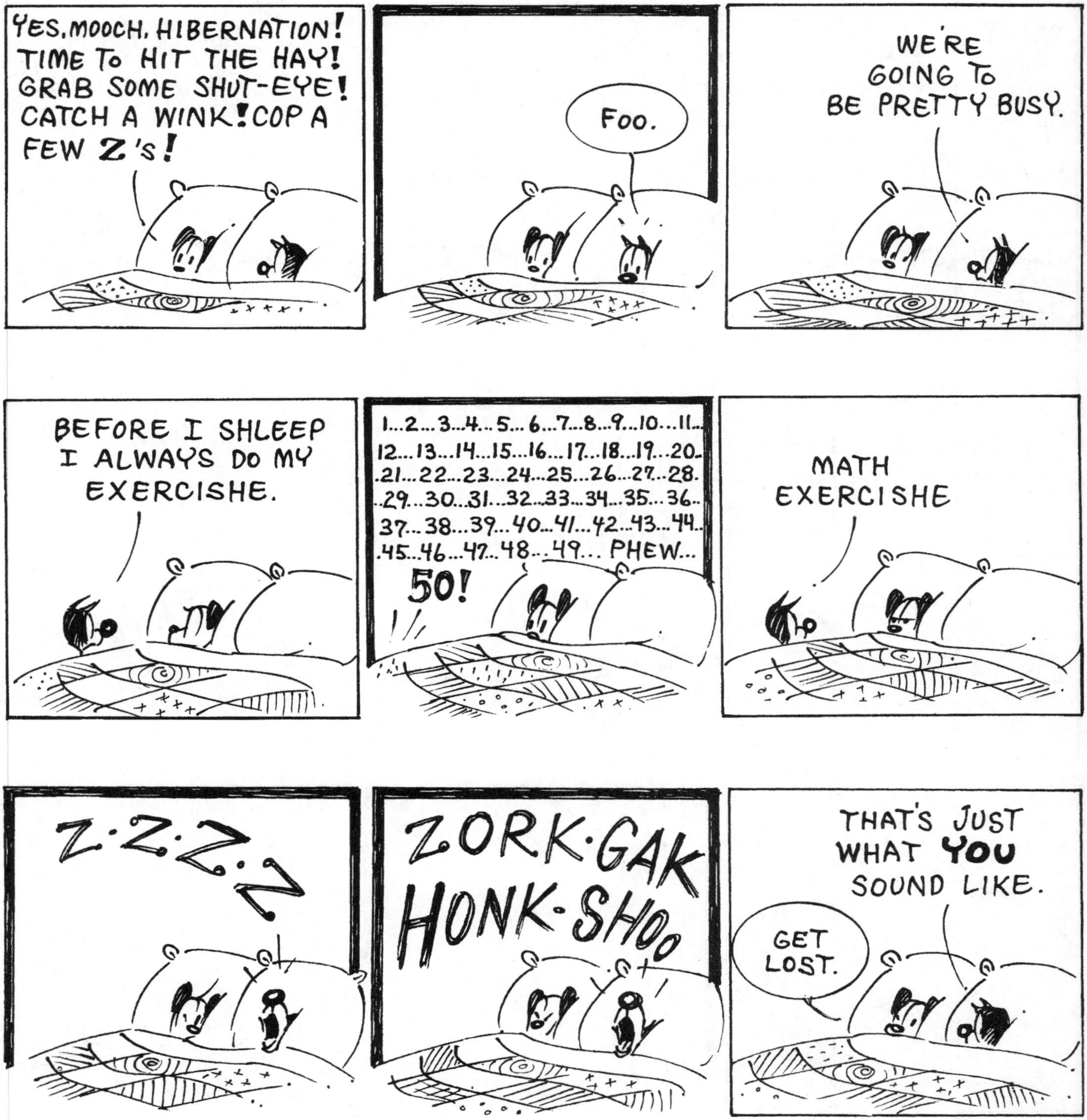
YES, MOOCH, HIBERNATION! TIME TO HIT THE HAY! GRAB SOME SHUT-EYE! CATCH A WINK! COP A FEW Z's!
FOO.
WE'RE GOING TO BE PRETTY BUSY.
BEFORE I SHLEEP I ALWAYS DO MY EXERCISHE.
1...2...3...4...5...6...7...8...9...10...11...12...13...14...15...16...17...18...19...20...21...22...23...24...25...26...27...28...29...30...31...32...33...34...35...36...37...38...39...40...41...42...43...44...45...46...47...48...49... PHEW...
50!
MATH EXERCISHE
Z·Z·Z·Z
ZORK·GAK HONK·SHOO
THAT'S JUST WHAT YOU SOUND LIKE.
GET LOST.

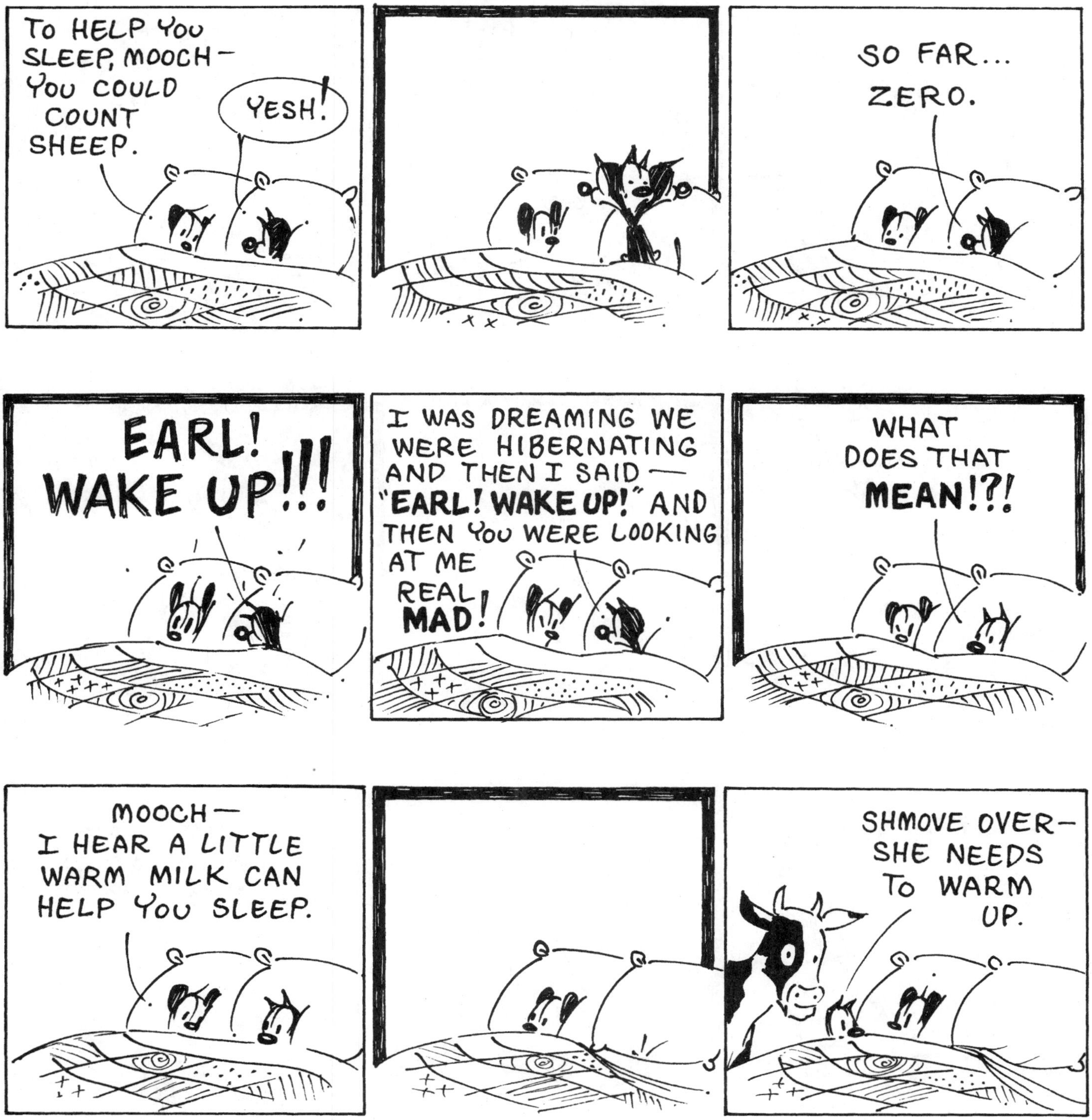

TO HELP YOU SLEEP, MOOCH— YOU COULD COUNT SHEEP.
YESH!
SO FAR... ZERO.
EARL! WAKE UP!!!
I WAS DREAMING WE WERE HIBERNATING AND THEN I SAID— "EARL! WAKE UP!" AND THEN YOU WERE LOOKING AT ME REAL MAD!
WHAT DOES THAT MEAN!?!
MOOCH— I HEAR A LITTLE WARM MILK CAN HELP YOU SLEEP.
SHMOVE OVER— SHE NEEDS TO WARM UP.

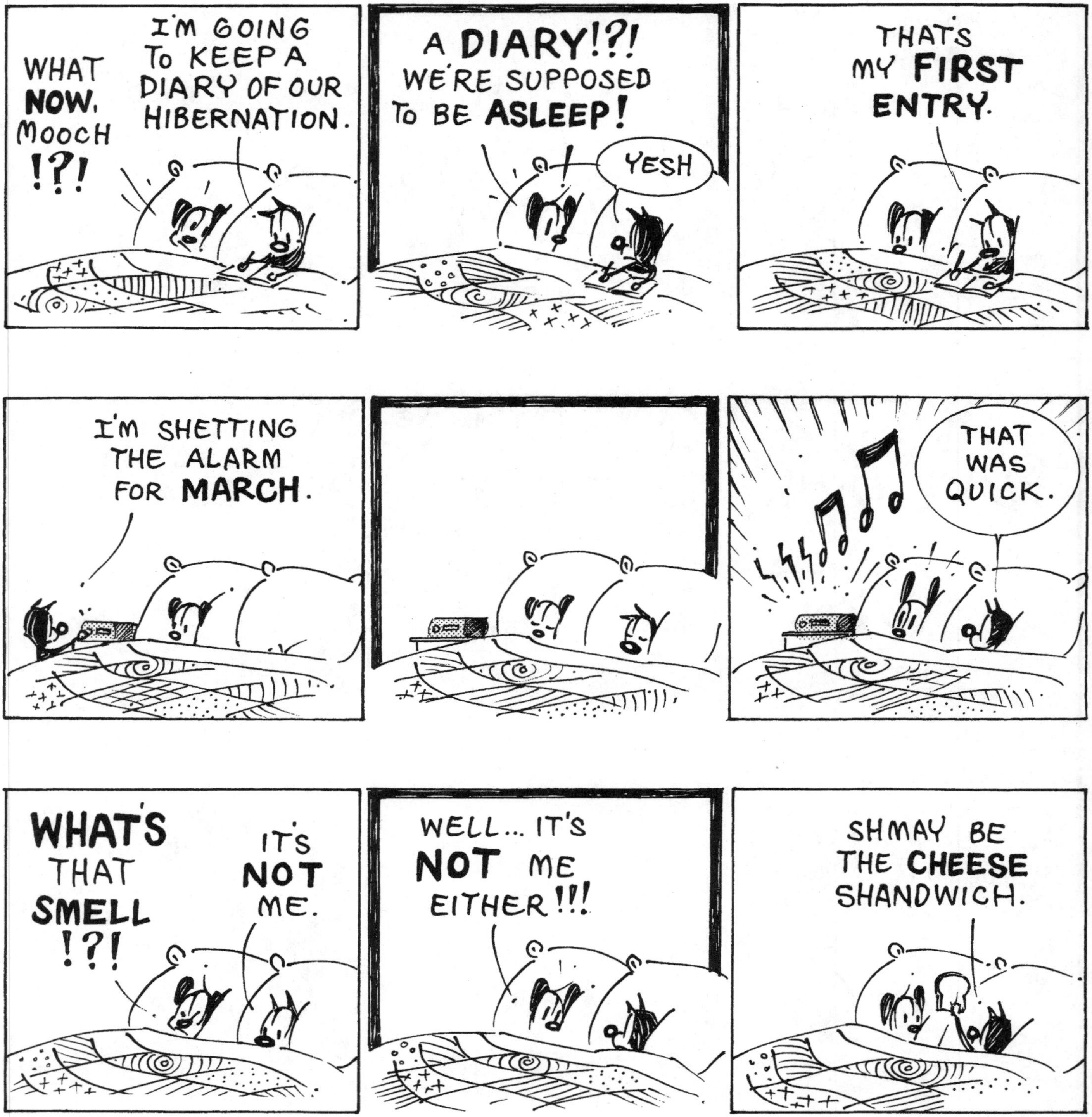
WHAT NOW, MOOCH !?!
I'M GOING TO KEEP A DIARY OF OUR HIBERNATION.
A DIARY!?! WE'RE SUPPOSED TO BE ASLEEP!
YESH
THAT'S MY FIRST ENTRY.
I'M SHETTING THE ALARM FOR MARCH.
THAT WAS QUICK.
WHAT'S THAT SMELL !?!
IT'S NOT ME.
WELL... IT'S NOT ME EITHER!!!
SHMAY BE THE CHEESE SHANDWICH.

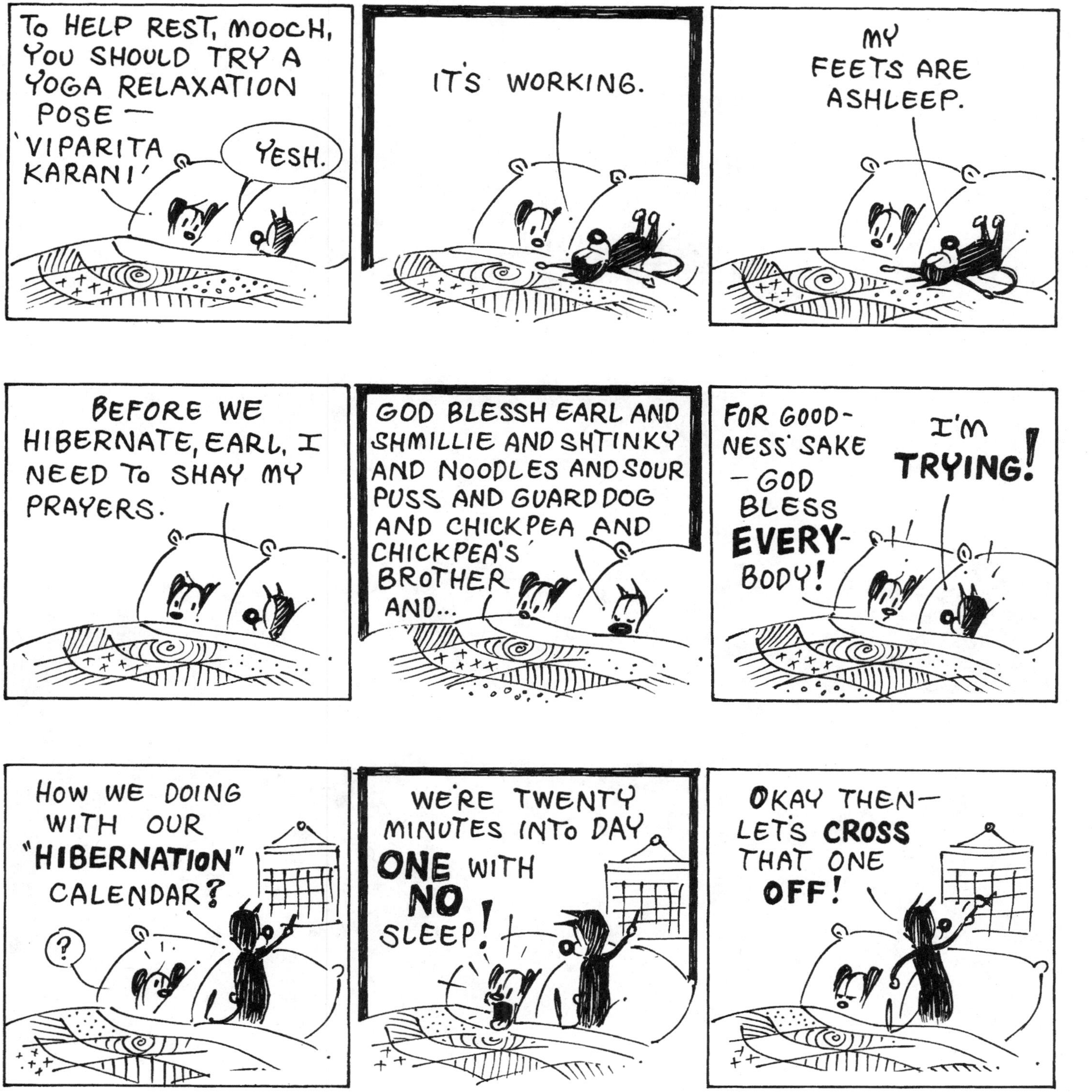
TO HELP REST, MOOCH, YOU SHOULD TRY A YOGA RELAXATION POSE — 'VIPARITA KARANI'
YESH.
IT'S WORKING.
MY FEETS ARE ASHLEEP.
BEFORE WE HIBERNATE, EARL, I NEED TO SHAY MY PRAYERS.
GOD BLESSH EARL AND SHMILLIE AND SHTINKY AND NOODLES AND SOUR PUSS AND GUARD DOG AND CHICKPEA AND CHICKPEA'S BROTHER AND...
FOR GOODNESS' SAKE — GOD BLESS EVERYBODY!
I'M TRYING!
HOW WE DOING WITH OUR "HIBERNATION" CALENDAR?
?
WE'RE TWENTY MINUTES INTO DAY ONE WITH NO SLEEP!
OKAY THEN— LET'S CROSS THAT ONE OFF!

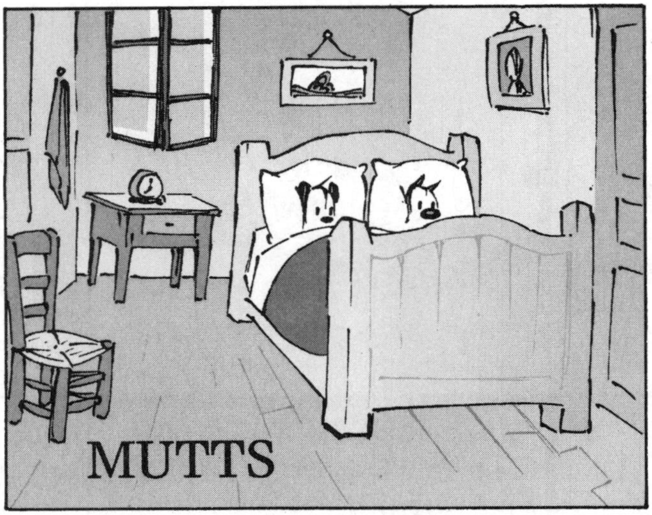
MUTTS

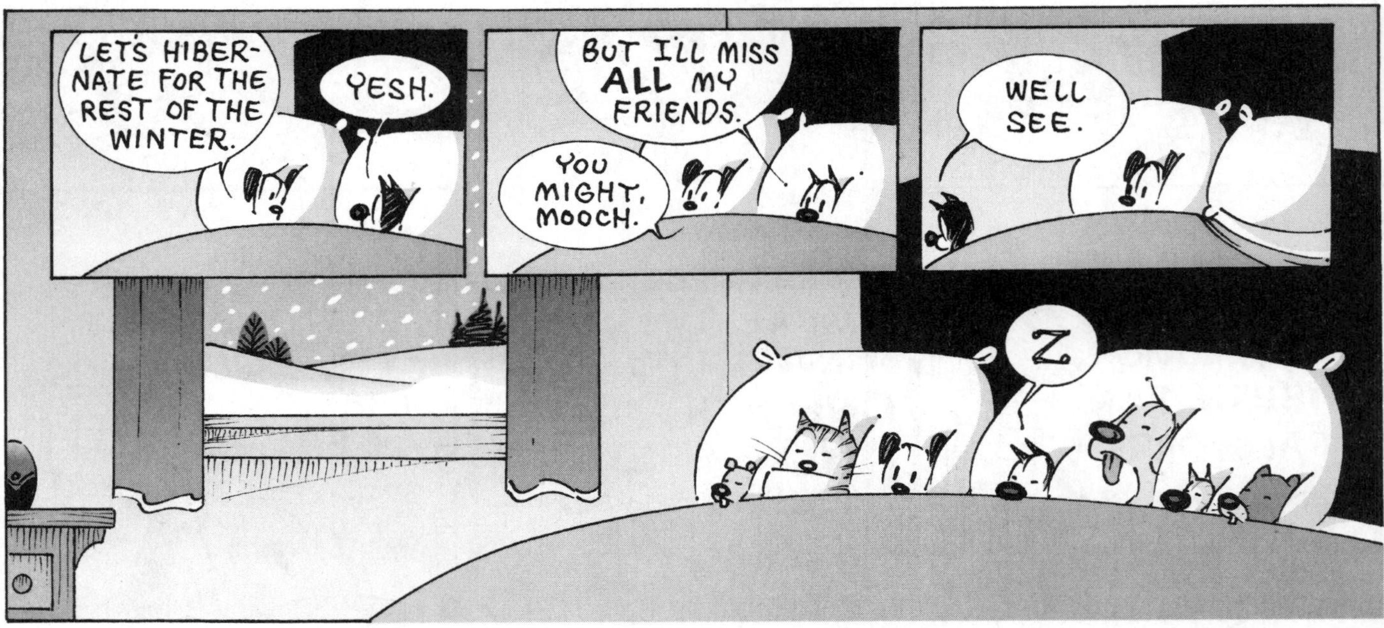
LET'S HIBER-NATE FOR THE REST OF THE WINTER.
YESH.
BUT I'LL MISS ALL MY FRIENDS.
YOU MIGHT, MOOCH.
WE'LL SEE.
Z

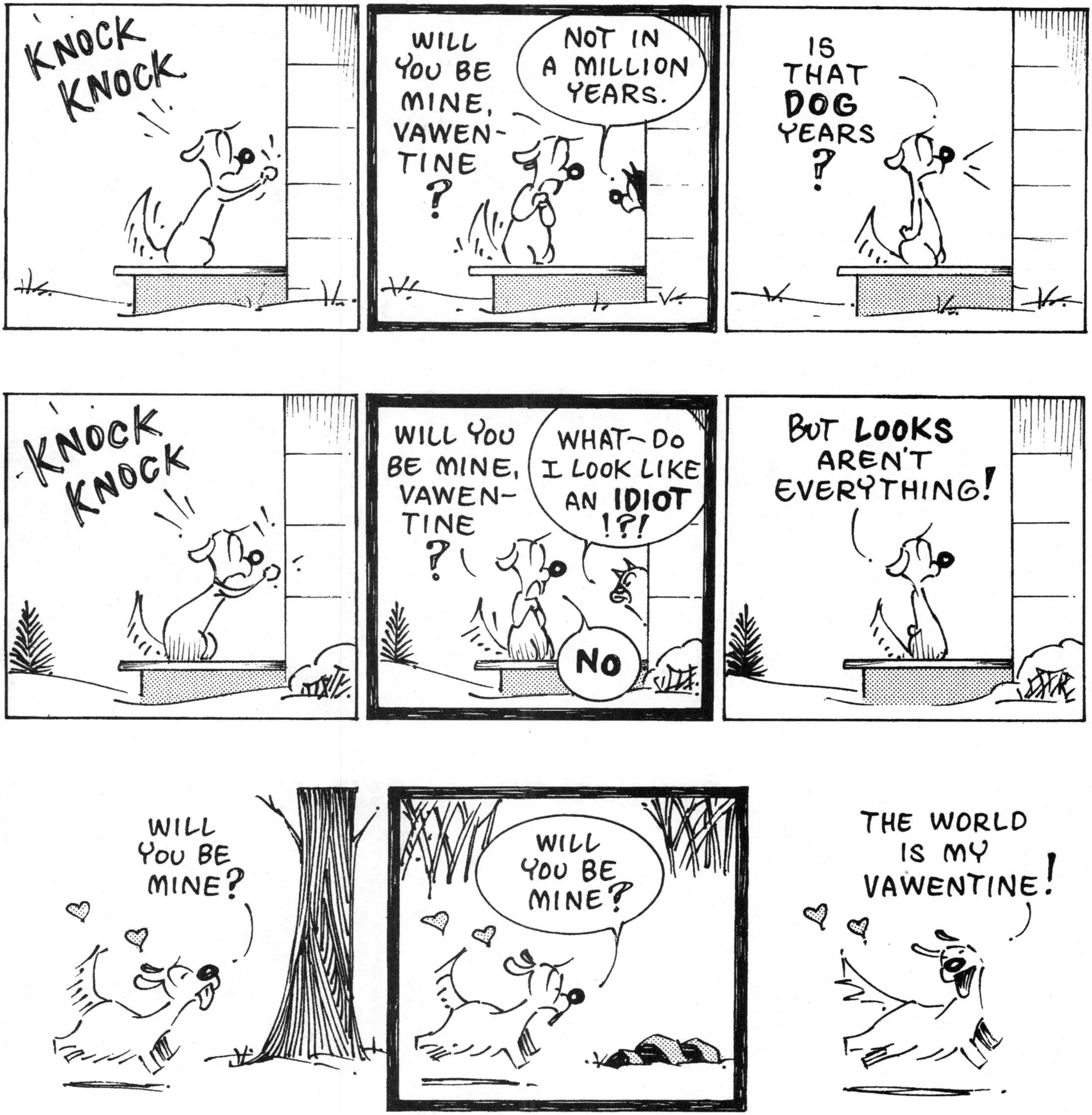
KNOCK KNOCK
WILL YOU BE MINE, VAWENTINE?
NOT IN A MILLION YEARS.
IS THAT DOG YEARS?
KNOCK KNOCK
WILL YOU BE MINE, VAWENTINE?
WHAT—DO I LOOK LIKE AN IDIOT!?!
NO
BUT LOOKS AREN'T EVERYTHING!
WILL YOU BE MINE?
WILL YOU BE MINE?
THE WORLD IS MY VAWENTINE!

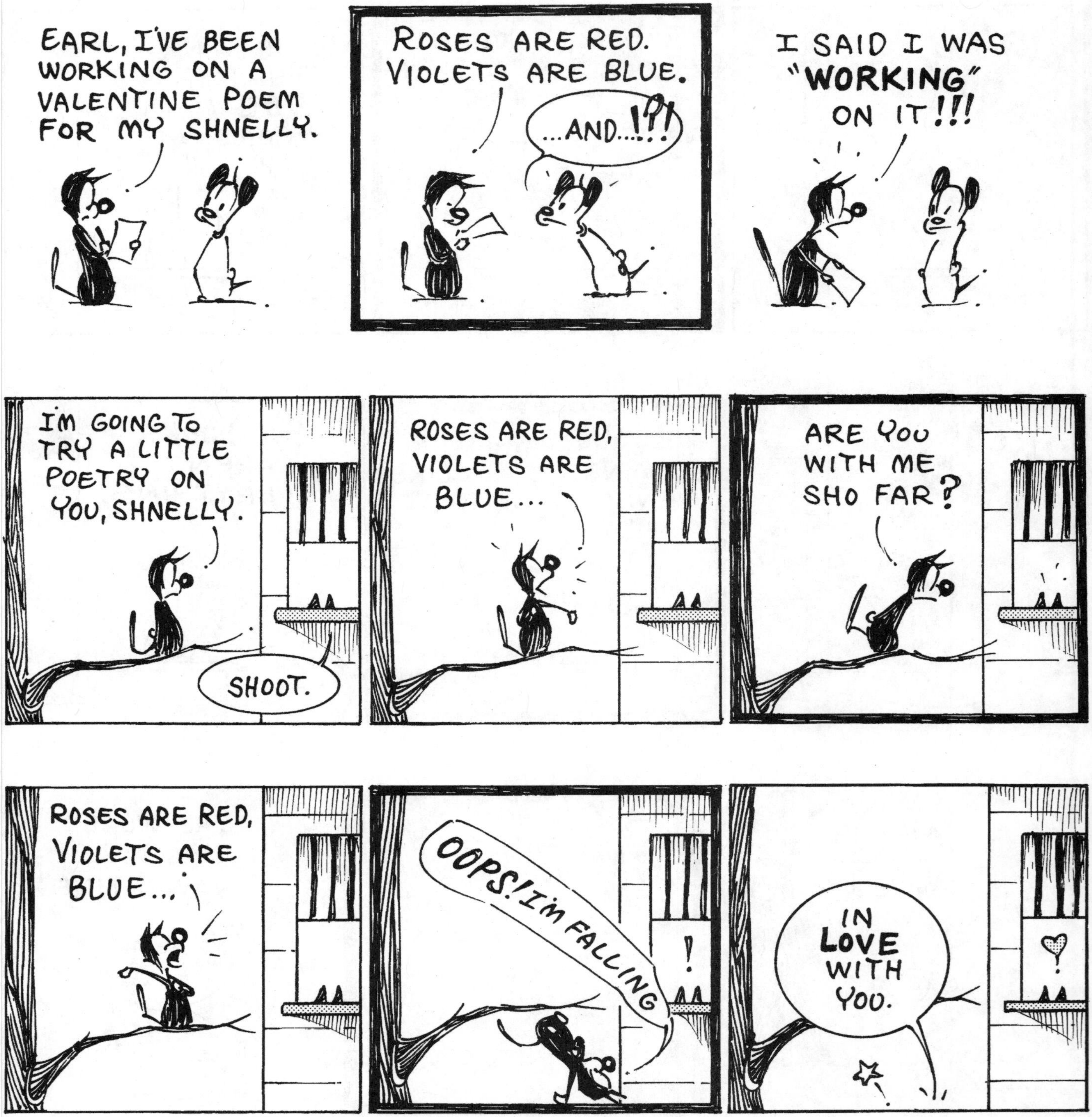
EARL, I'VE BEEN WORKING ON A VALENTINE POEM FOR MY SHNELLY.
ROSES ARE RED. VIOLETS ARE BLUE.
...AND...!?!
I SAID I WAS "WORKING" ON IT!!!
I'M GOING TO TRY A LITTLE POETRY ON YOU, SHNELLY.
SHOOT.
ROSES ARE RED, VIOLETS ARE BLUE...
ARE YOU WITH ME SHO FAR?
ROSES ARE RED, VIOLETS ARE BLUE...
OOPS! I'M FALLING
!
IN LOVE WITH YOU.

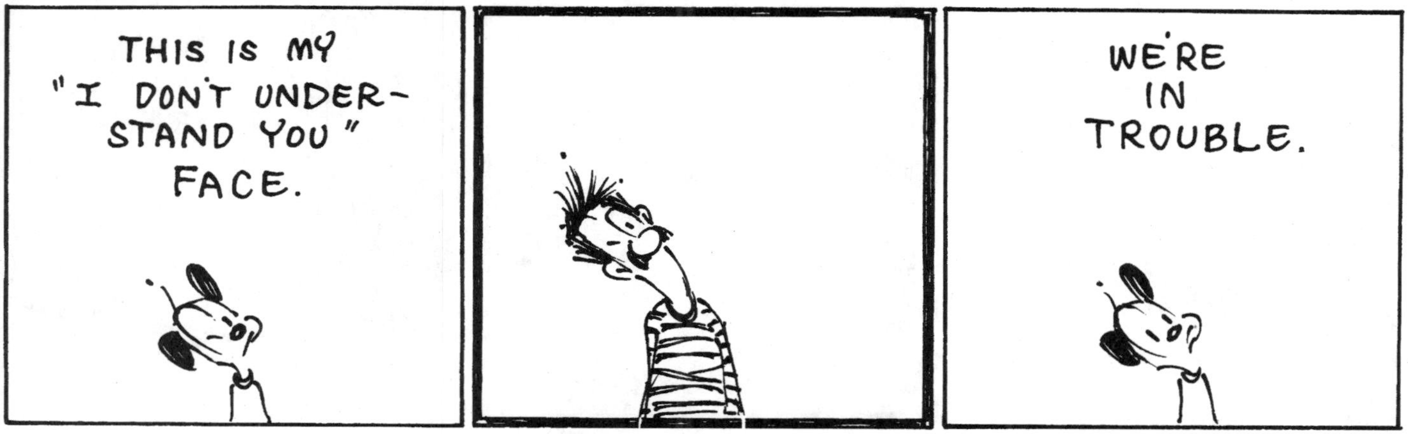
THIS IS MY "I DON'T UNDER-STAND YOU" FACE.
WE'RE IN TROUBLE.

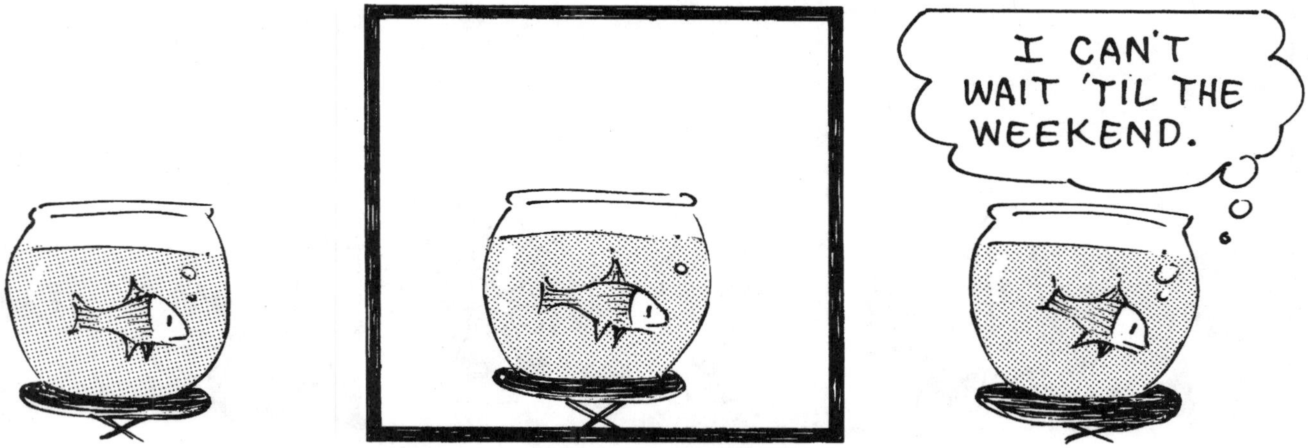
I CAN'T WAIT 'TIL THE WEEKEND.

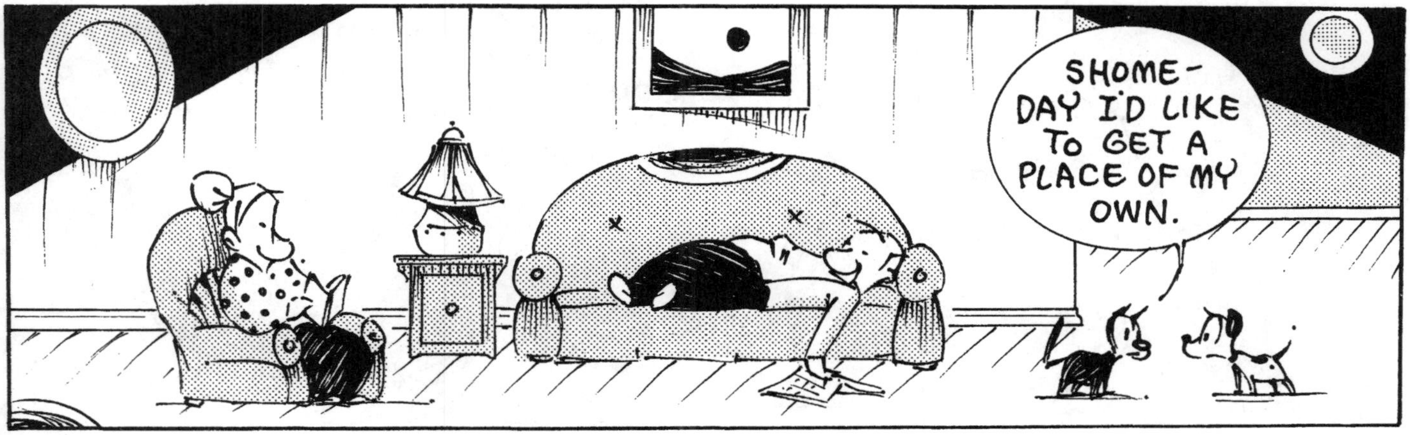
SHOME-DAY I'D LIKE TO GET A PLACE OF MY OWN.

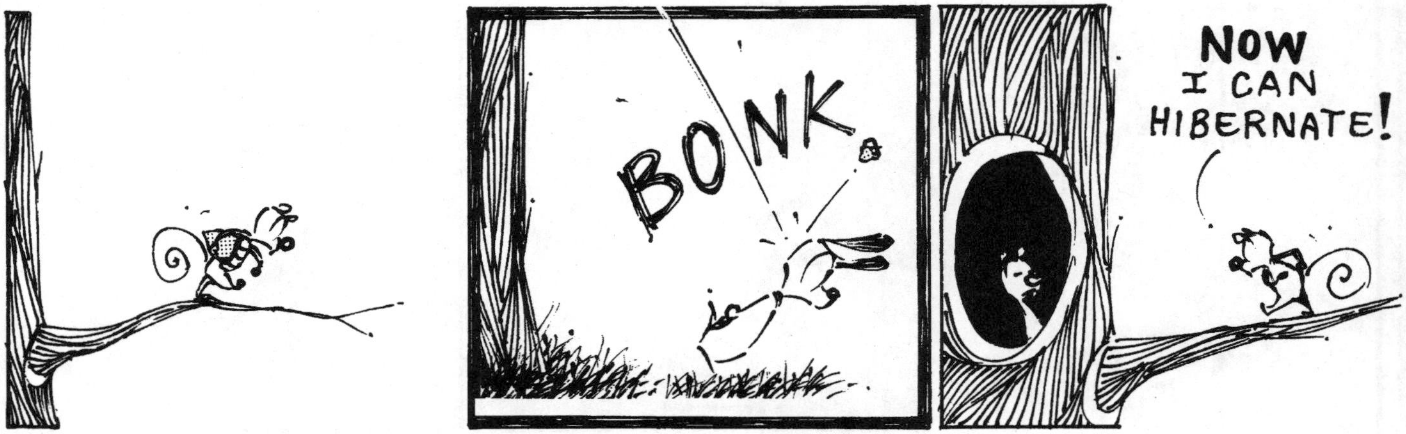
BONK
NOW I CAN HIBERNATE!

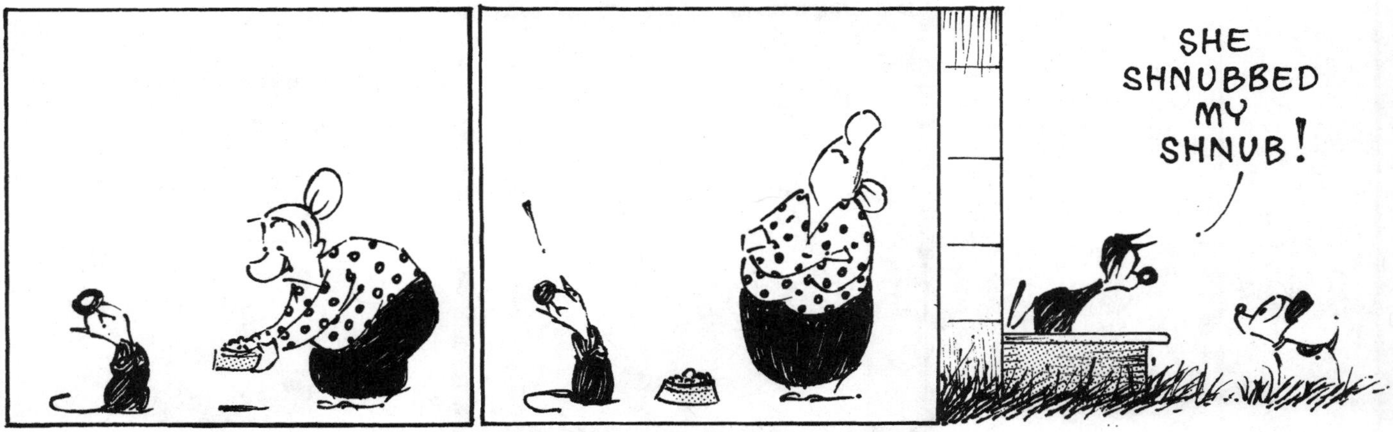
SHE SHNUBBED MY SHNUB!

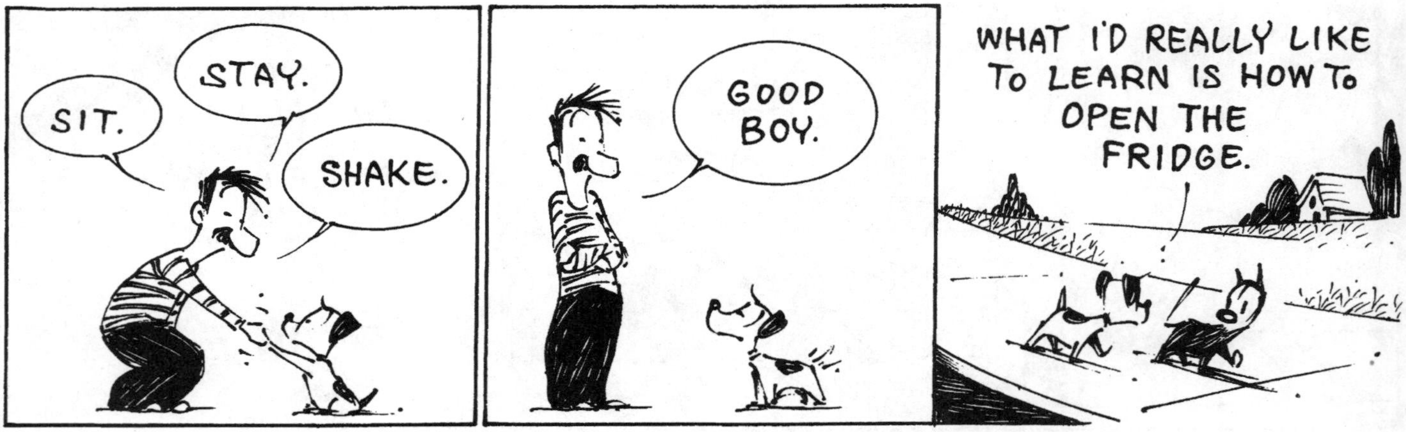
SIT.
STAY.
SHAKE.
GOOD BOY.
WHAT I'D REALLY LIKE TO LEARN IS HOW TO OPEN THE FRIDGE.

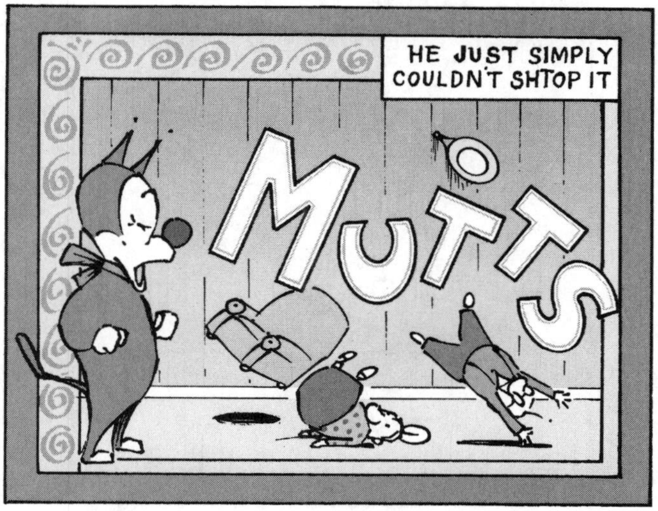
HE JUST SIMPLY COULDN'T SHTOP IT
MUTTS

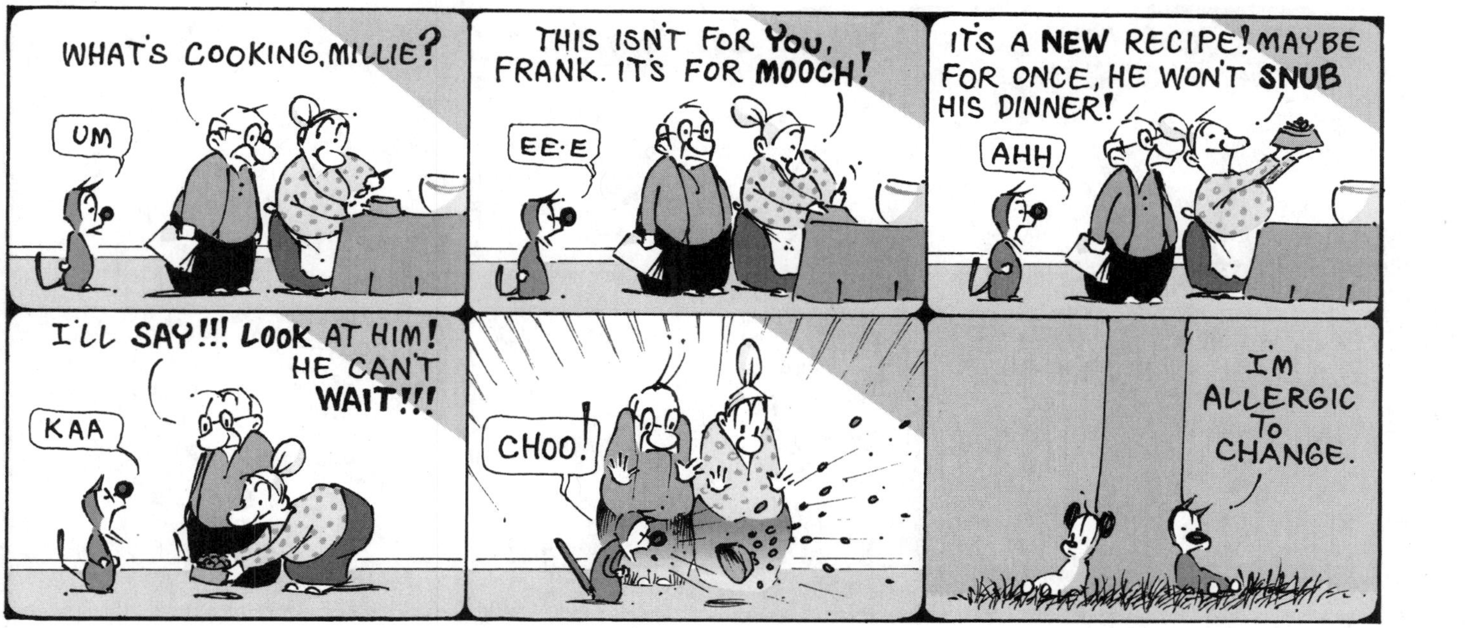
WHAT'S COOKING, MILLIE?
UM
THIS ISN'T FOR YOU, FRANK. IT'S FOR MOOCH!
EE·E
IT'S A NEW RECIPE! MAYBE FOR ONCE, HE WON'T SNUB HIS DINNER!
AHH
I'LL SAY!!! LOOK AT HIM! HE CAN'T WAIT!!!
KAA
CHOO!
I'M ALLERGIC TO CHANGE.

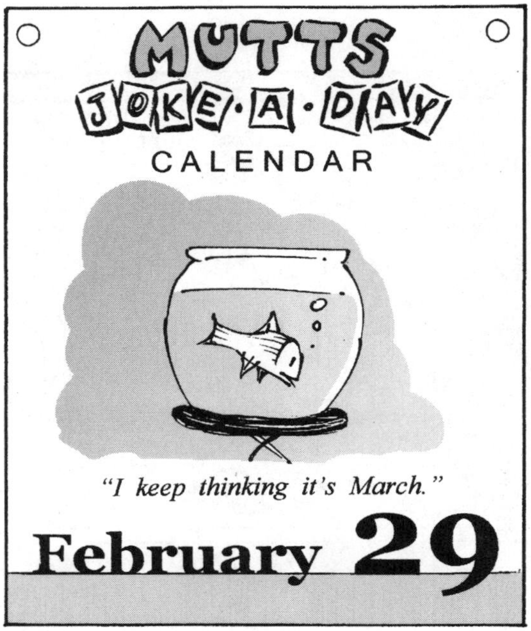
MUTTS
JOKE·A·DAY
CALENDAR
"I keep thinking it's March."
February 29

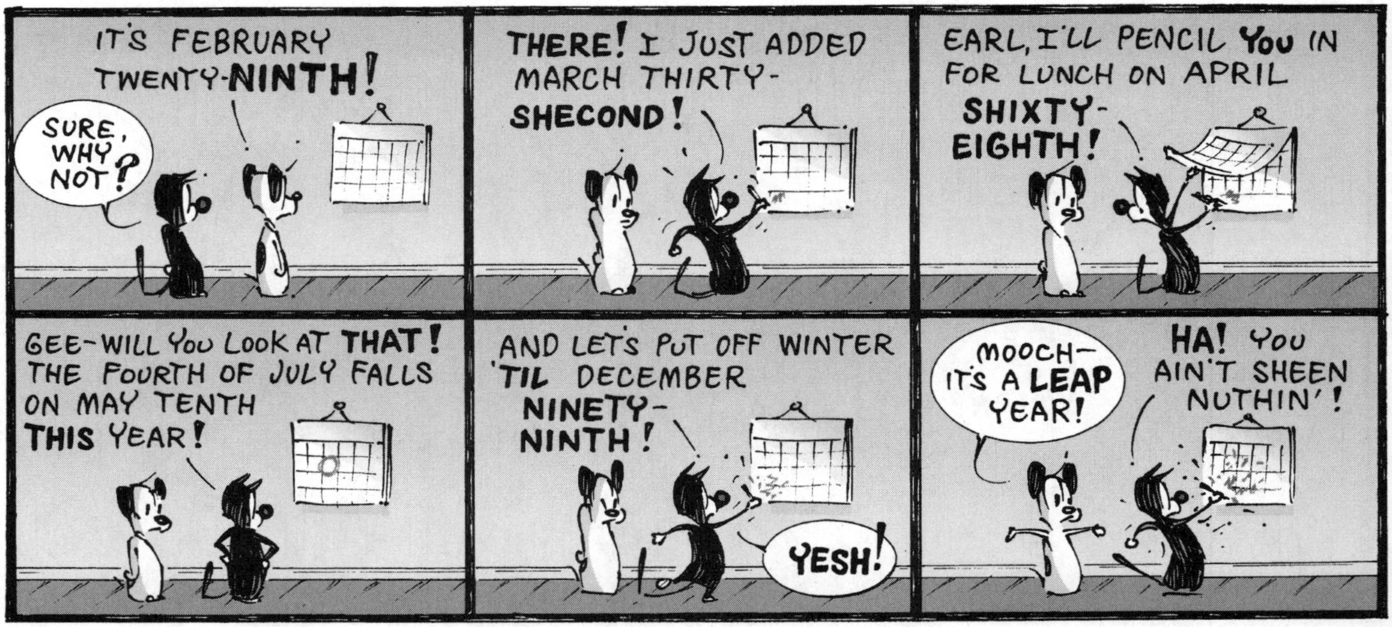
IT'S FEBRUARY TWENTY-NINTH!
SURE, WHY NOT?
THERE! I JUST ADDED MARCH THIRTY-SHECOND!
EARL, I'LL PENCIL YOU IN FOR LUNCH ON APRIL SHIXTY-EIGHTH!
GEE-WILL YOU LOOK AT THAT! THE FOURTH OF JULY FALLS ON MAY TENTH THIS YEAR!
AND LET'S PUT OFF WINTER 'TIL DECEMBER NINETY-NINTH!
YESH!
MOOCH-IT'S A LEAP YEAR!
HA! YOU AIN'T SHEEN NUTHIN'!

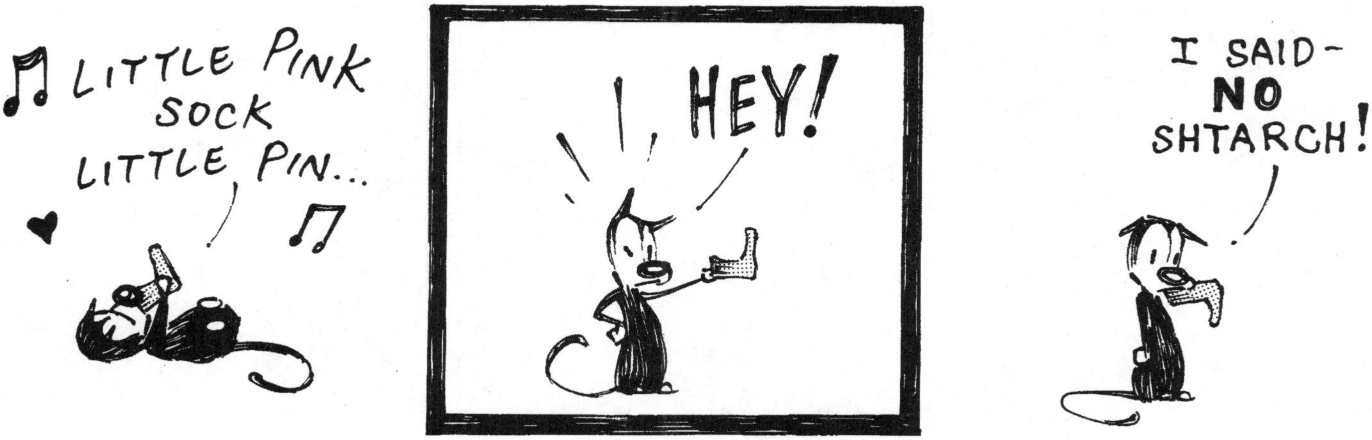
LITTLE PINK SOCK LITTLE PIN...
HEY!
I SAID- NO SHTARCH!

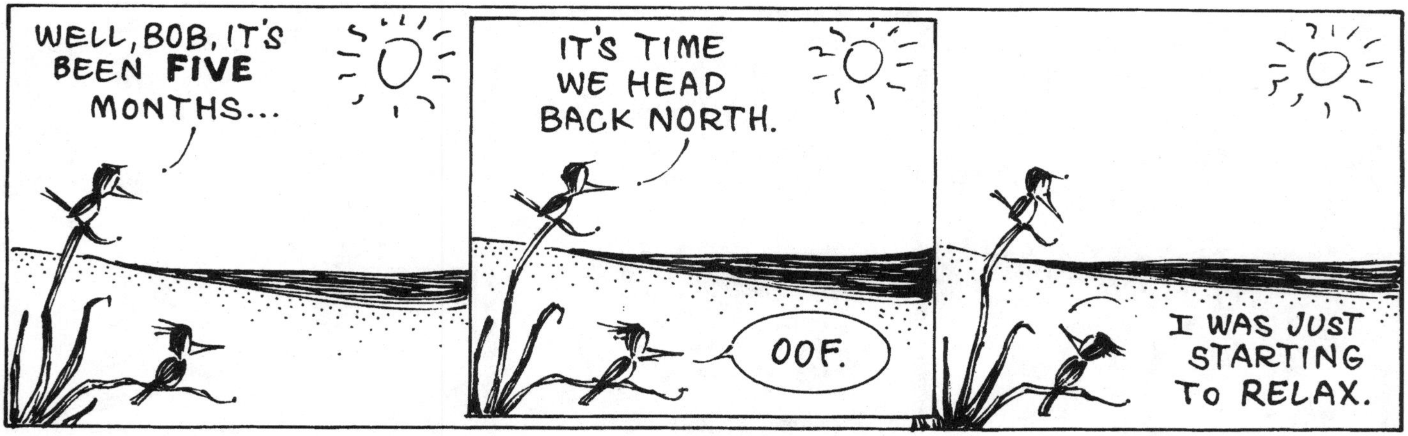
WELL, BOB, IT'S BEEN FIVE MONTHS...
IT'S TIME WE HEAD BACK NORTH.
OOF.
I WAS JUST STARTING TO RELAX.

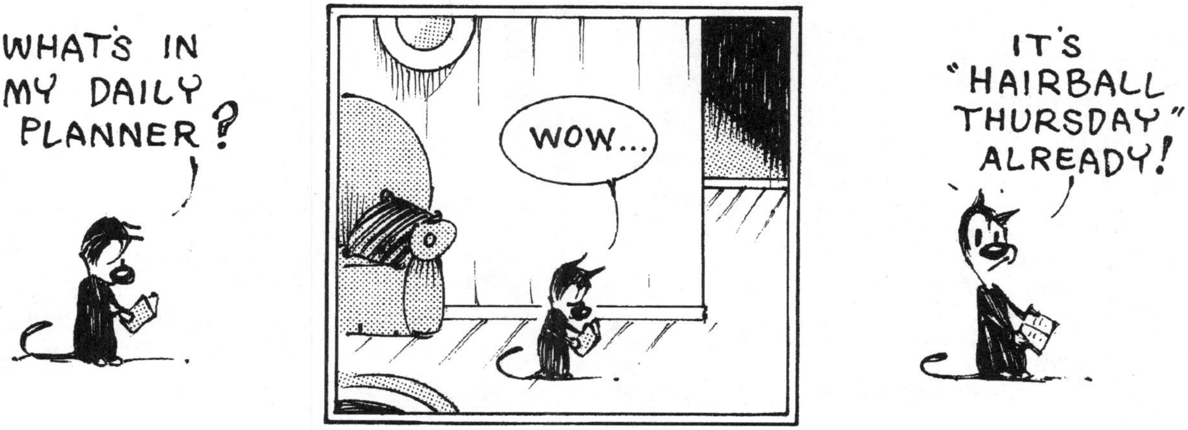
WHAT'S IN MY DAILY PLANNER?
WOW...
IT'S "HAIRBALL THURSDAY" ALREADY!

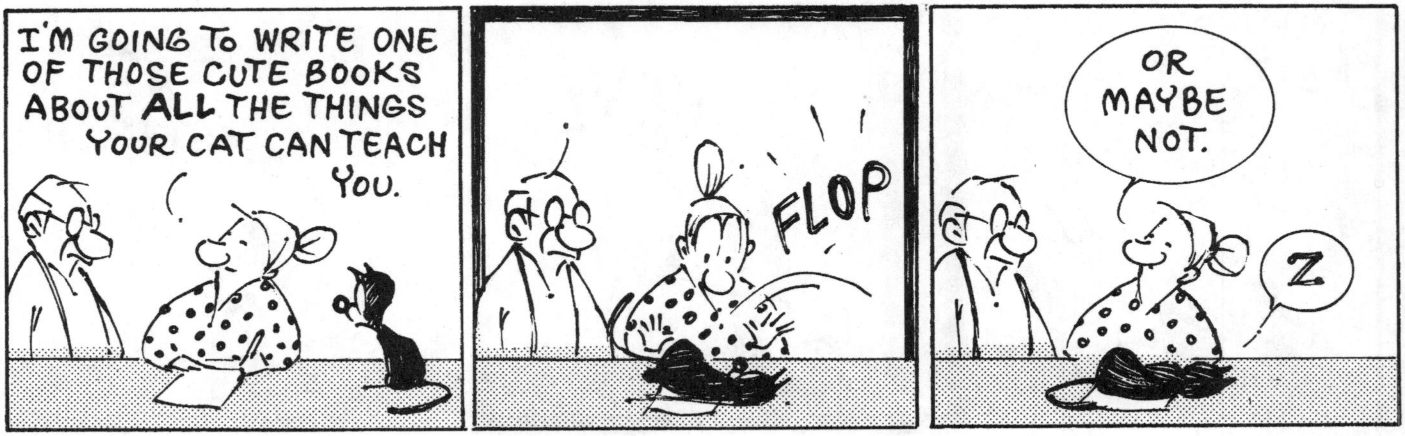
I'M GOING TO WRITE ONE OF THOSE CUTE BOOKS ABOUT ALL THE THINGS YOUR CAT CAN TEACH YOU.
FLOP
OR MAYBE NOT.
Z

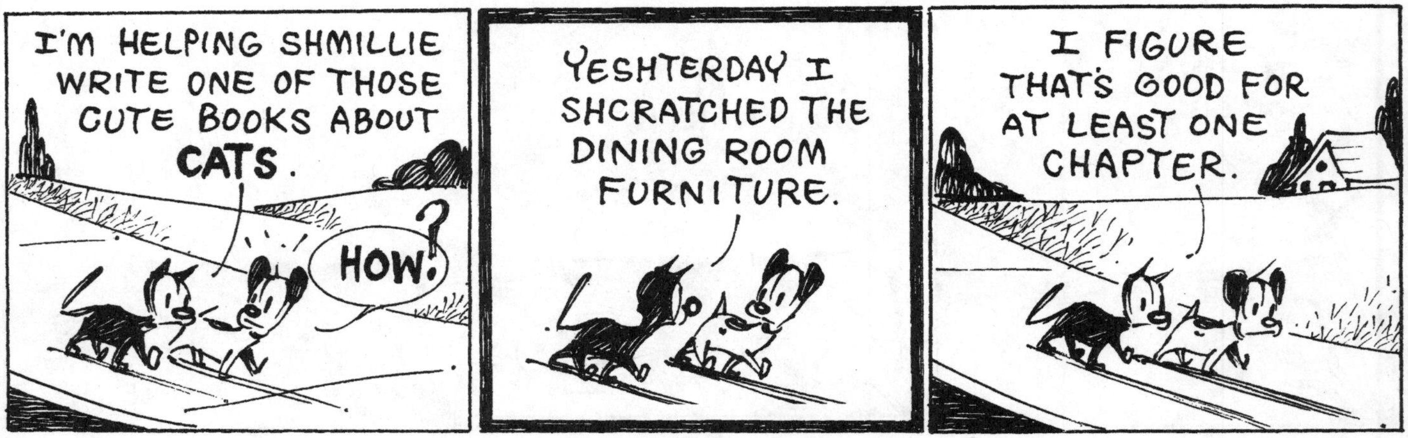
I'M HELPING SHMILLIE WRITE ONE OF THOSE CUTE BOOKS ABOUT CATS.
HOW?
YESHTERDAY I SHCRATCHED THE DINING ROOM FURNITURE.
I FIGURE THAT'S GOOD FOR AT LEAST ONE CHAPTER.

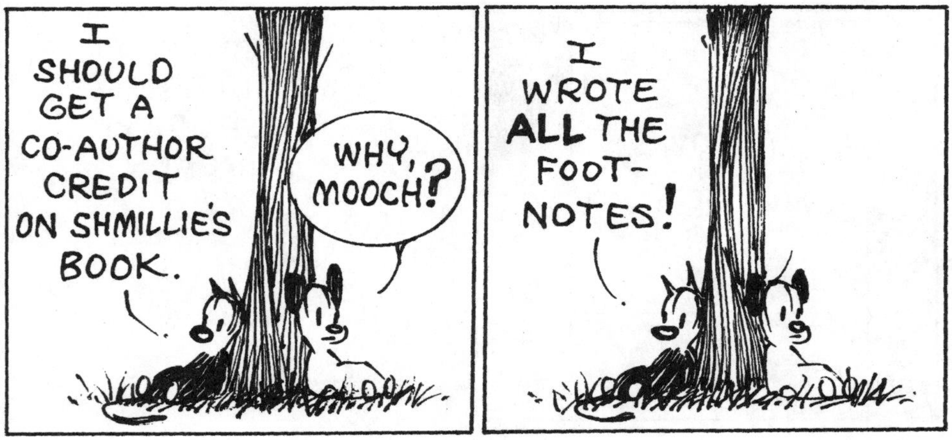
I SHOULD GET A CO-AUTHOR CREDIT ON SHMILLIE'S BOOK.
WHY, MOOCH?
I WROTE ALL THE FOOT-NOTES!

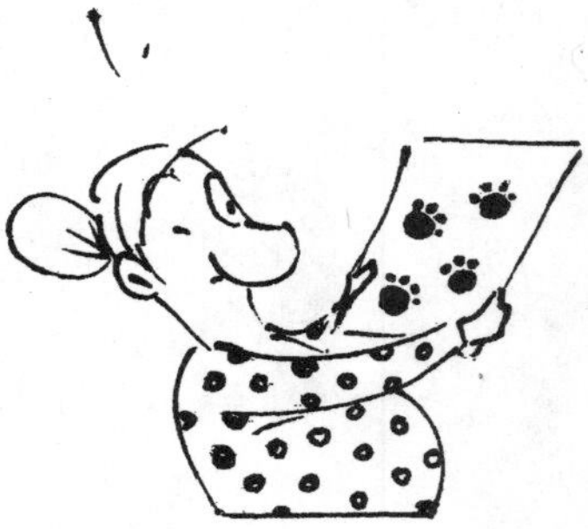

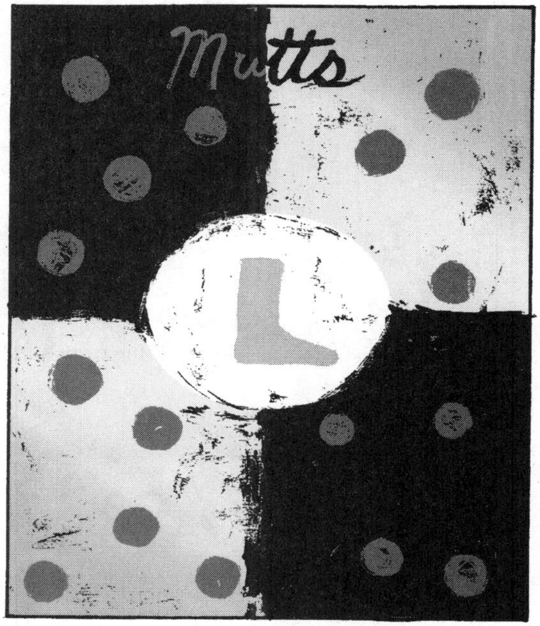
Mutts

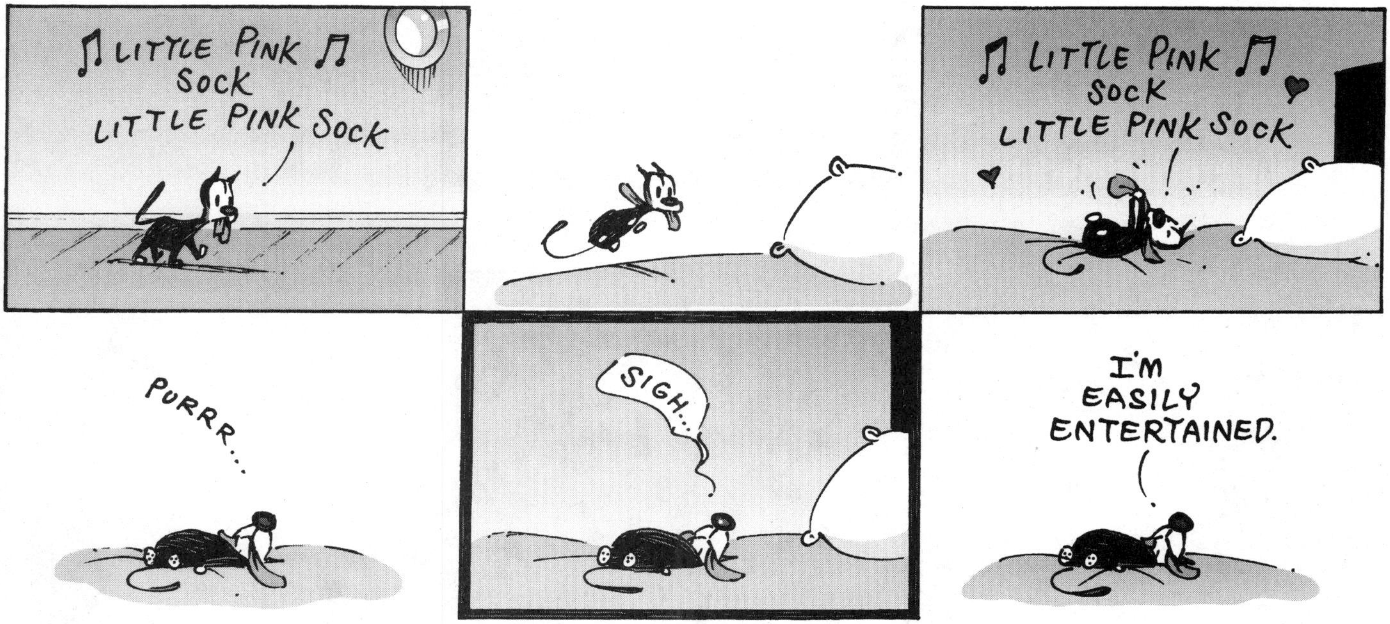
♫ LITTLE PINK ♫ SOCK LITTLE PINK SOCK
♫ LITTLE PINK ♫ SOCK LITTLE PINK SOCK
PURRR...
SIGH...
I'M EASILY ENTERTAINED.

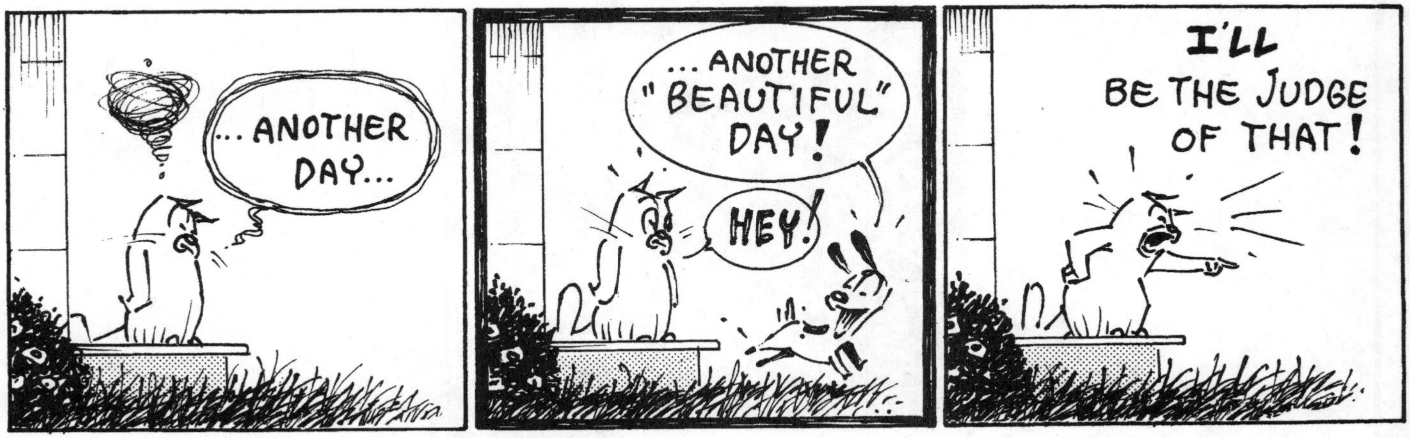
... ANOTHER DAY...
... ANOTHER "BEAUTIFUL" DAY!
HEY!
I'LL BE THE JUDGE OF THAT!

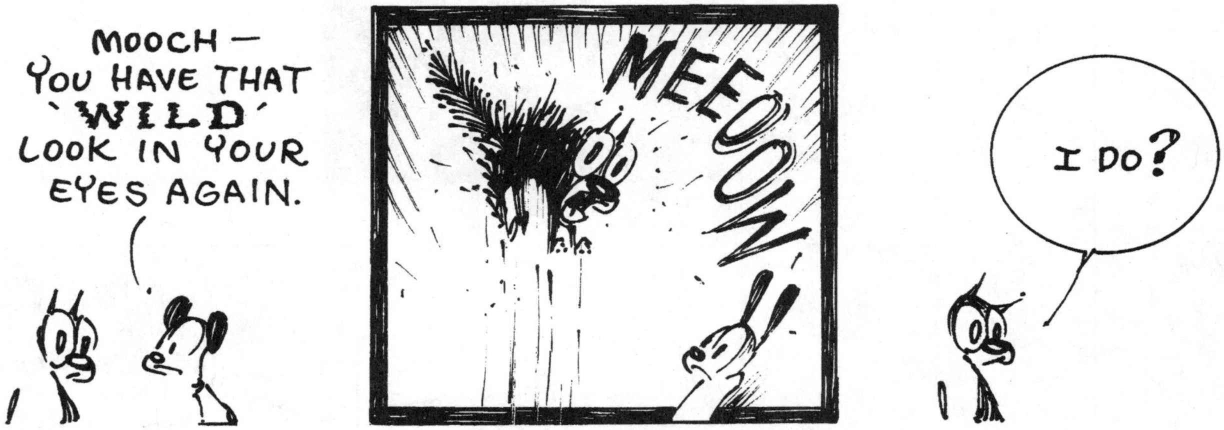
MOOCH — YOU HAVE THAT WILD LOOK IN YOUR EYES AGAIN.
MEEOOOW!!
I DO?

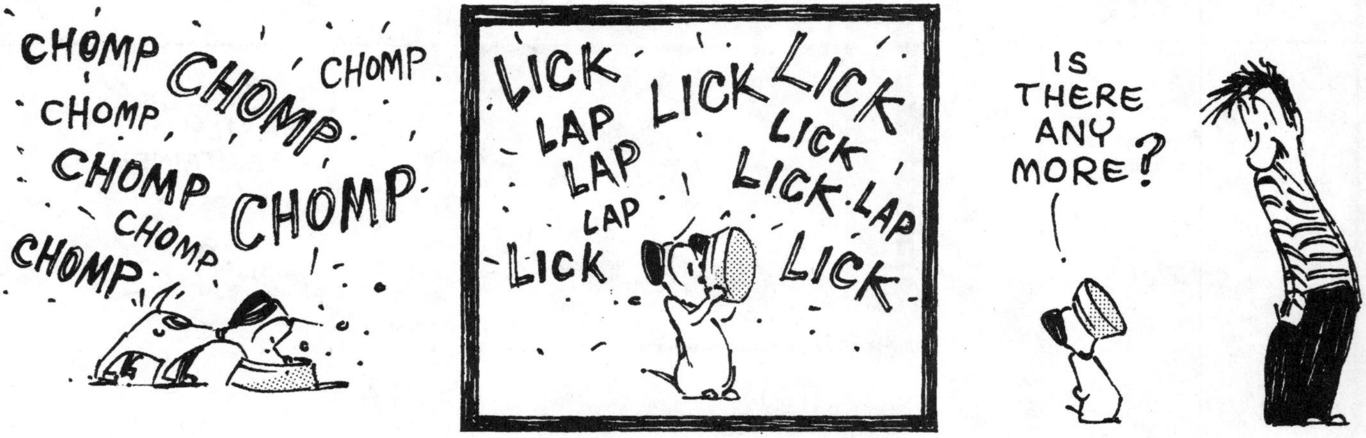
CHOMP CHOMP CHOMP
CHOMP
CHOMP CHOMP
CHOMP
CHOMP
LICK LICK LICK
LAP LAP LAP
LICK LICK LAP
LICK LICK
IS THERE ANY MORE?

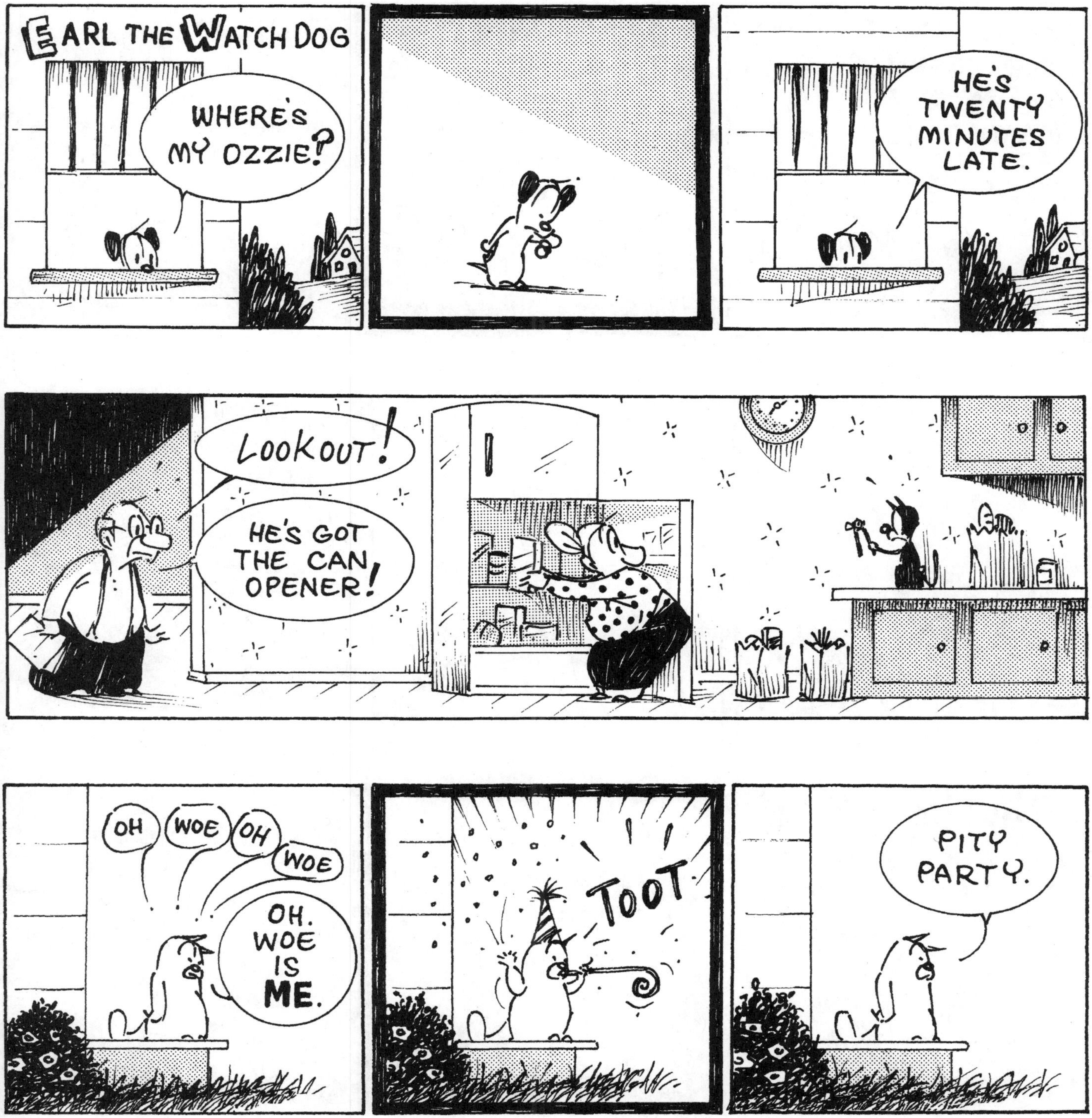
EARL THE WATCH DOG
WHERE'S MY OZZIE?
HE'S TWENTY MINUTES LATE.
LOOKOUT!
HE'S GOT THE CAN OPENER!
OH
WOE
OH
WOE
OH. WOE IS ME.
TOOT
PITY PARTY.

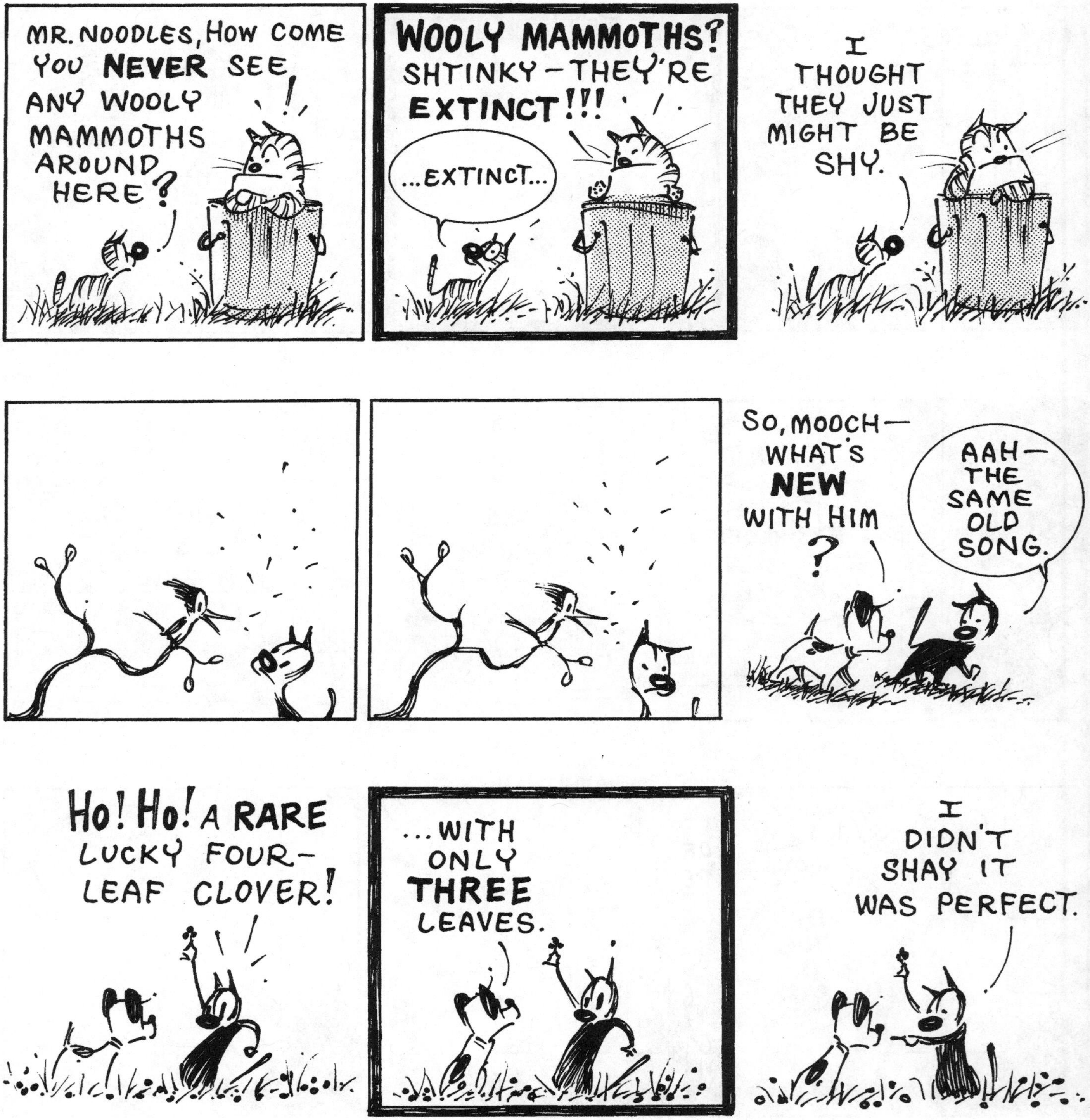

MR. NOODLES, HOW COME YOU **NEVER** SEE ANY WOOLY MAMMOTHS AROUND HERE?
WOOLY MAMMOTHS? SHTINKY – THEY'RE **EXTINCT!!!**
...EXTINCT...
I THOUGHT THEY JUST MIGHT BE SHY.
SO, MOOCH – WHAT'S **NEW** WITH HIM?
AAH – THE SAME OLD SONG.
HO! HO! A **RARE** LUCKY FOUR-LEAF CLOVER!
...WITH ONLY **THREE** LEAVES.
I DIDN'T SHAY IT WAS PERFECT.

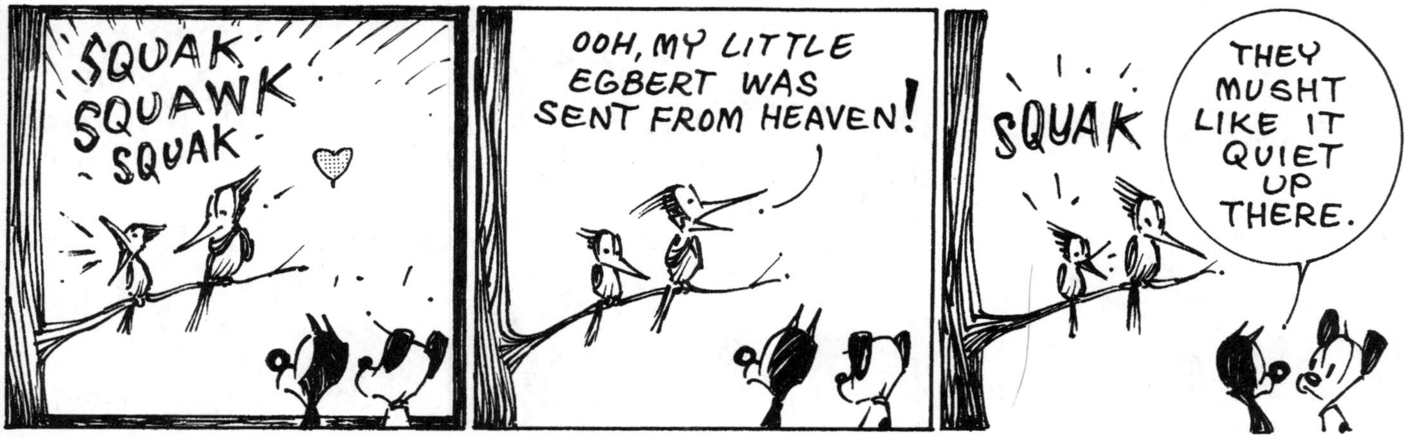
SQUAK SQUAWK SQUAK
OOH, MY LITTLE EGBERT WAS SENT FROM HEAVEN!
SQUAK
THEY MUSHT LIKE IT QUIET UP THERE.

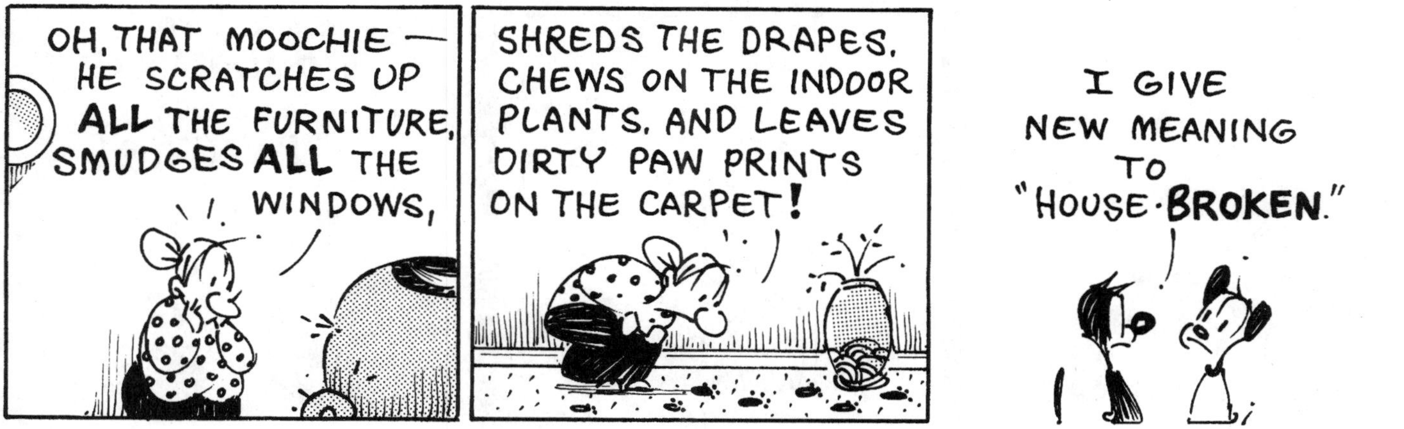
OH, THAT MOOCHIE — HE SCRATCHES UP ALL THE FURNITURE, SMUDGES ALL THE WINDOWS,
SHREDS THE DRAPES, CHEWS ON THE INDOOR PLANTS, AND LEAVES DIRTY PAW PRINTS ON THE CARPET!
I GIVE NEW MEANING TO "HOUSE-BROKEN."

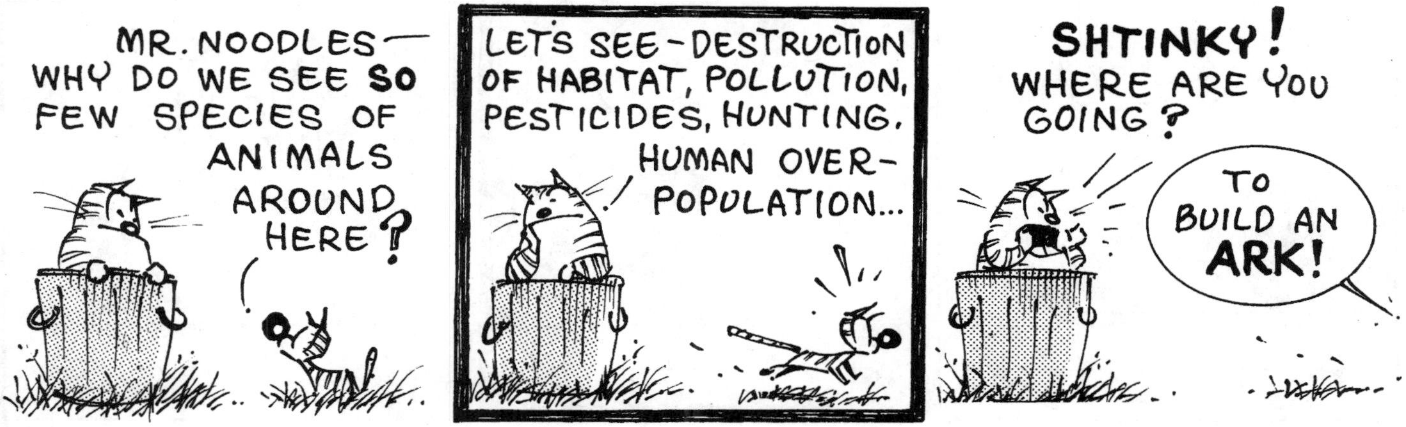
MR. NOODLES — WHY DO WE SEE SO FEW SPECIES OF ANIMALS AROUND HERE?
LET'S SEE – DESTRUCTION OF HABITAT, POLLUTION, PESTICIDES, HUNTING, HUMAN OVER-POPULATION...
SHTINKY! WHERE ARE YOU GOING?
TO BUILD AN ARK!

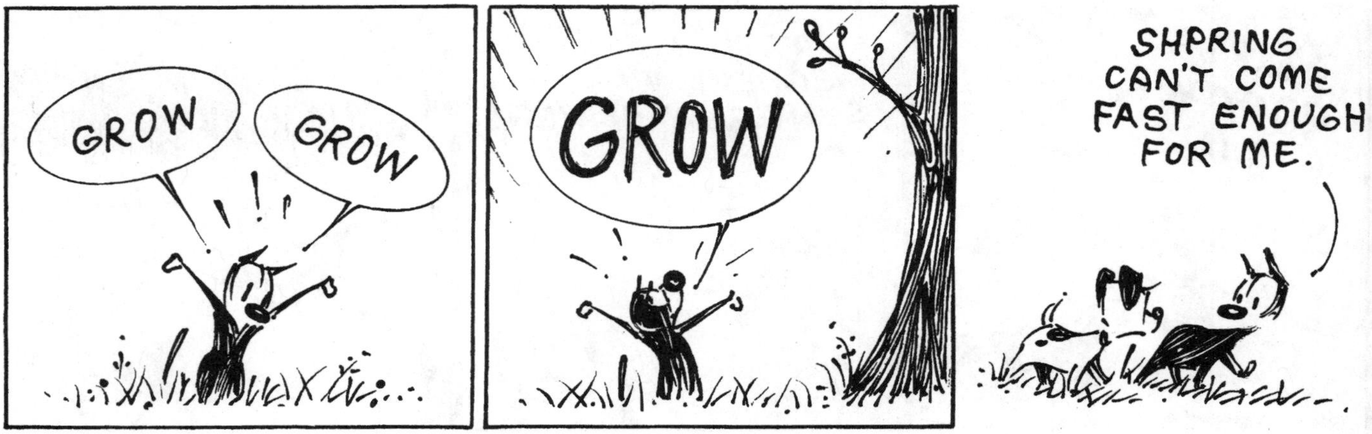
GROW
GROW
GROW
SHPRING CAN'T COME FAST ENOUGH FOR ME.

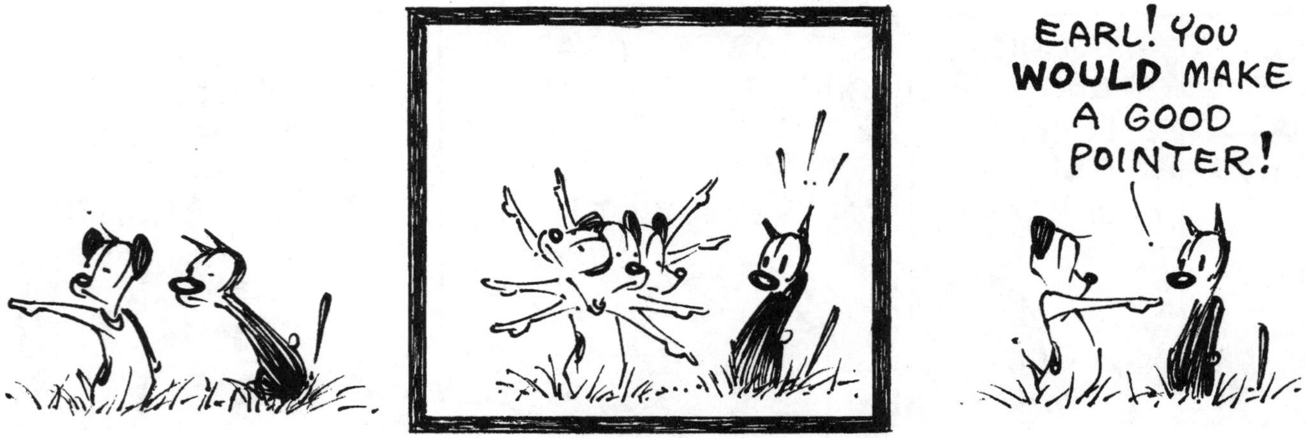
EARL! YOU **WOULD** MAKE A GOOD POINTER!

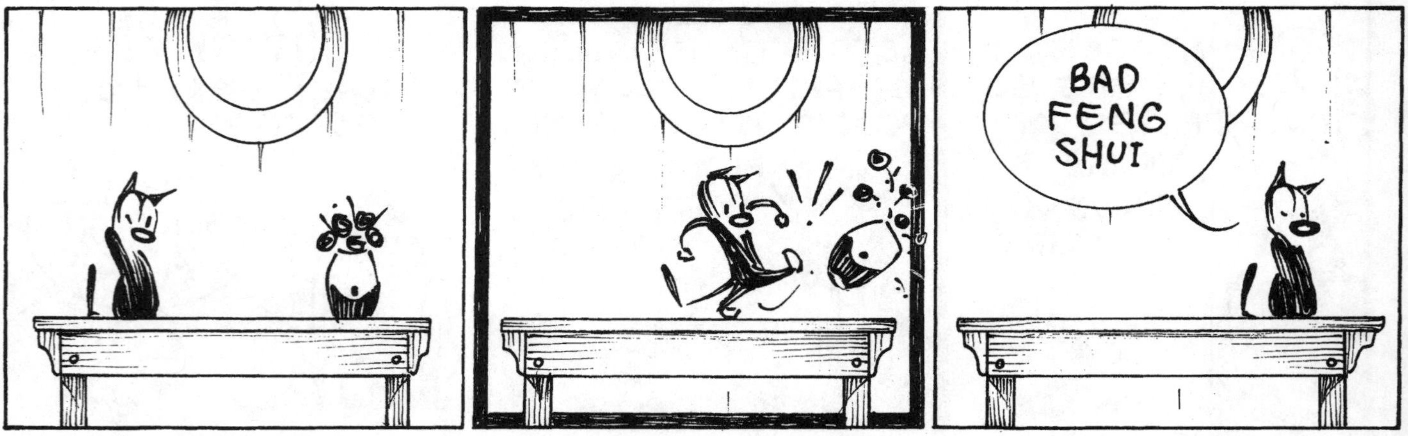
BAD FENG SHUI

MUTTS
PATRICK McDONNELL

KNOCK KNOCK
ARE YOU "EARL"?
YES?
WELL...
THERE IT IS!
IF YOU'LL JUST SIGN HERE.
THANK YOU...
NO PROBLEM. ENJOY!
EVERY DOG HAS HIS DAY.

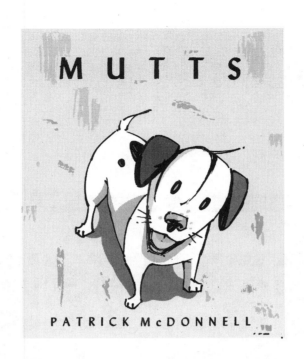

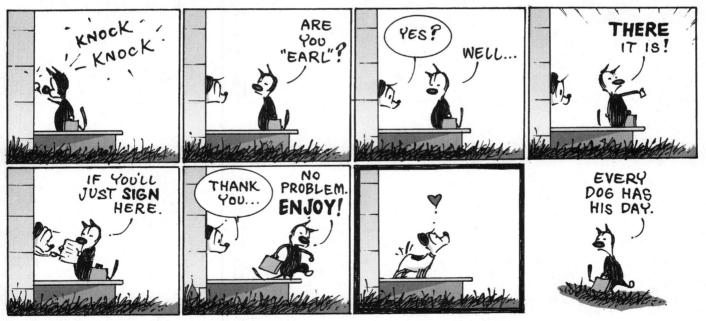

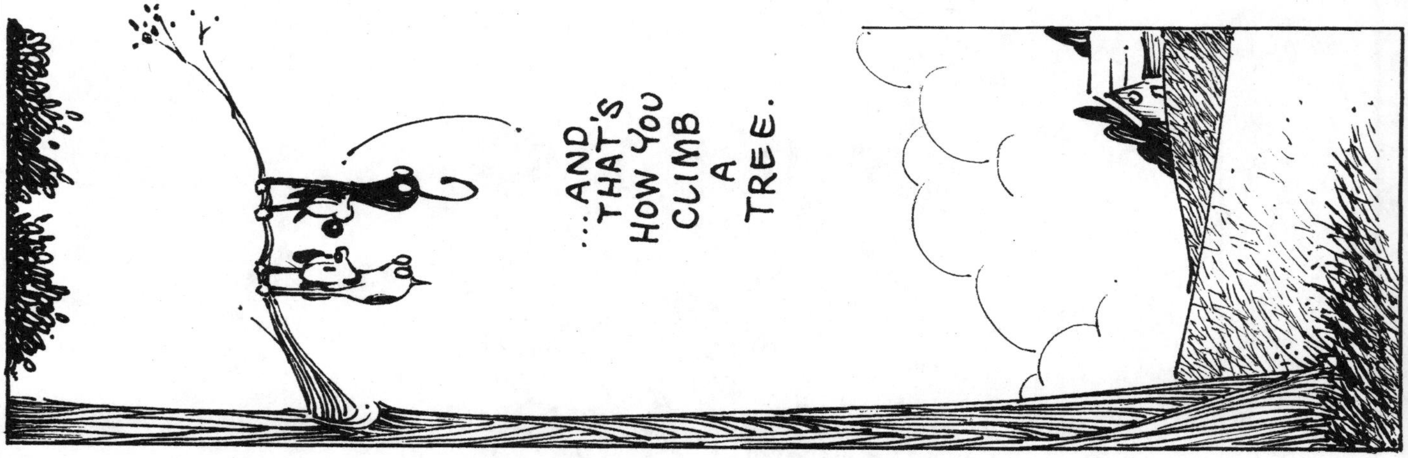
...AND THAT'S HOW YOU CLIMB A TREE.

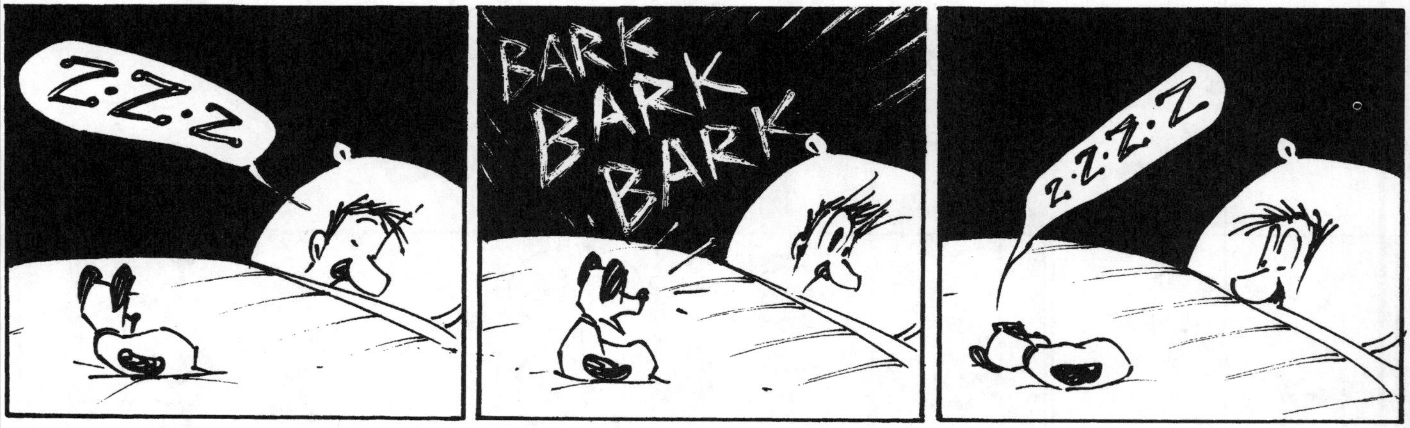
Z-Z-Z
BARK BARK BARK BARK
Z-Z-Z-Z

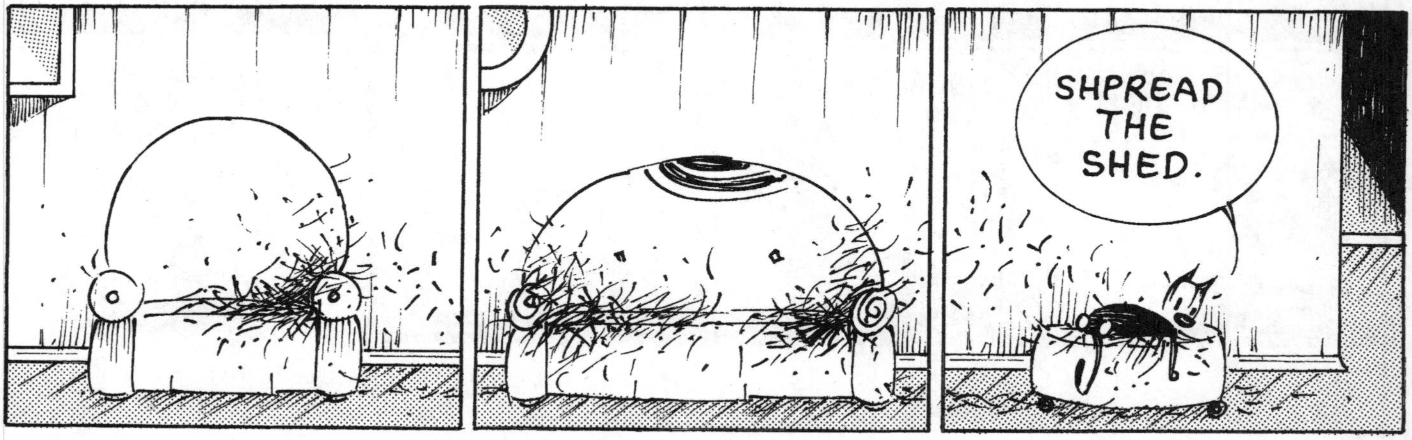
SHPREAD THE SHED.

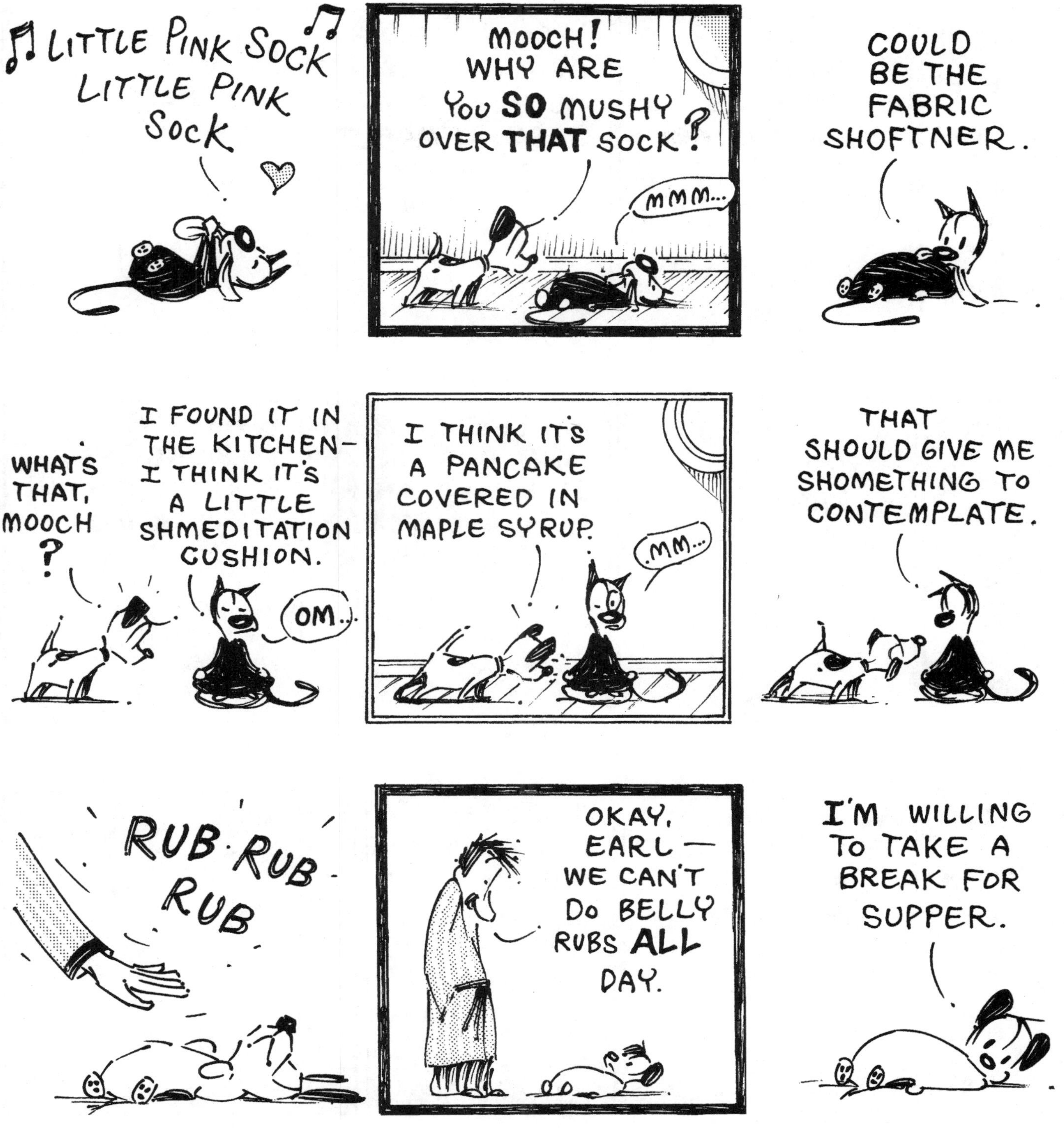
LITTLE PINK SOCK LITTLE PINK SOCK
MOOCH! WHY ARE YOU SO MUSHY OVER THAT SOCK?
MMM...
COULD BE THE FABRIC SHOFTNER.
WHATS THAT, MOOCH?
I FOUND IT IN THE KITCHEN- I THINK IT'S A LITTLE SHMEDITATION CUSHION.
OM...
I THINK ITS A PANCAKE COVERED IN MAPLE SYRUP.
MM...
THAT SHOULD GIVE ME SHOMETHING TO CONTEMPLATE.
RUB RUB RUB
OKAY, EARL— WE CAN'T DO BELLY RUBS ALL DAY.
I'M WILLING TO TAKE A BREAK FOR SUPPER.

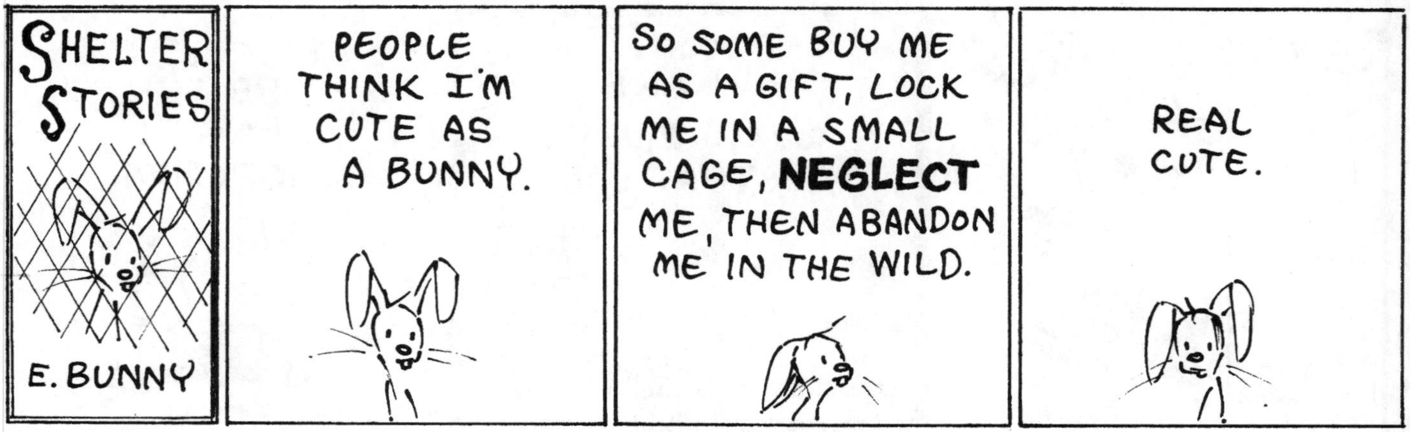
SHELTER STORIES
E. BUNNY
PEOPLE THINK I'M CUTE AS A BUNNY.
SO SOME BUY ME AS A GIFT, LOCK ME IN A SMALL CAGE, NEGLECT ME, THEN ABANDON ME IN THE WILD.
REAL CUTE.

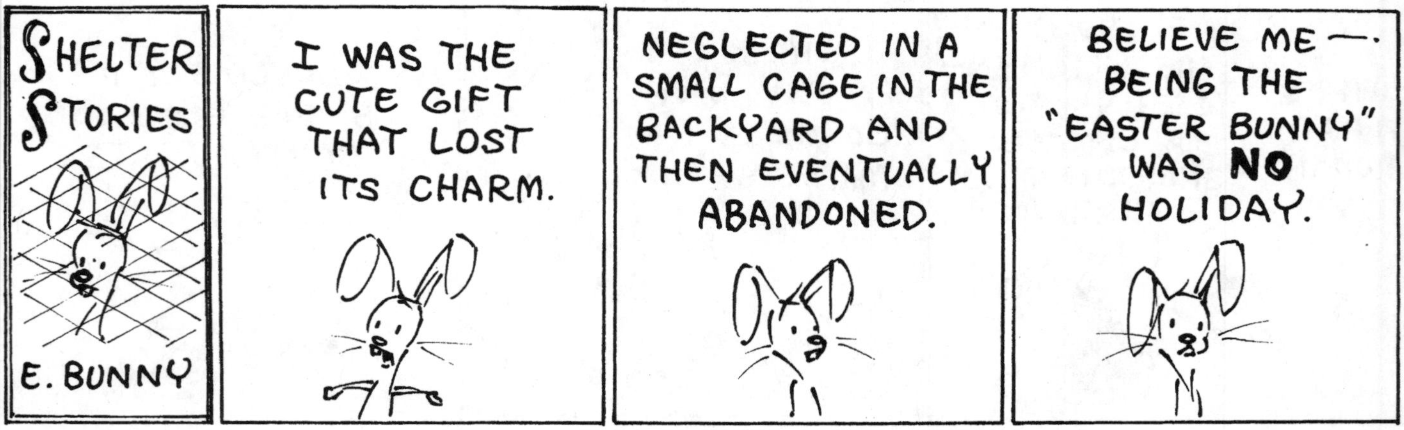
SHELTER STORIES
E. BUNNY
I WAS THE CUTE GIFT THAT LOST ITS CHARM.
NEGLECTED IN A SMALL CAGE IN THE BACKYARD AND THEN EVENTUALLY ABANDONED.
BELIEVE ME— BEING THE "EASTER BUNNY" WAS NO HOLIDAY.

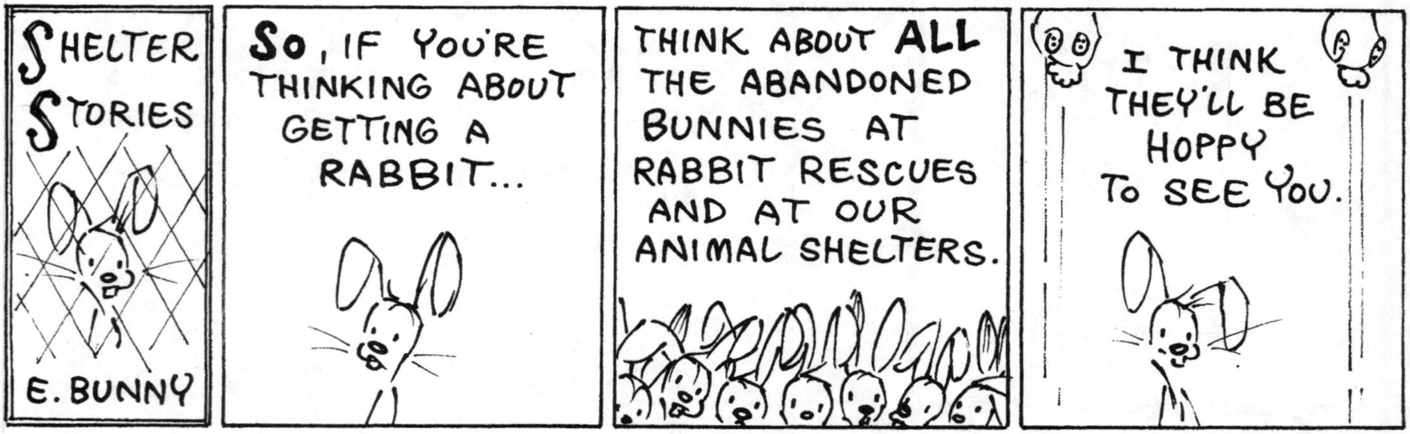
SHELTER STORIES
E. BUNNY
SO, IF YOU'RE THINKING ABOUT GETTING A RABBIT...
THINK ABOUT ALL THE ABANDONED BUNNIES AT RABBIT RESCUES AND AT OUR ANIMAL SHELTERS.
I THINK THEY'LL BE HOPPY TO SEE YOU.

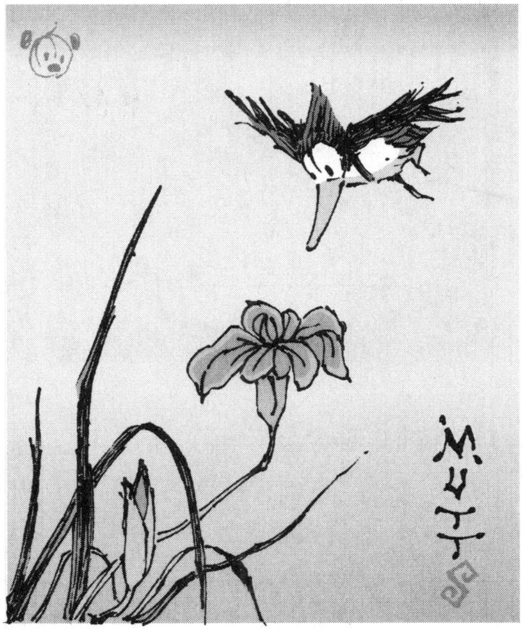
MUTT

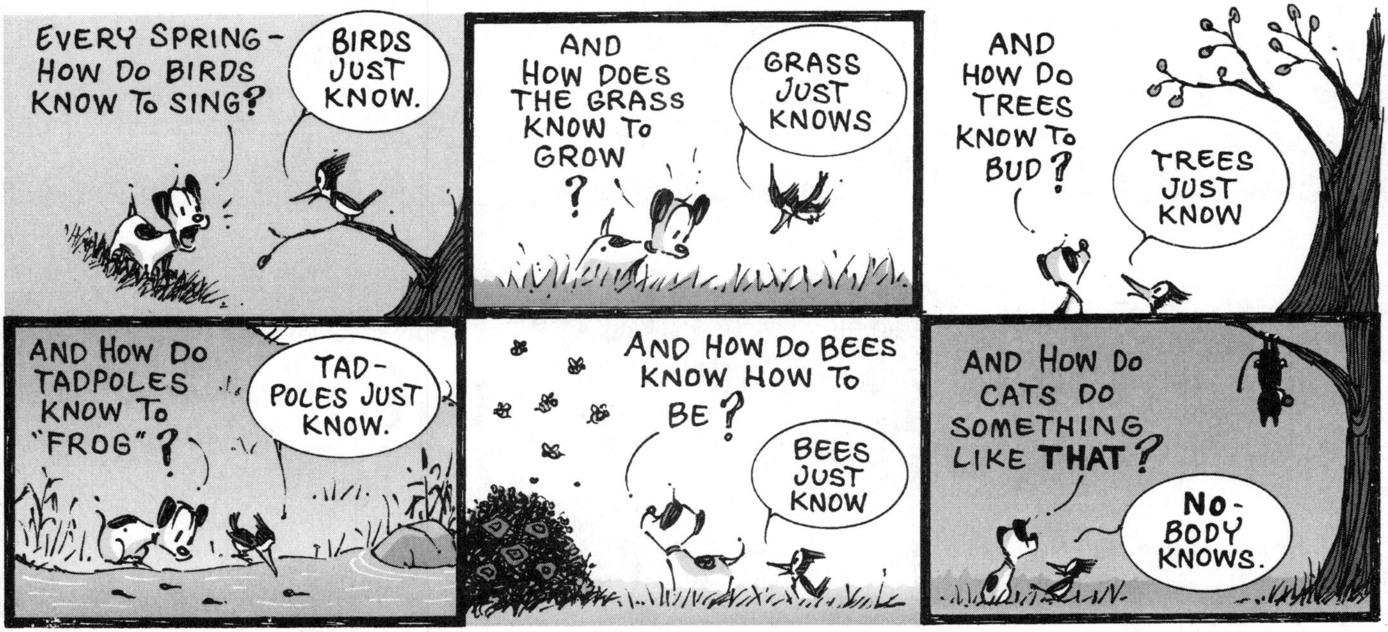
EVERY SPRING - HOW DO BIRDS KNOW TO SING?
BIRDS JUST KNOW.
AND HOW DOES THE GRASS KNOW TO GROW ?
GRASS JUST KNOWS
AND HOW DO TREES KNOW TO BUD?
TREES JUST KNOW
AND HOW DO TADPOLES KNOW TO "FROG"?
TAD-POLES JUST KNOW.
AND HOW DO BEES KNOW HOW TO BE?
BEES JUST KNOW
AND HOW DO CATS DO SOMETHING LIKE THAT?
NO-BODY KNOWS.

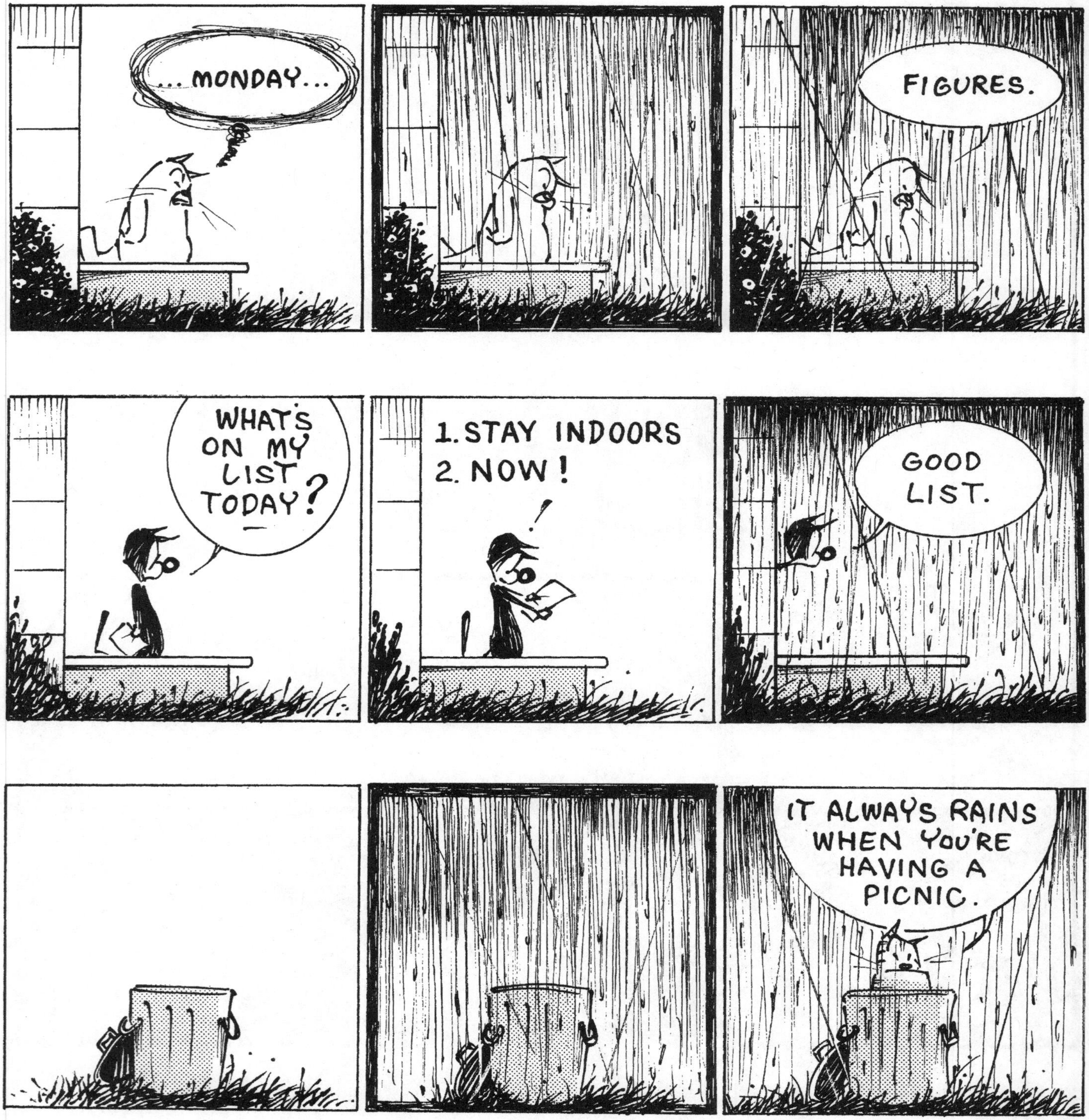
...MONDAY...
FIGURES.
WHAT'S ON MY LIST TODAY?
1. STAY INDOORS
2. NOW!
GOOD LIST.
IT ALWAYS RAINS WHEN YOU'RE HAVING A PICNIC.

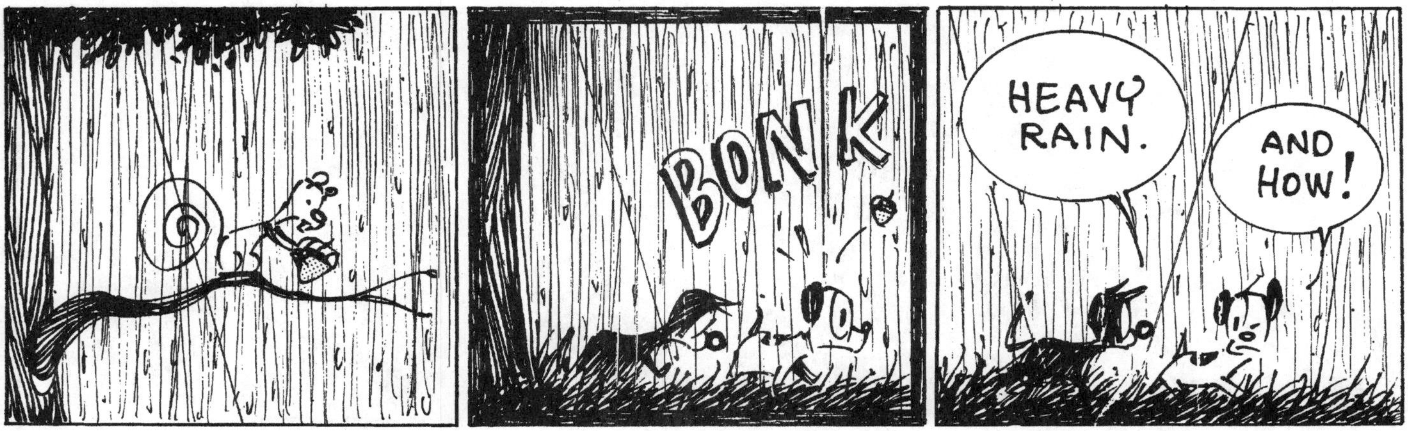
BONK
HEAVY RAIN.
AND HOW!

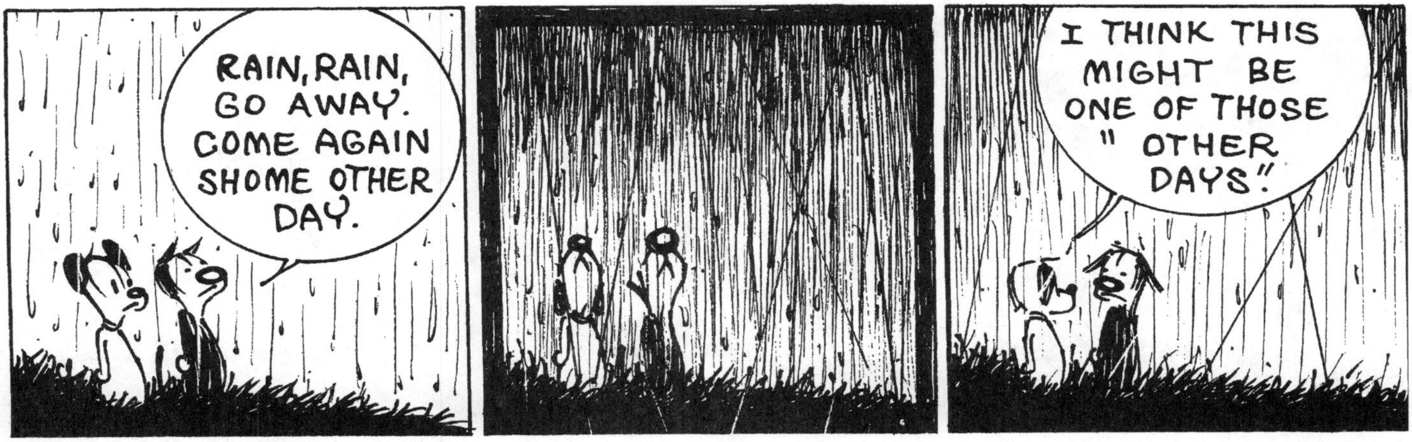
RAIN, RAIN, GO AWAY. COME AGAIN SHOME OTHER DAY.
I THINK THIS MIGHT BE ONE OF THOSE " OTHER DAYS."

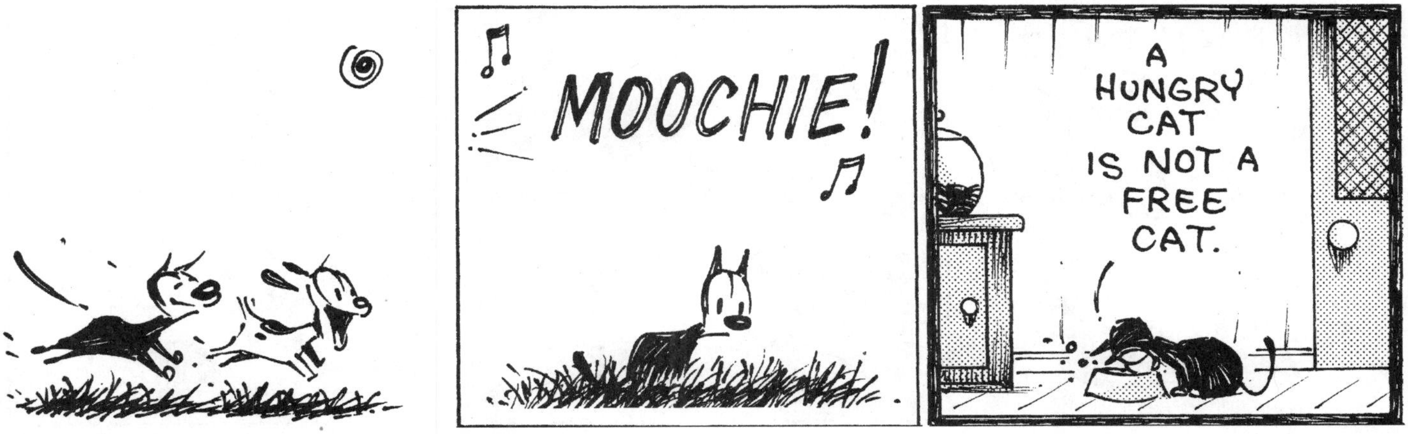
MOOCHIE!
A HUNGRY CAT IS NOT A FREE CAT.

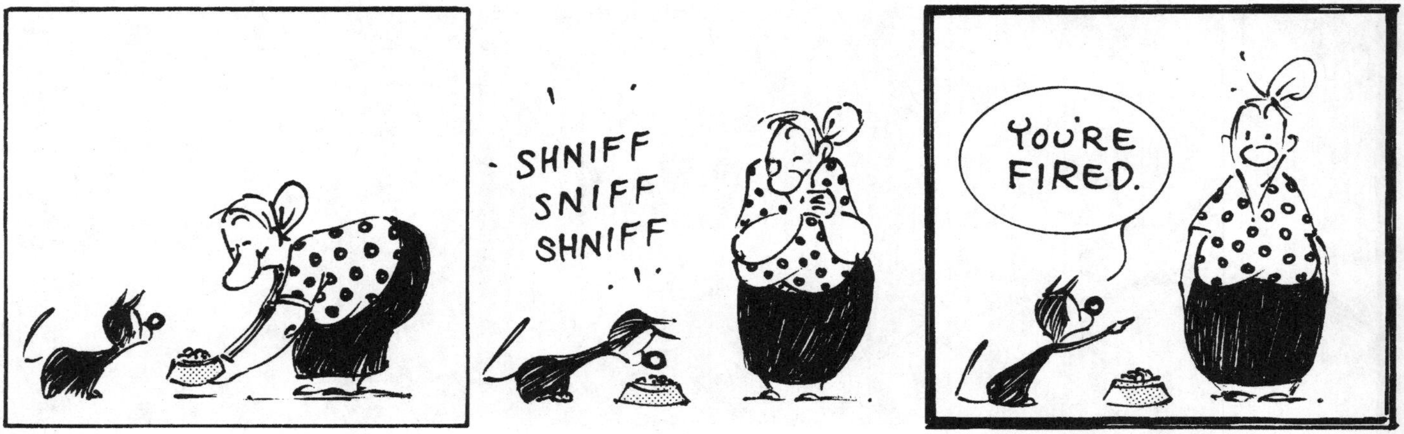
SHNIFF
SNIFF
SHNIFF
YOU'RE FIRED.

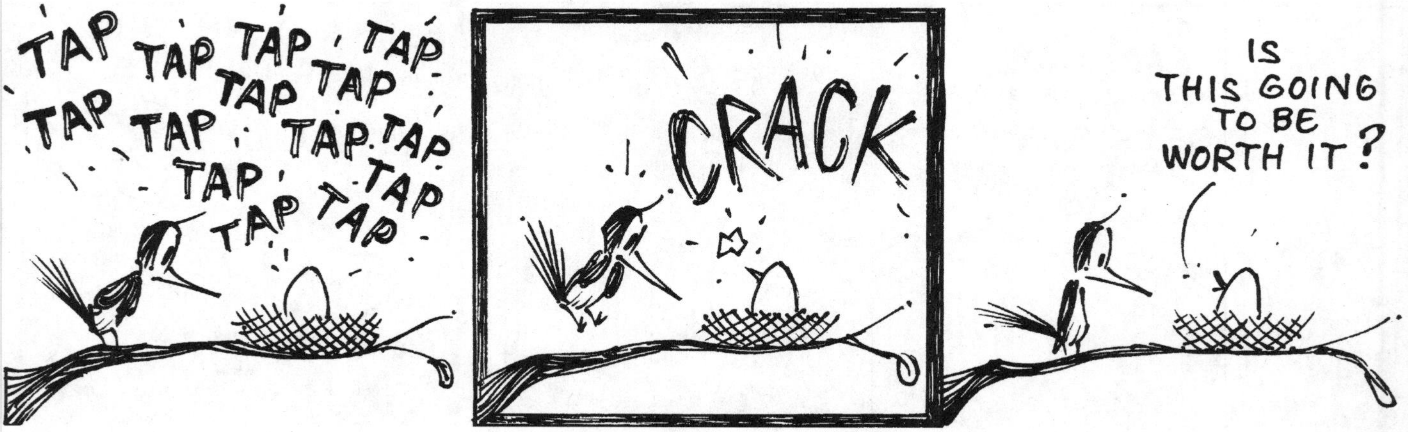
TAP TAP TAP TAP TAP TAP TAP TAP TAP TAP TAP TAP TAP TAP
CRACK
IS THIS GOING TO BE WORTH IT?

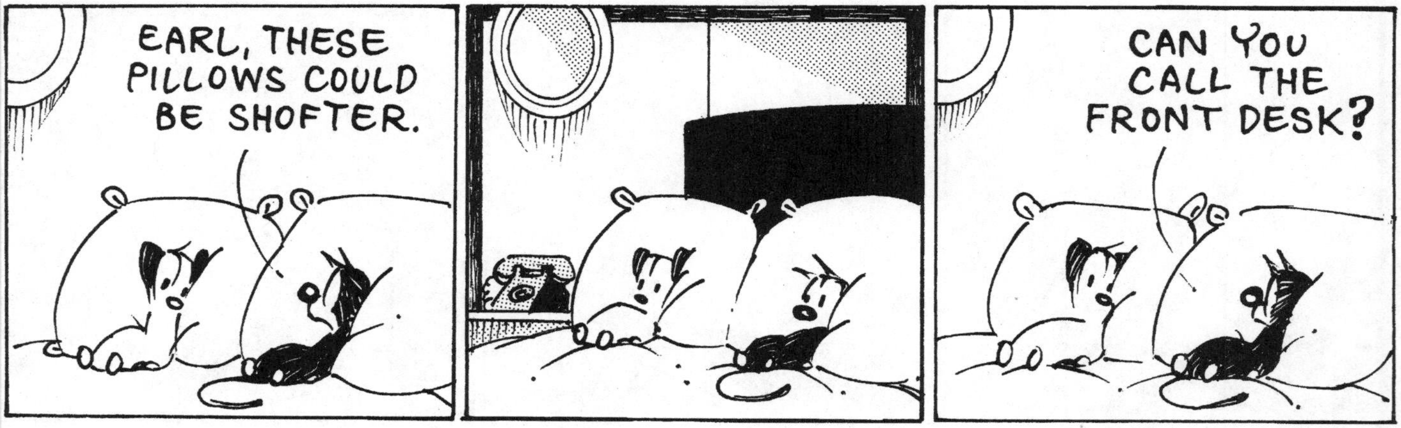
EARL, THESE PILLOWS COULD BE SHOFTER.
CAN YOU CALL THE FRONT DESK?

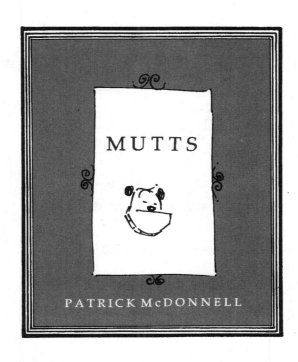

MUTTS
PATRICK McDONNELL

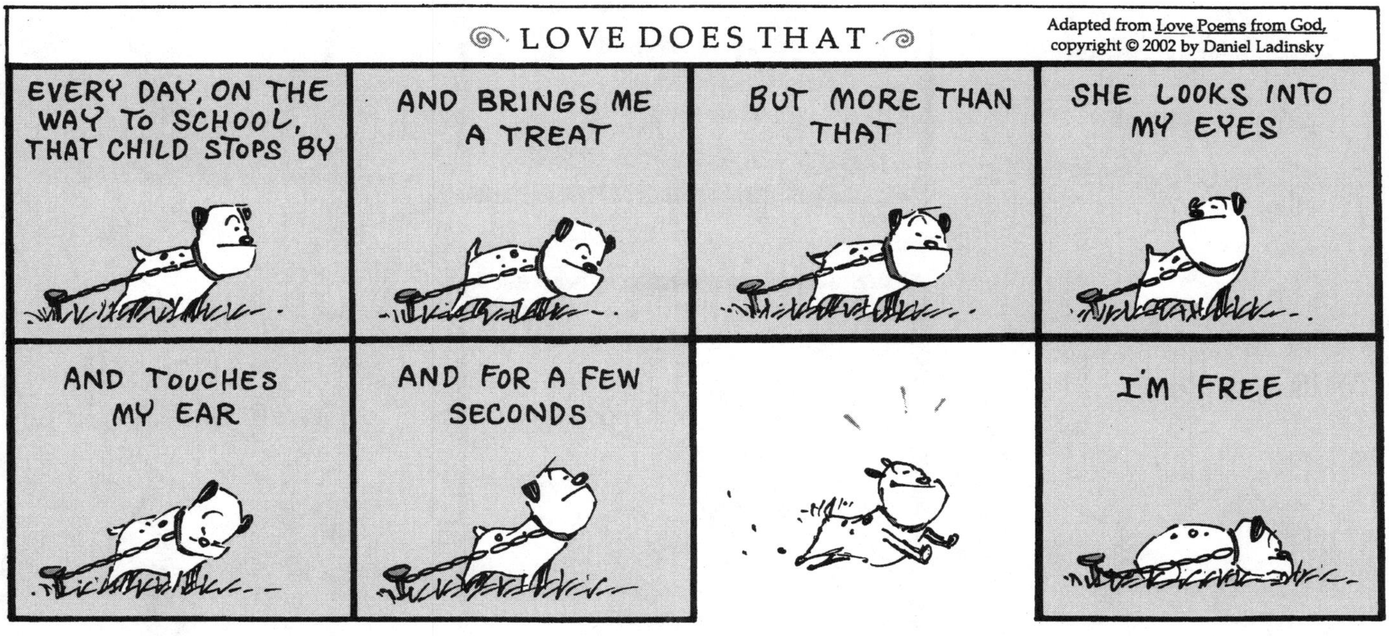

LOVE DOES THAT
Adapted from Love Poems from God, copyright © 2002 by Daniel Ladinsky
EVERY DAY, ON THE WAY TO SCHOOL, THAT CHILD STOPS BY
AND BRINGS ME A TREAT
BUT MORE THAN THAT
SHE LOOKS INTO MY EYES
AND TOUCHES MY EAR
AND FOR A FEW SECONDS
I'M FREE

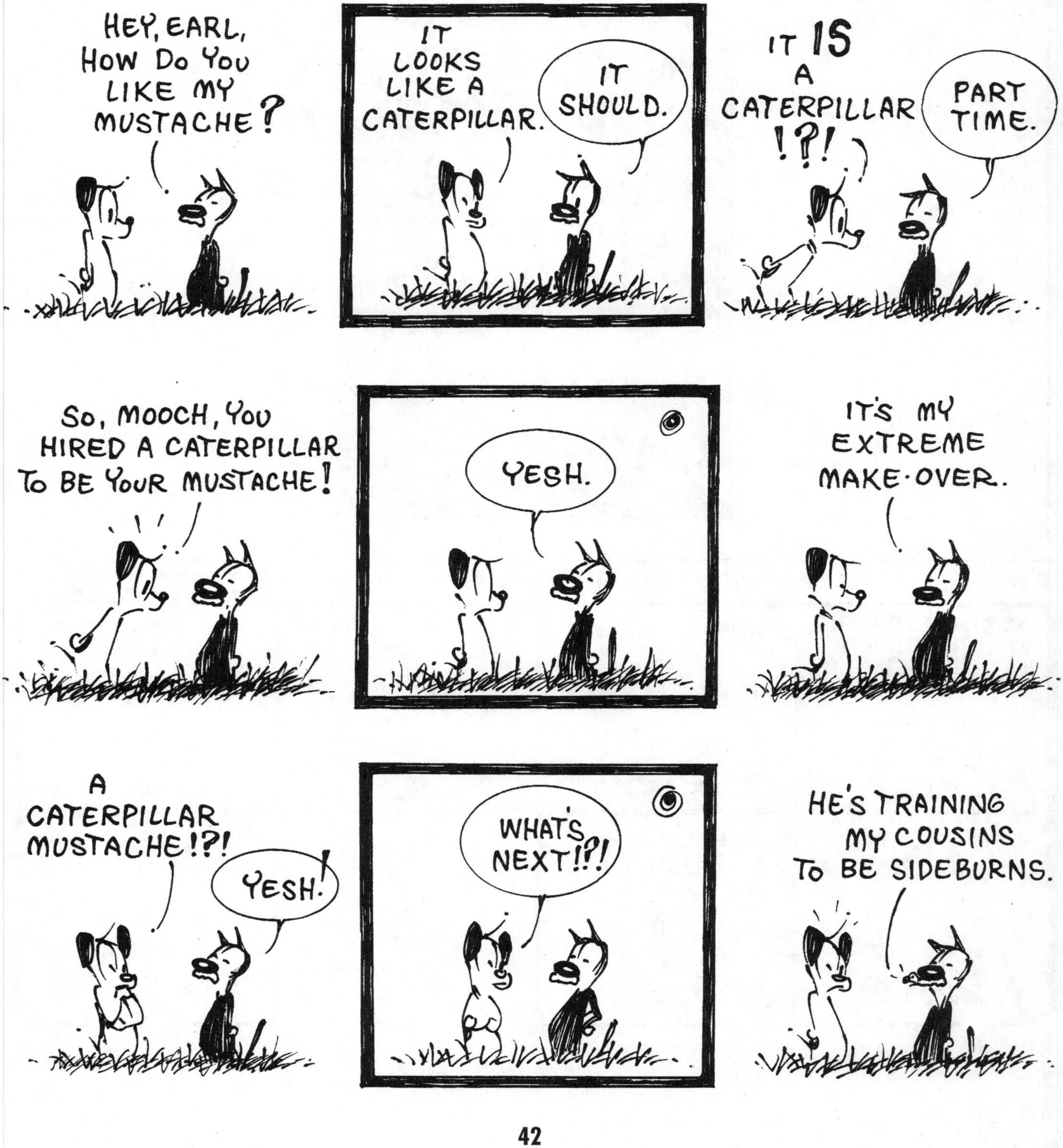
HEY, EARL, HOW DO YOU LIKE MY MUSTACHE?
IT LOOKS LIKE A CATERPILLAR.
IT SHOULD.
IT IS A CATERPILLAR !?!
PART TIME.
SO, MOOCH, YOU HIRED A CATERPILLAR TO BE YOUR MUSTACHE!
YESH.
IT'S MY EXTREME MAKE-OVER.
A CATERPILLAR MUSTACHE!?!
YESH!
WHAT'S NEXT!?!
HE'S TRAINING MY COUSINS TO BE SIDEBURNS.

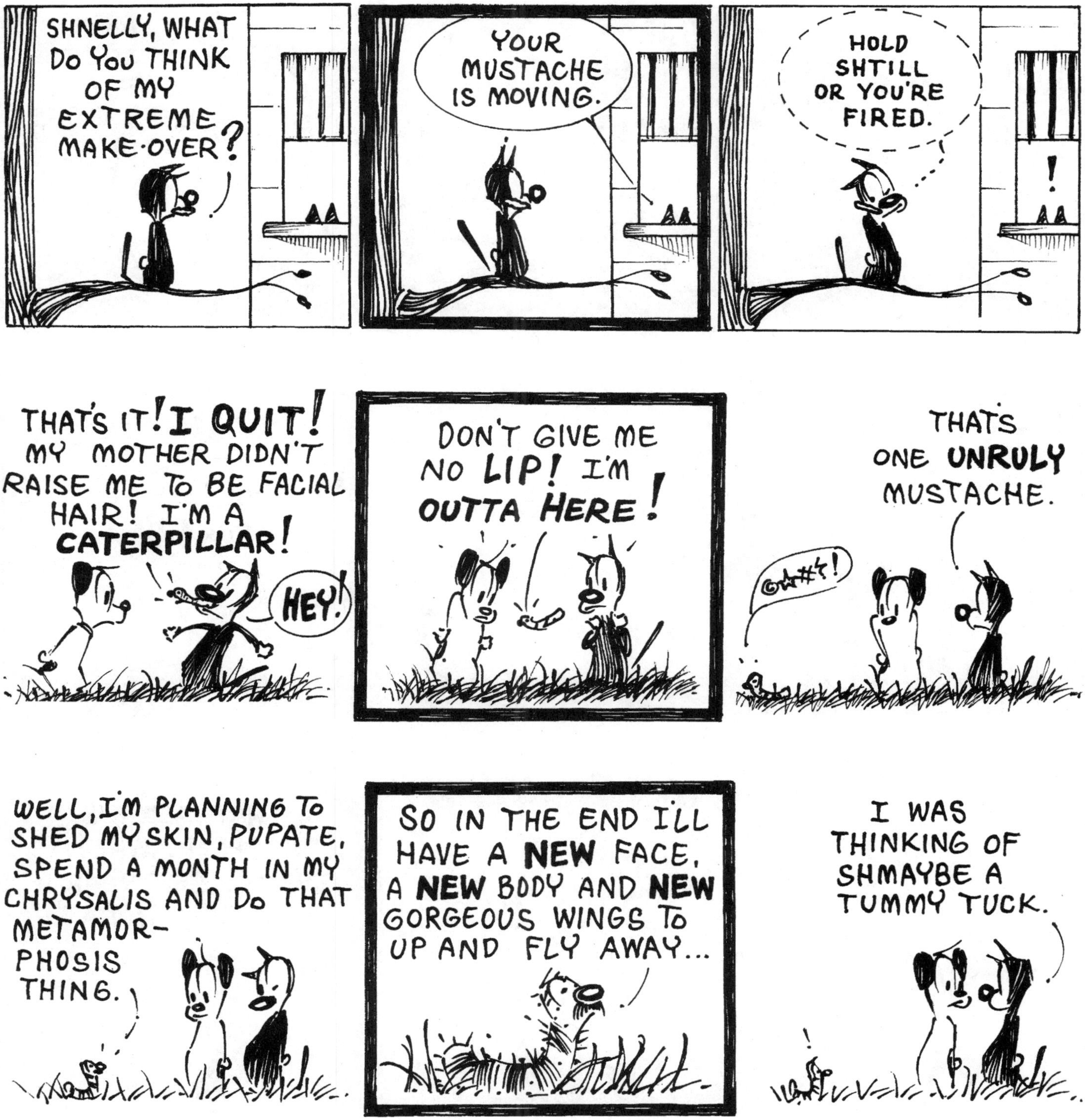
SHNELLY, WHAT DO YOU THINK OF MY EXTREME MAKE-OVER?
YOUR MUSTACHE IS MOVING.
HOLD SHTILL OR YOU'RE FIRED.
!
THAT'S IT! I QUIT! MY MOTHER DIDN'T RAISE ME TO BE FACIAL HAIR! I'M A CATERPILLAR!
HEY!
DON'T GIVE ME NO LIP! I'M OUTTA HERE!
THAT'S ONE UNRULY MUSTACHE.
WELL, I'M PLANNING TO SHED MY SKIN, PUPATE, SPEND A MONTH IN MY CHRYSALIS AND DO THAT METAMOR-PHOSIS THING.
SO IN THE END I'LL HAVE A NEW FACE, A NEW BODY AND NEW GORGEOUS WINGS TO UP AND FLY AWAY...
I WAS THINKING OF SHMAYBE A TUMMY TUCK.
!

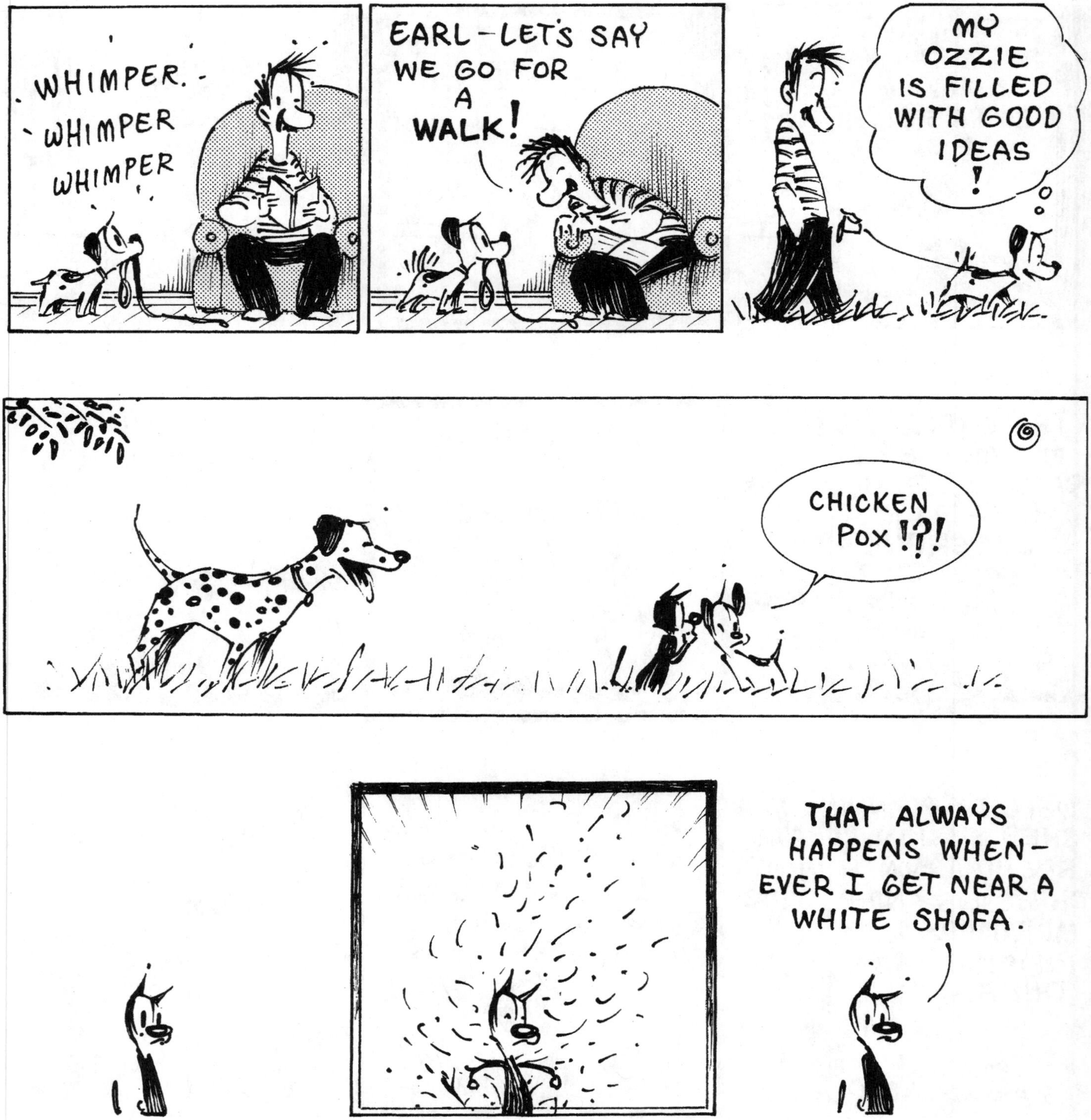
WHIMPER. WHIMPER WHIMPER
EARL - LET'S SAY WE GO FOR A WALK!
MY OZZIE IS FILLED WITH GOOD IDEAS!
CHICKEN POX!?!
THAT ALWAYS HAPPENS WHENEVER I GET NEAR A WHITE SHOFA.

MUTTS
McDONNELL

!
?
ARF!
ARF!
ARF!
ONLY A DOG CAN GET HOMESICK IN HIS OWN BACKYARD.

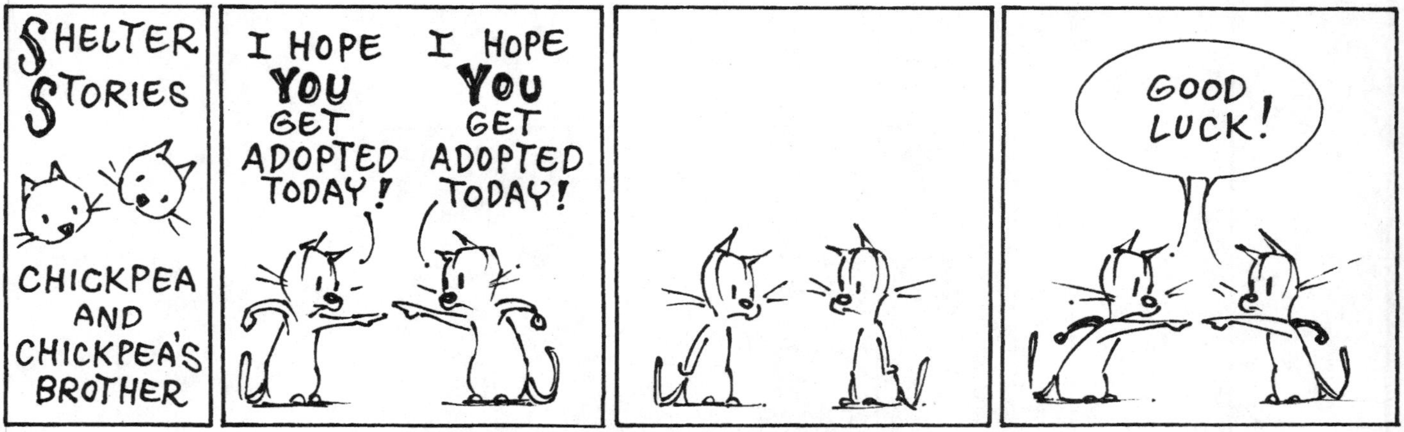
SHELTER STORIES
CHICKPEA AND CHICKPEA'S BROTHER
I HOPE YOU GET ADOPTED TODAY!
I HOPE YOU GET ADOPTED TODAY!
GOOD LUCK!

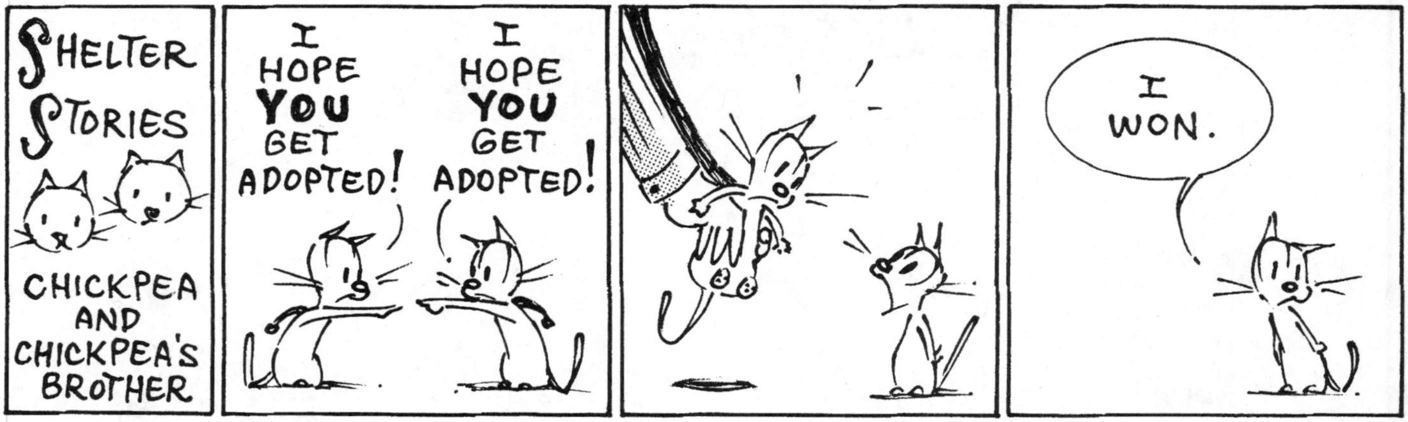
SHELTER STORIES
CHICKPEA AND CHICKPEA'S BROTHER
I HOPE YOU GET ADOPTED!
I HOPE YOU GET ADOPTED!
I WON.

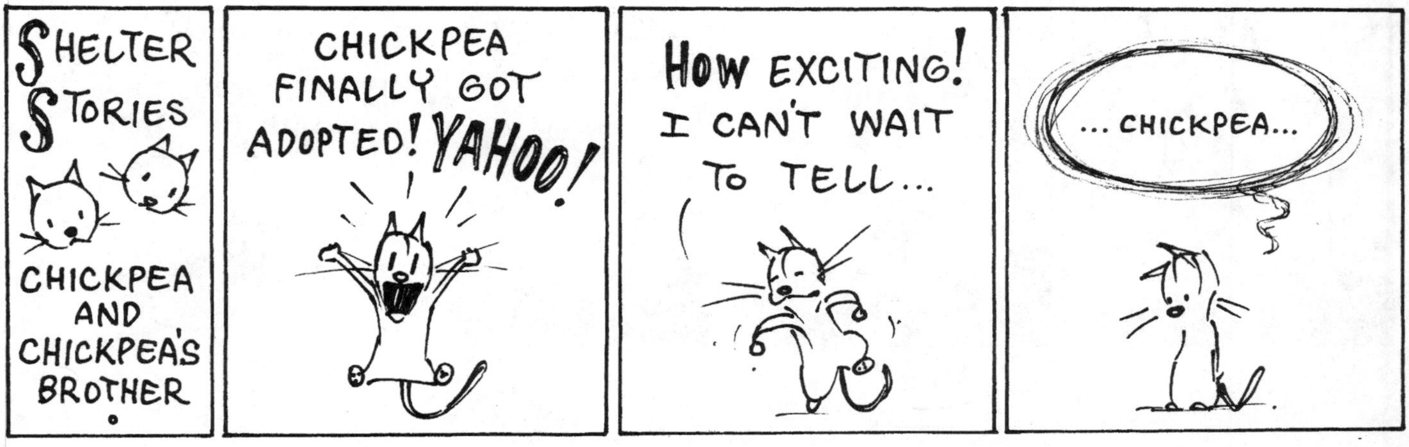
SHELTER STORIES
CHICKPEA AND CHICKPEA'S BROTHER
CHICKPEA FINALLY GOT ADOPTED! YAHOO!
HOW EXCITING! I CAN'T WAIT TO TELL...
... CHICKPEA...

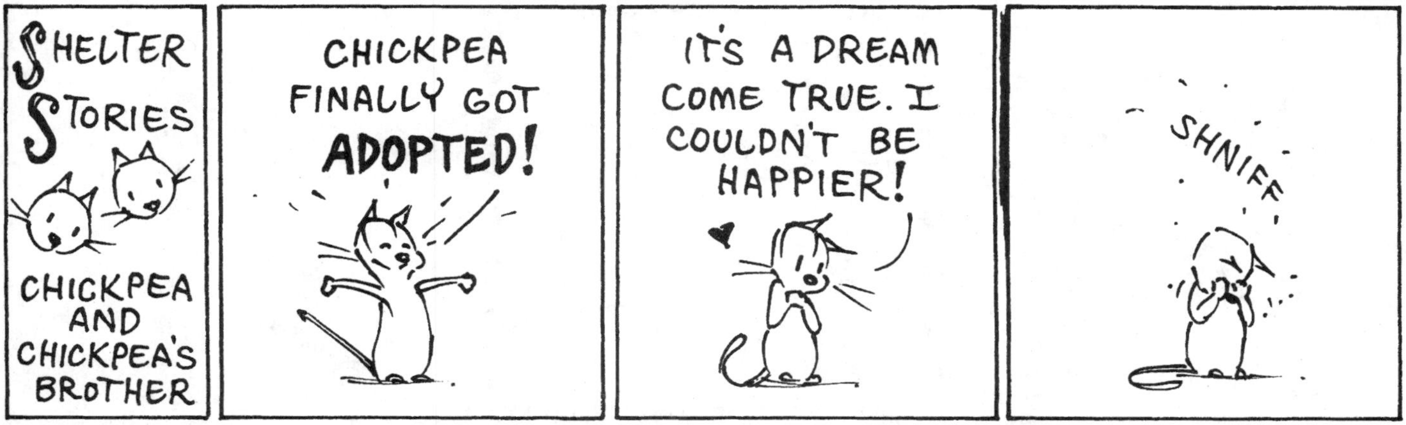
SHELTER STORIES
CHICKPEA AND CHICKPEA'S BROTHER
CHICKPEA FINALLY GOT ADOPTED!
IT'S A DREAM COME TRUE. I COULDN'T BE HAPPIER!
SHNIFF

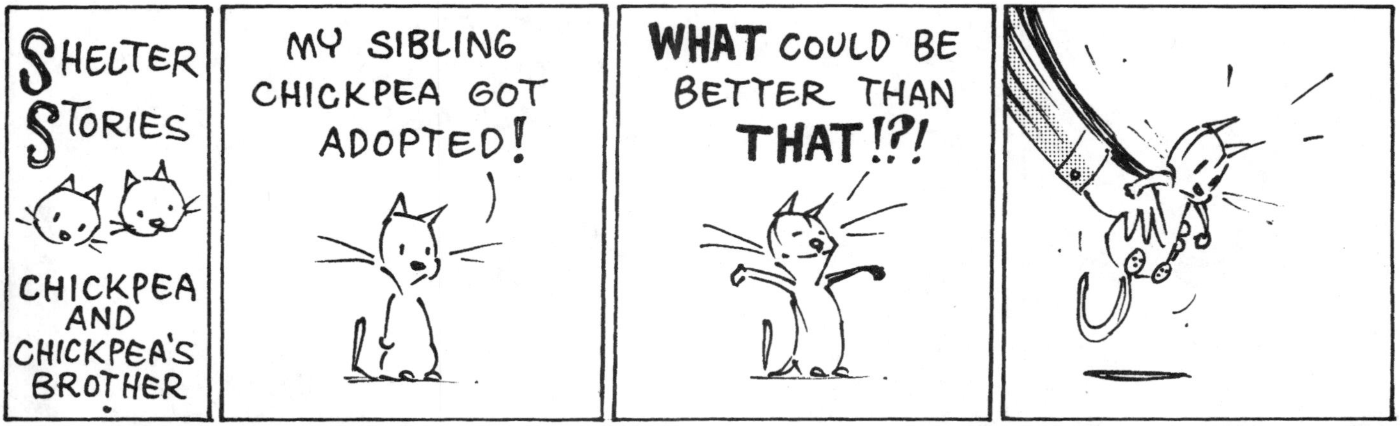
SHELTER STORIES
CHICKPEA AND CHICKPEA'S BROTHER
MY SIBLING CHICKPEA GOT ADOPTED!
WHAT COULD BE BETTER THAN THAT!?!

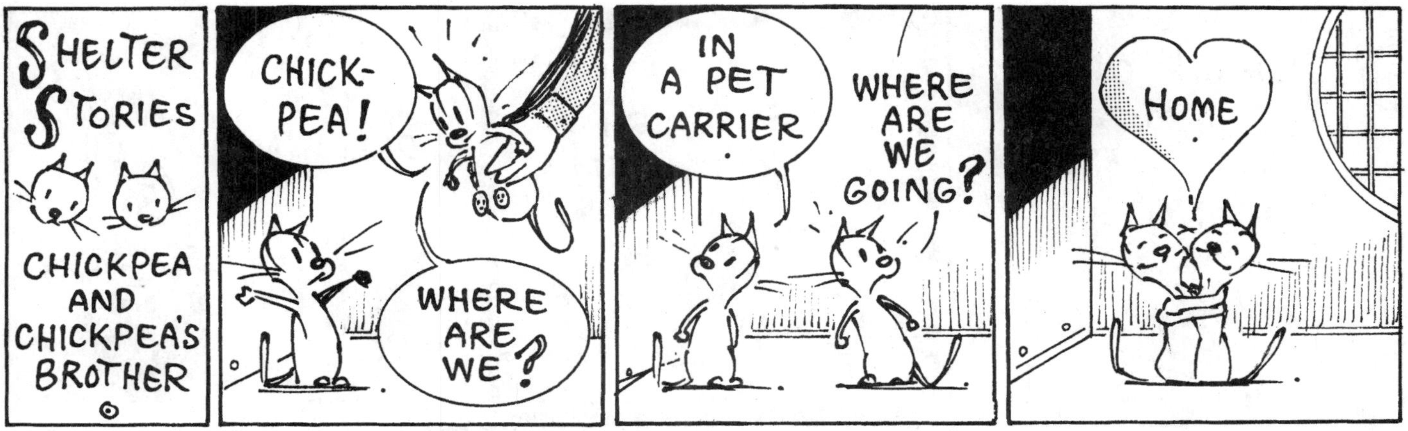
SHELTER STORIES
CHICKPEA AND CHICKPEA'S BROTHER
CHICK-PEA!
WHERE ARE WE?
IN A PET CARRIER
WHERE ARE WE GOING?
HOME

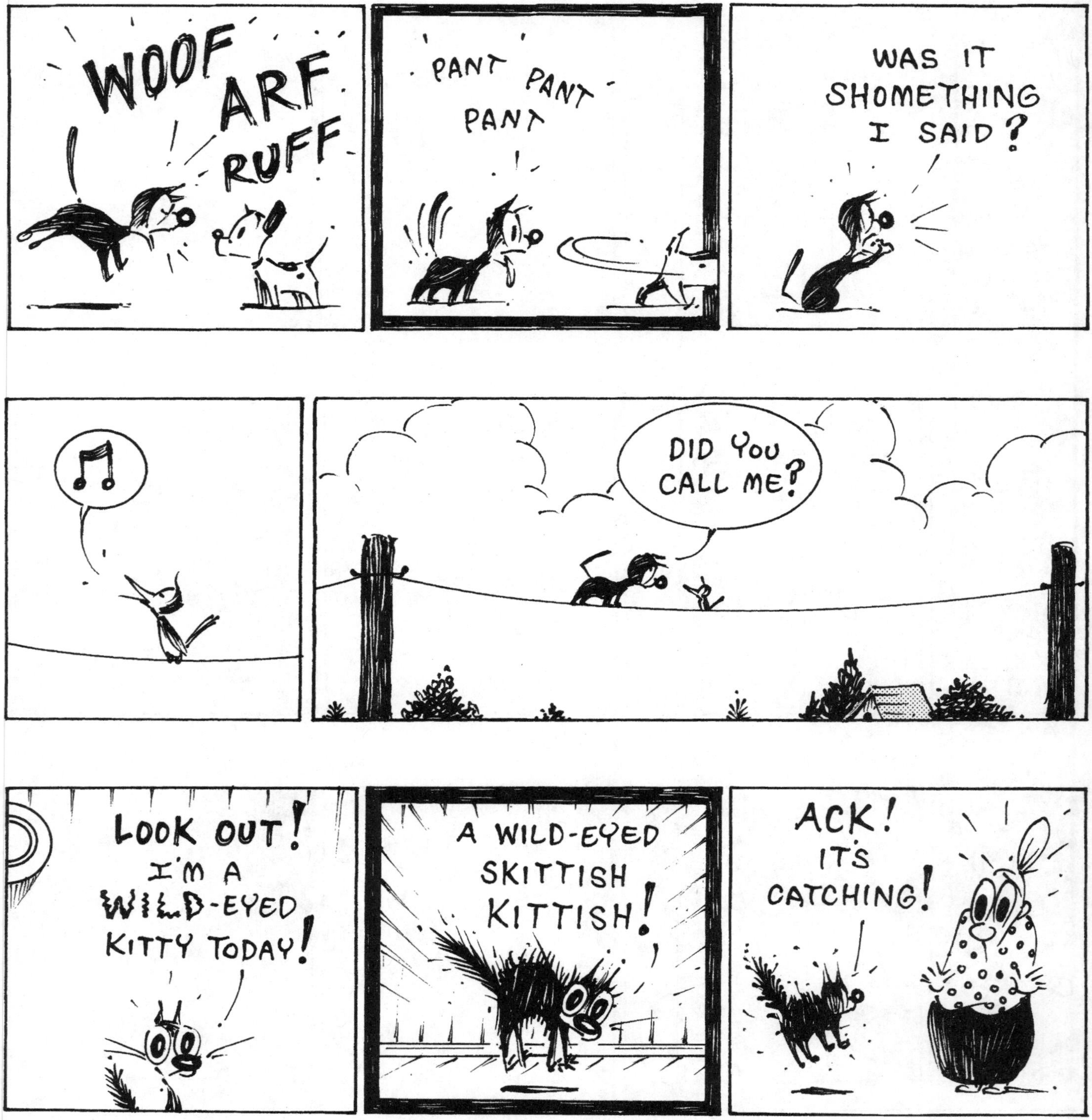
WOOF
ARF
RUFF
PANT PANT
PANT
WAS IT SHOMETHING I SAID?
DID YOU CALL ME?
LOOK OUT! I'M A WILD-EYED KITTY TODAY!
A WILD-EYED SKITTISH KITTISH!
ACK! IT'S CATCHING!

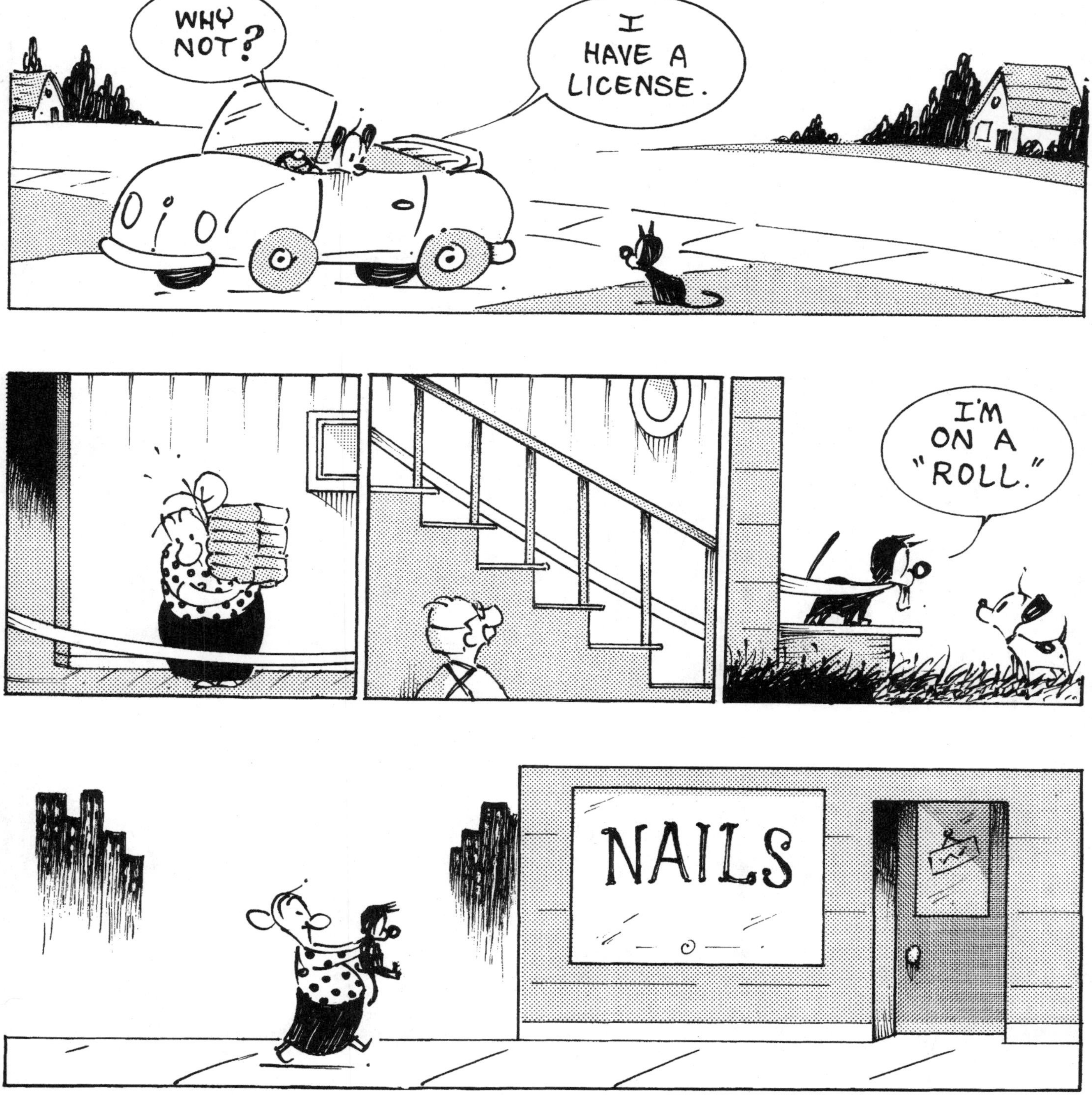
WHY NOT?
I HAVE A LICENSE.
I'M ON A "ROLL."
NAILS

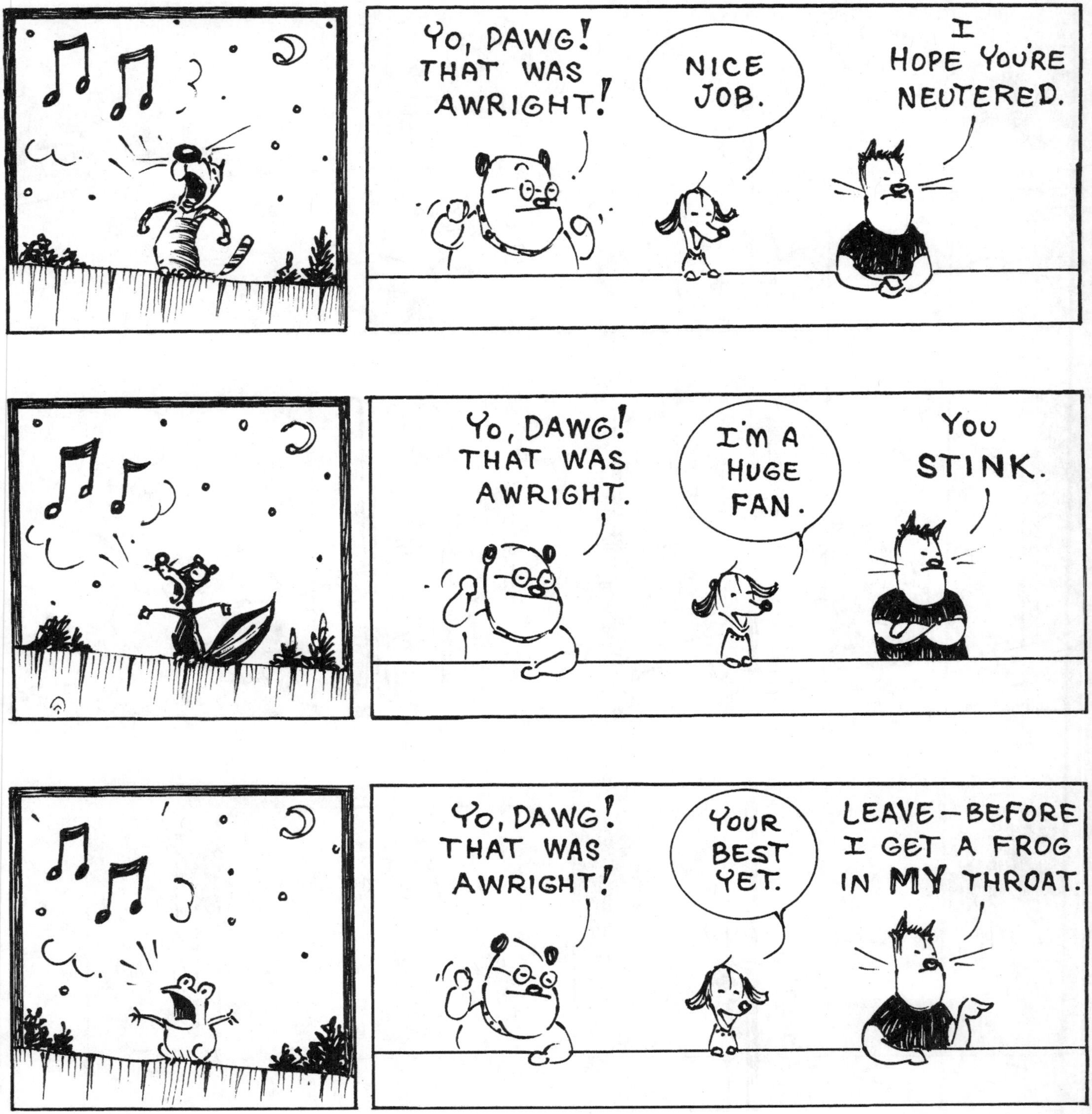
YO, DAWG! THAT WAS AWRIGHT!
NICE JOB.
I HOPE YOU'RE NEUTERED.
YO, DAWG! THAT WAS AWRIGHT.
I'M A HUGE FAN.
YOU STINK.
YO, DAWG! THAT WAS AWRIGHT!
YOUR BEST YET.
LEAVE—BEFORE I GET A FROG IN MY THROAT.

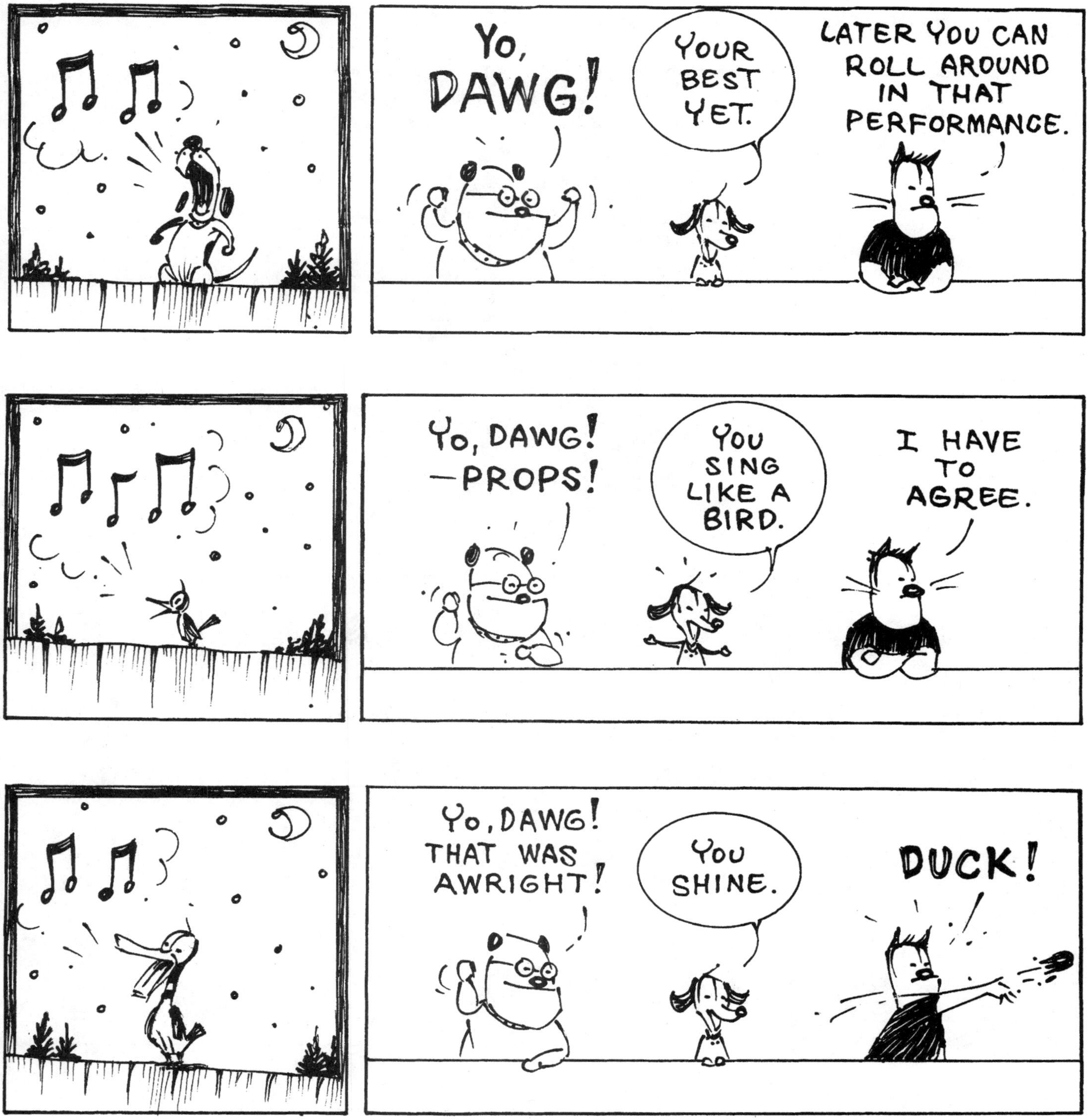
YO, DAWG!
YOUR BEST YET.
LATER YOU CAN ROLL AROUND IN THAT PERFORMANCE.
YO, DAWG! —PROPS!
YOU SING LIKE A BIRD.
I HAVE TO AGREE.
YO, DAWG! THAT WAS AWRIGHT!
YOU SHINE.
DUCK!

MUTTS
McD.
OH, MIGHTY SHPHINX- WHY DID THE CHICKEN CROSS THE ROAD?
SHTAY RIGHT THERE!
NONE OF YOUR BUSINESSH.

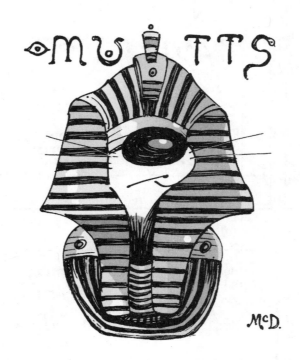

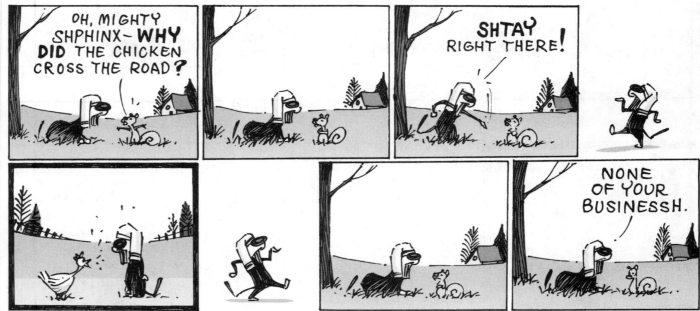

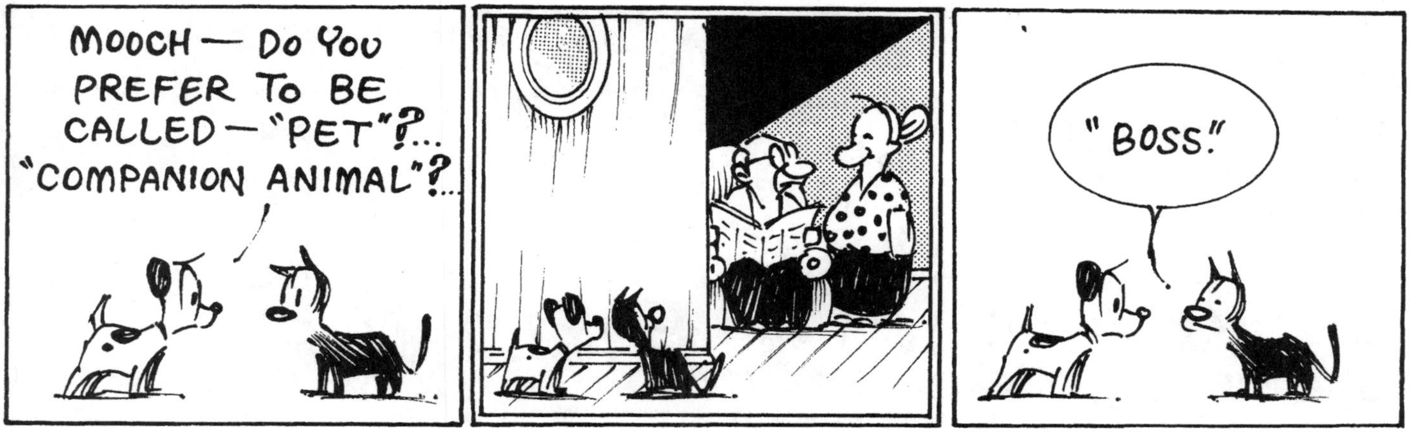
MOOCH — DO YOU PREFER TO BE CALLED — "PET"?... "COMPANION ANIMAL"?...
"BOSS."

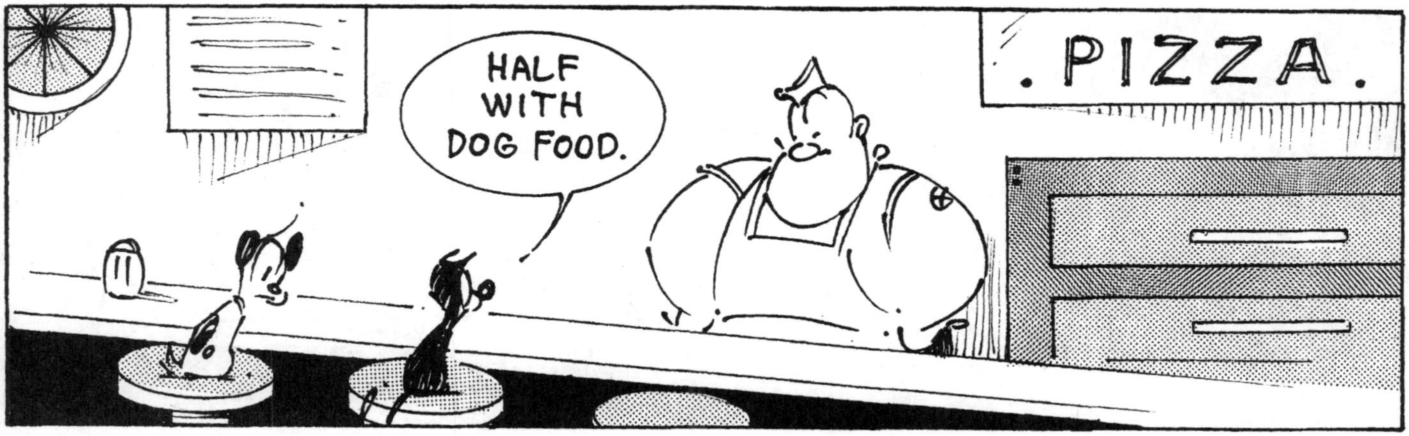
. PIZZA .
HALF WITH DOG FOOD.

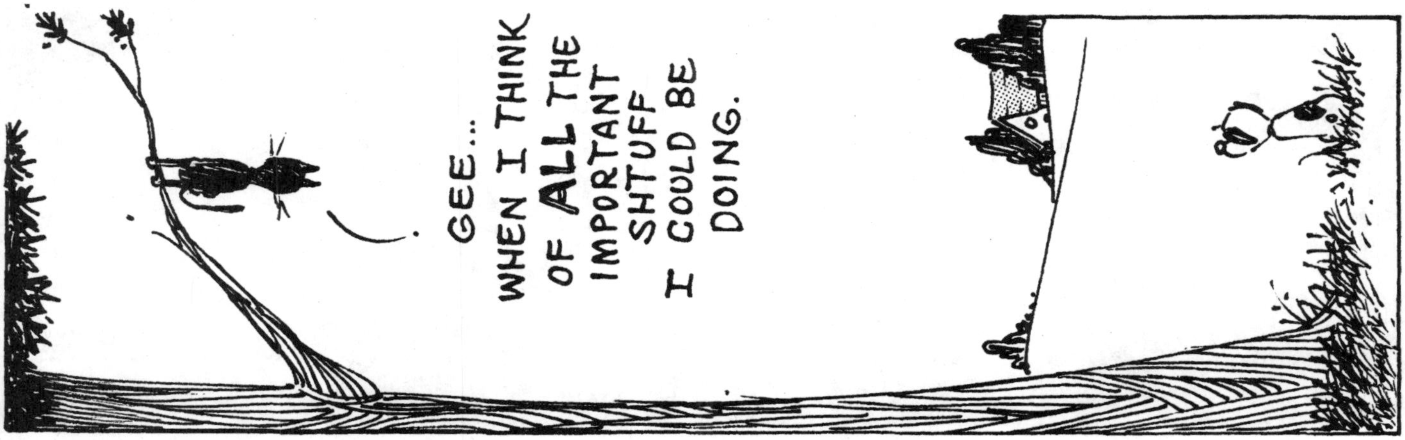
GEE... WHEN I THINK OF ALL THE IMPORTANT SHTUFF I COULD BE DOING.

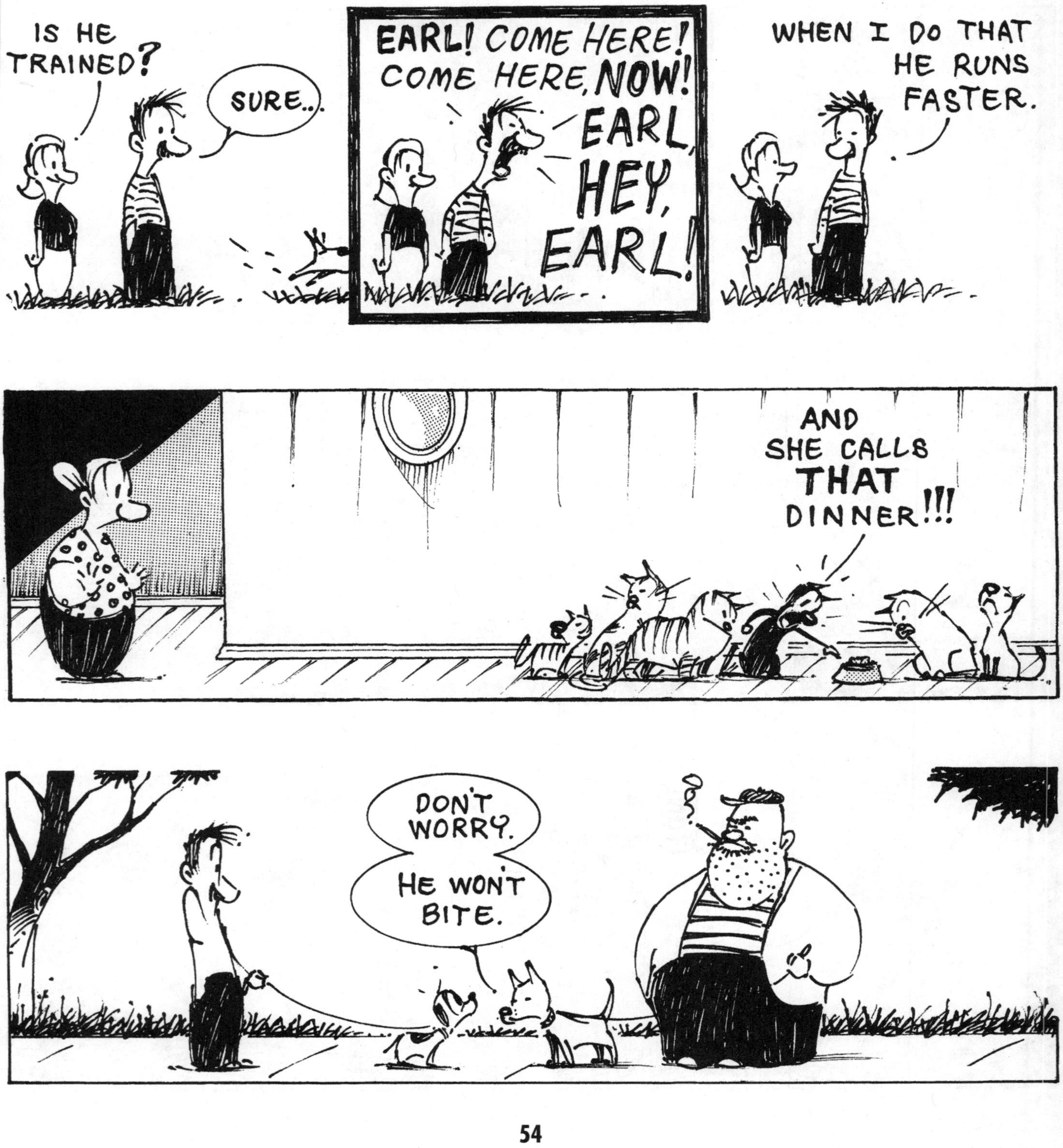
IS HE TRAINED?
SURE...
EARL! COME HERE! COME HERE, NOW! EARL, HEY, EARL!
WHEN I DO THAT HE RUNS FASTER.
AND SHE CALLS THAT DINNER!!!
DON'T WORRY.
HE WON'T BITE.

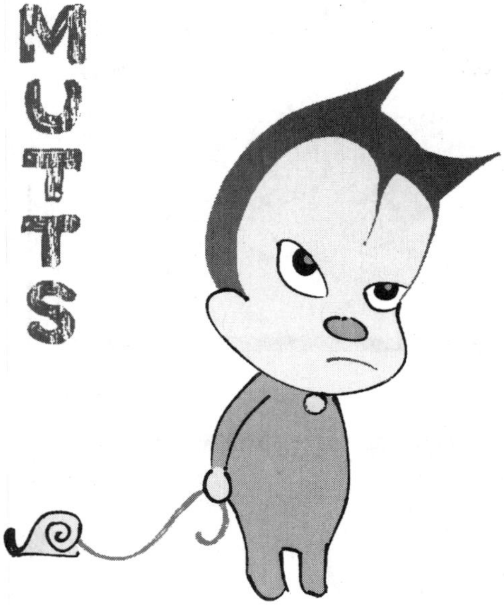
MUTTS

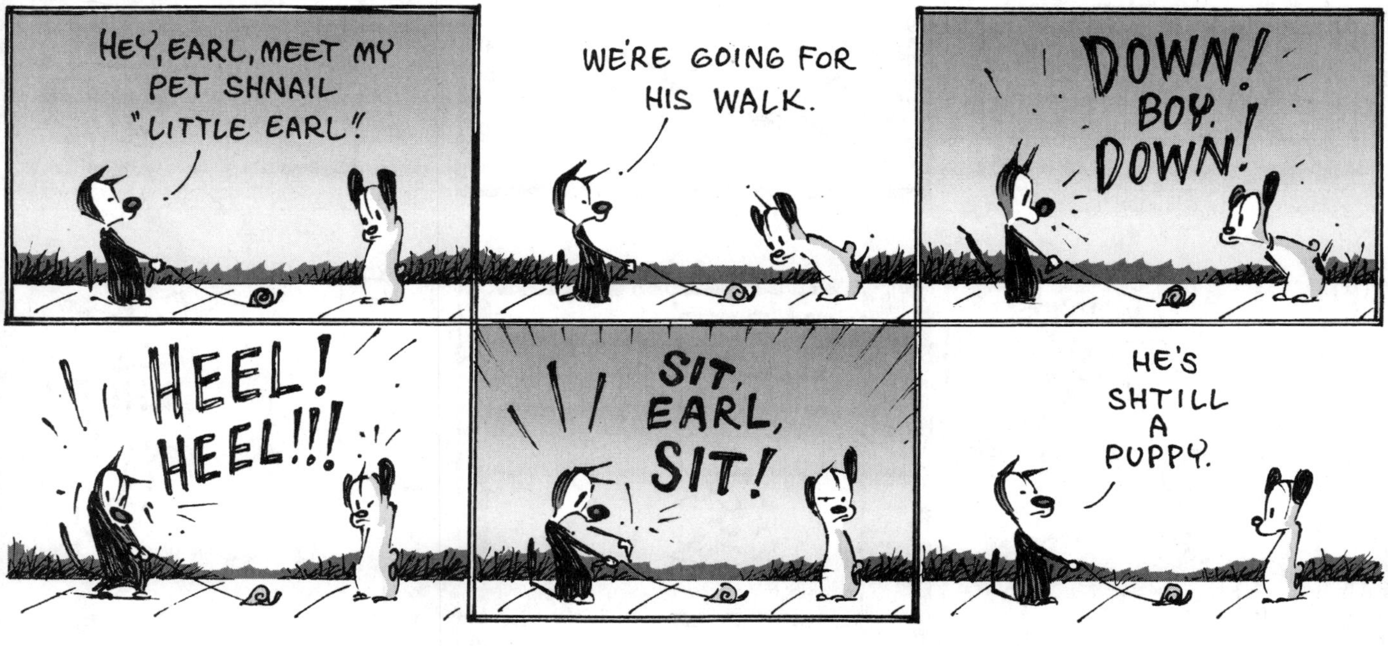
HEY, EARL, MEET MY PET SHNAIL "LITTLE EARL."
WE'RE GOING FOR HIS WALK.
DOWN! BOY. DOWN!
HEEL! HEEL!!!
SIT, EARL, SIT!
HE'S SHTILL A PUPPY.

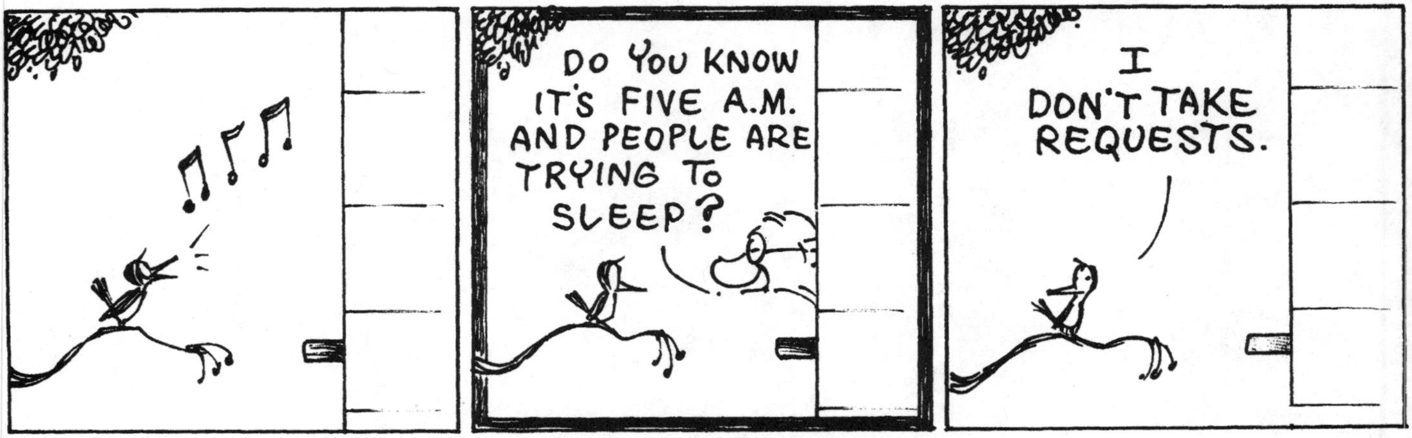
DO YOU KNOW IT'S FIVE A.M. AND PEOPLE ARE TRYING TO SLEEP?
I DON'T TAKE REQUESTS.

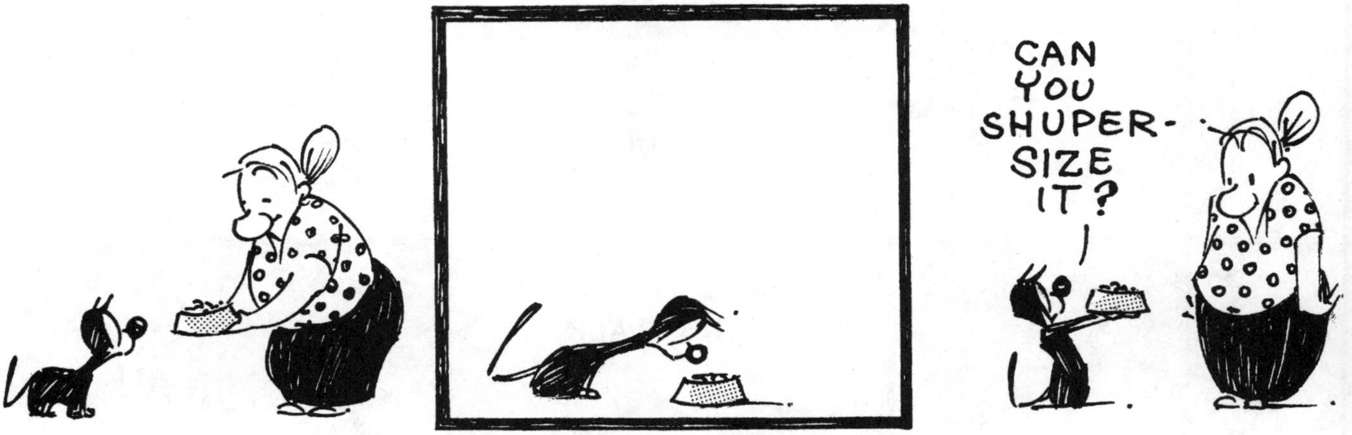
CAN YOU SHUPER-SIZE IT?

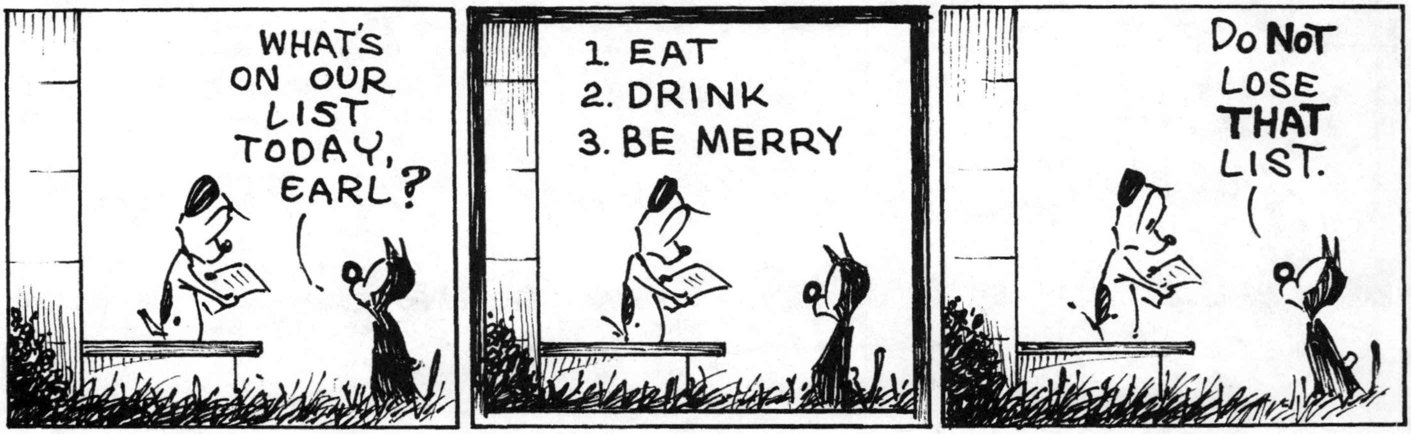
WHAT'S ON OUR LIST TODAY, EARL?
1. EAT
2. DRINK
3. BE MERRY
DO **NOT** LOSE **THAT** LIST.

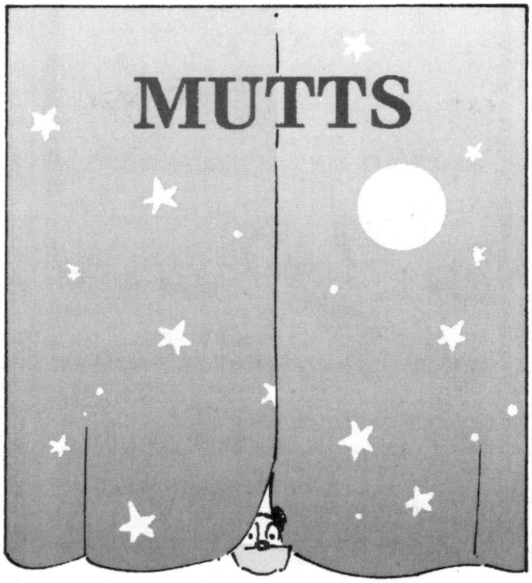
MUTTS

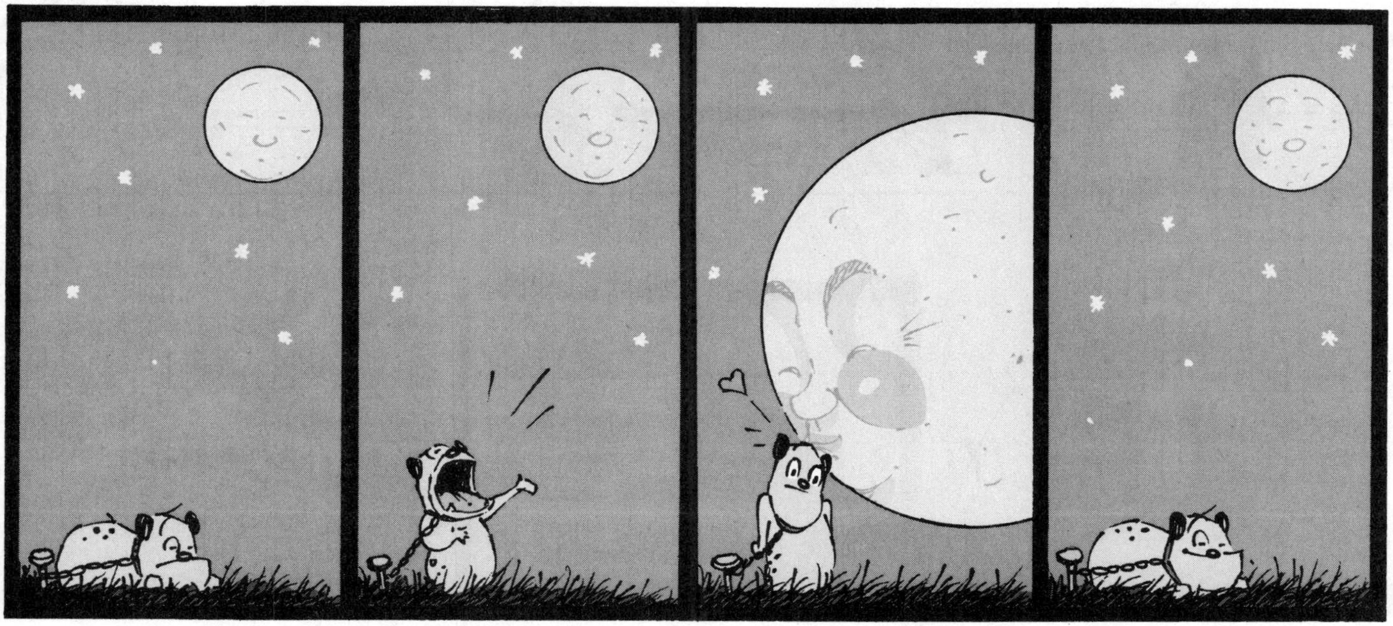

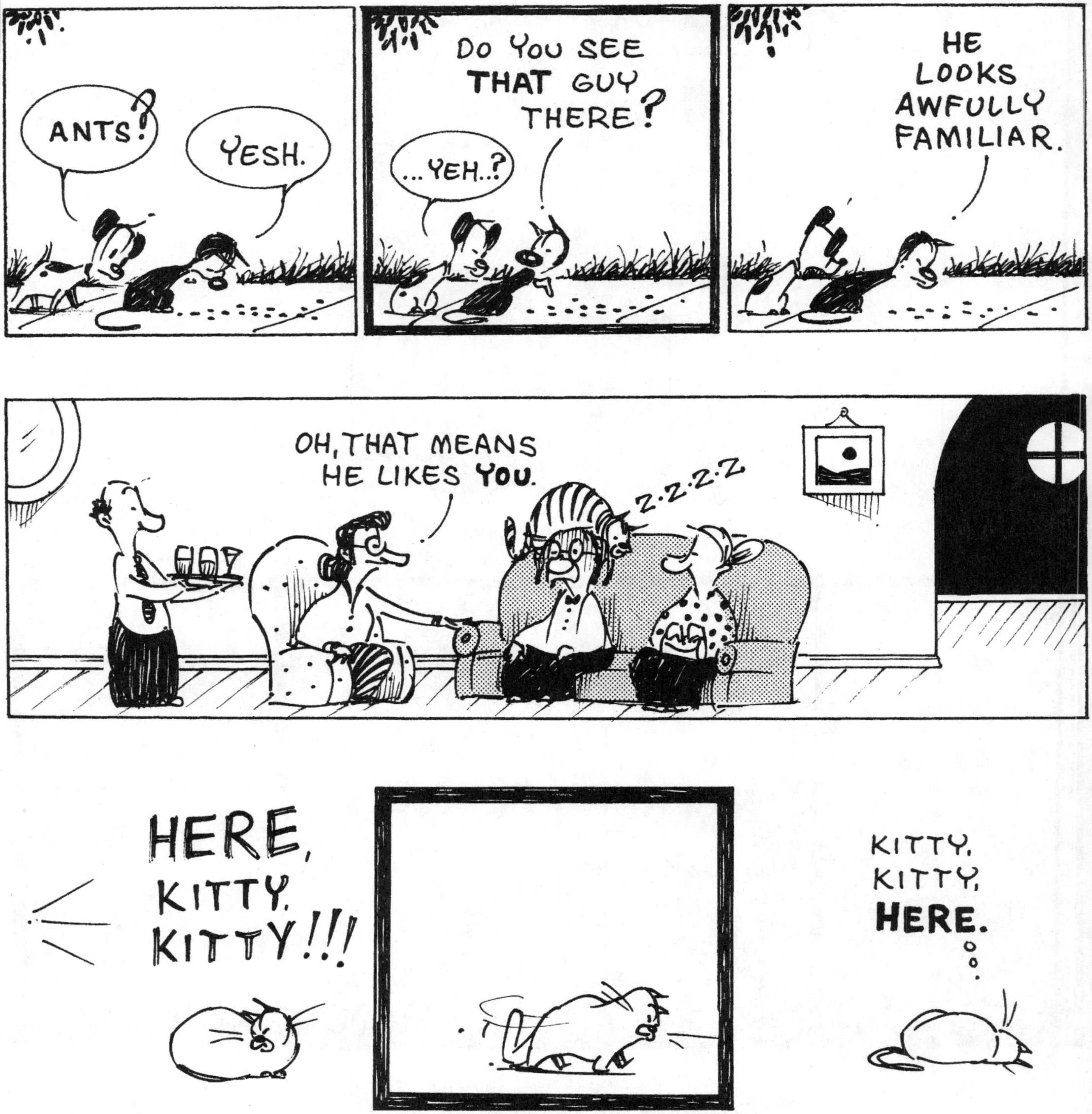
ANTS?
YESH.
DO YOU SEE THAT GUY THERE?
...YEH..?
HE LOOKS AWFULLY FAMILIAR.
OH, THAT MEANS HE LIKES YOU.
Z·Z·Z·Z
HERE, KITTY, KITTY!!!
KITTY, KITTY, HERE.

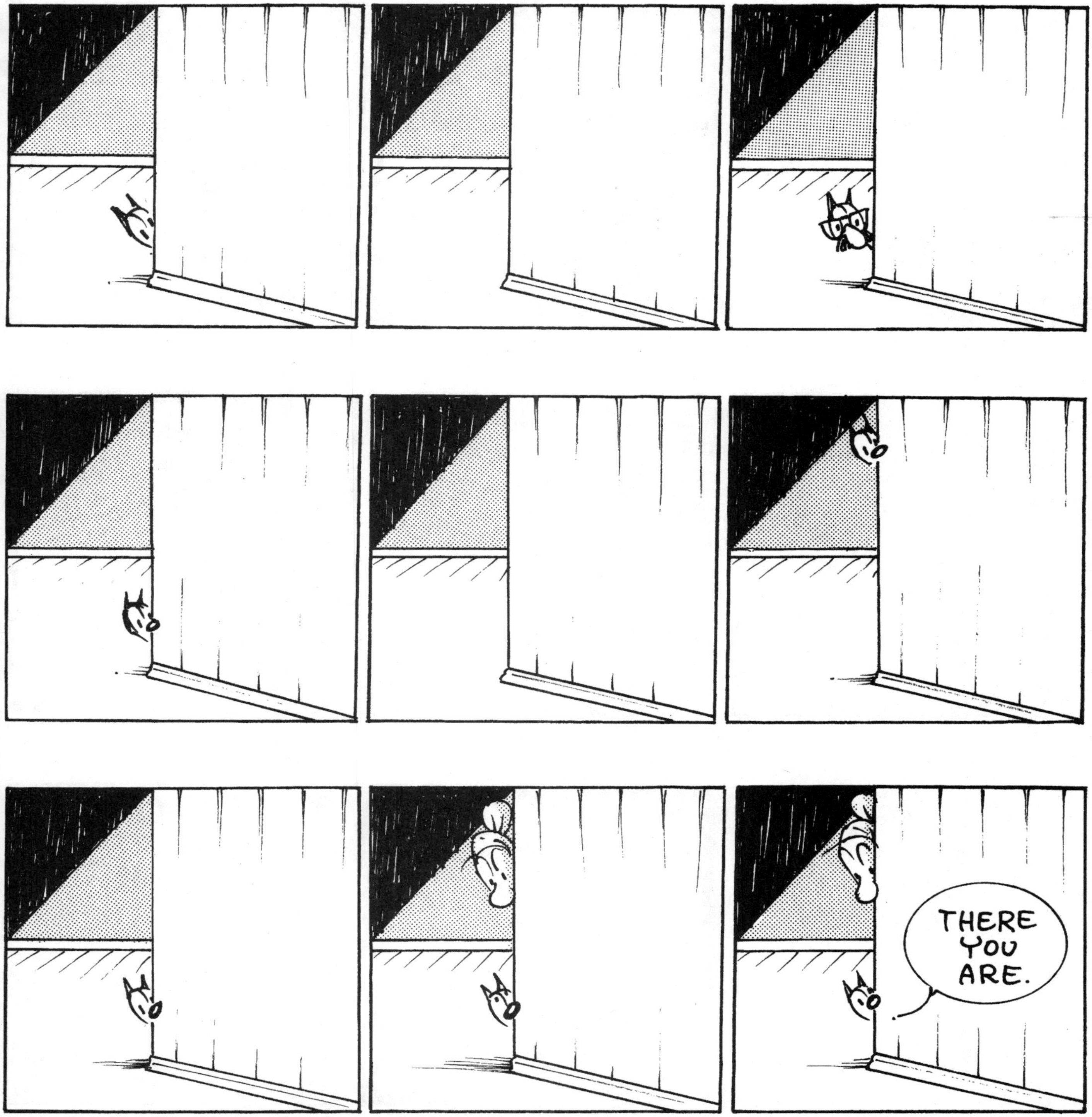
THERE YOU ARE.

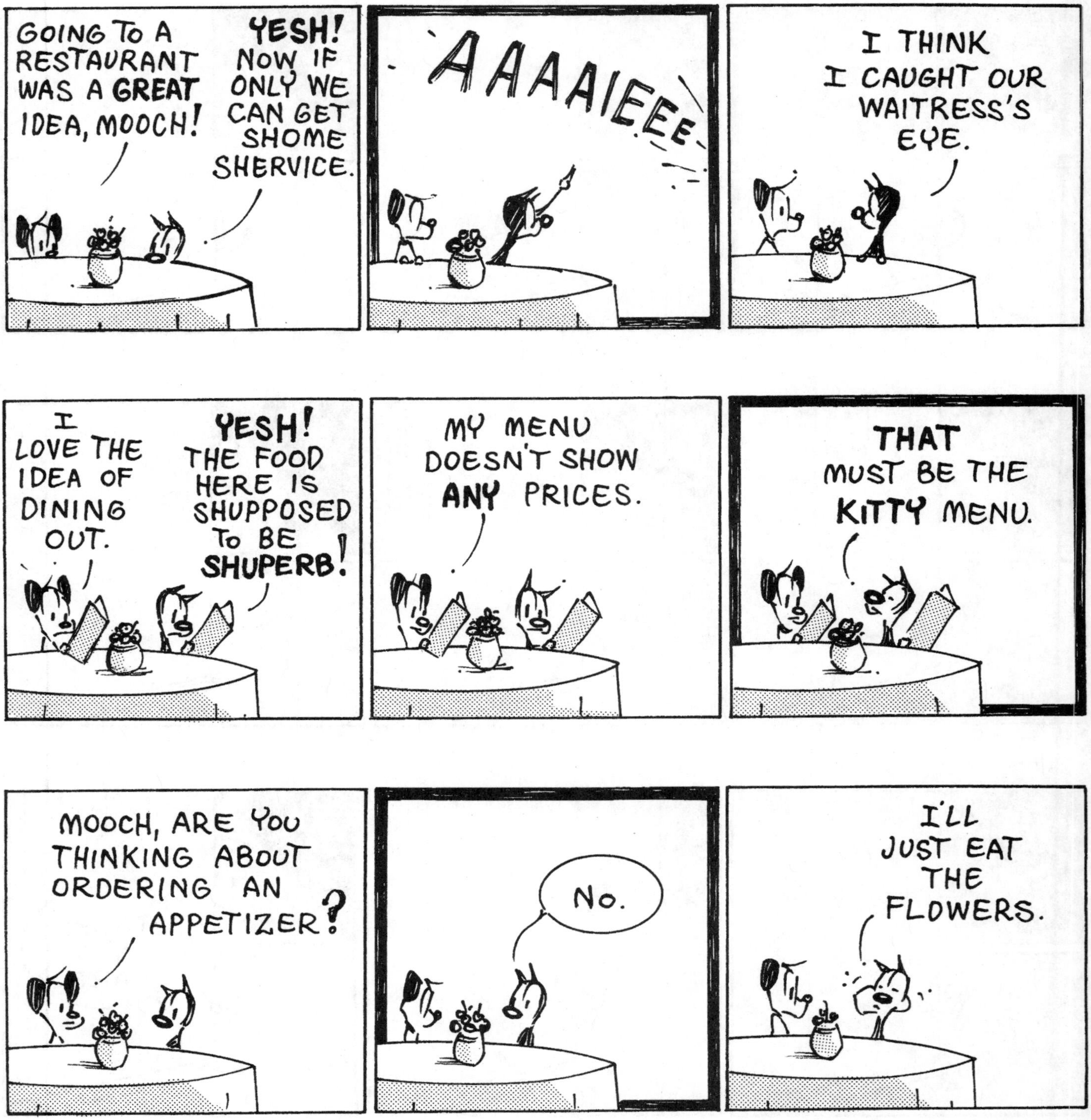
GOING TO A RESTAURANT WAS A GREAT IDEA, MOOCH!
YESH! NOW IF ONLY WE CAN GET SHOME SHERVICE.
AAAAIEEEE
I THINK I CAUGHT OUR WAITRESS'S EYE.
I LOVE THE IDEA OF DINING OUT.
YESH! THE FOOD HERE IS SHUPPOSED TO BE SHUPERB!
MY MENU DOESN'T SHOW ANY PRICES.
THAT MUST BE THE KITTY MENU.
MOOCH, ARE YOU THINKING ABOUT ORDERING AN APPETIZER?
No.
I'LL JUST EAT THE FLOWERS.

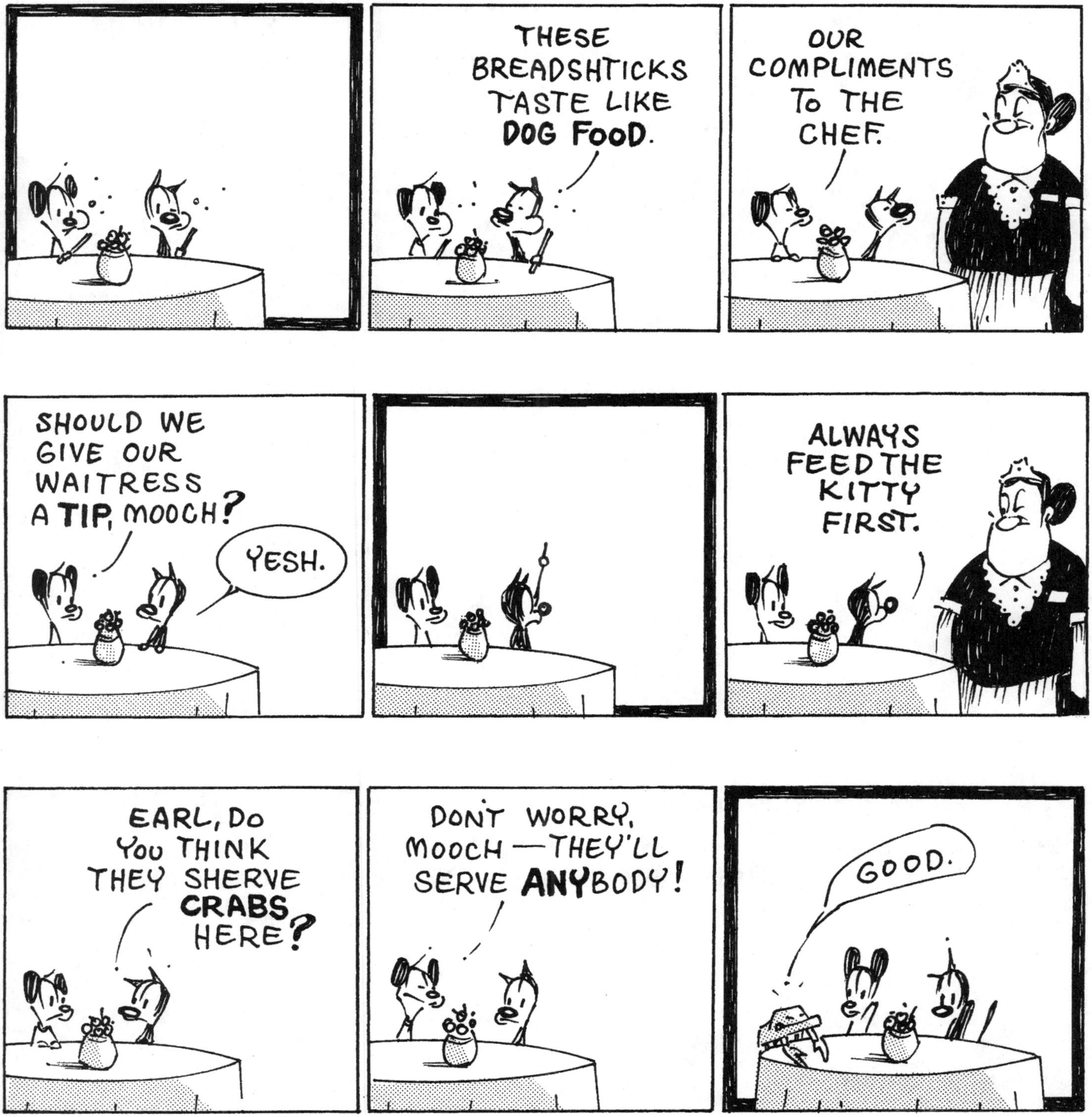
THESE BREADSHTICKS TASTE LIKE **DOG FOOD**.
OUR COMPLIMENTS TO THE CHEF.
SHOULD WE GIVE OUR WAITRESS A **TIP**, MOOCH?
YESH.
ALWAYS FEED THE KITTY FIRST.
EARL, DO YOU THINK THEY SHERVE **CRABS** HERE?
DON'T WORRY, MOOCH—THEY'LL SERVE **ANY**BODY!
GOOD.

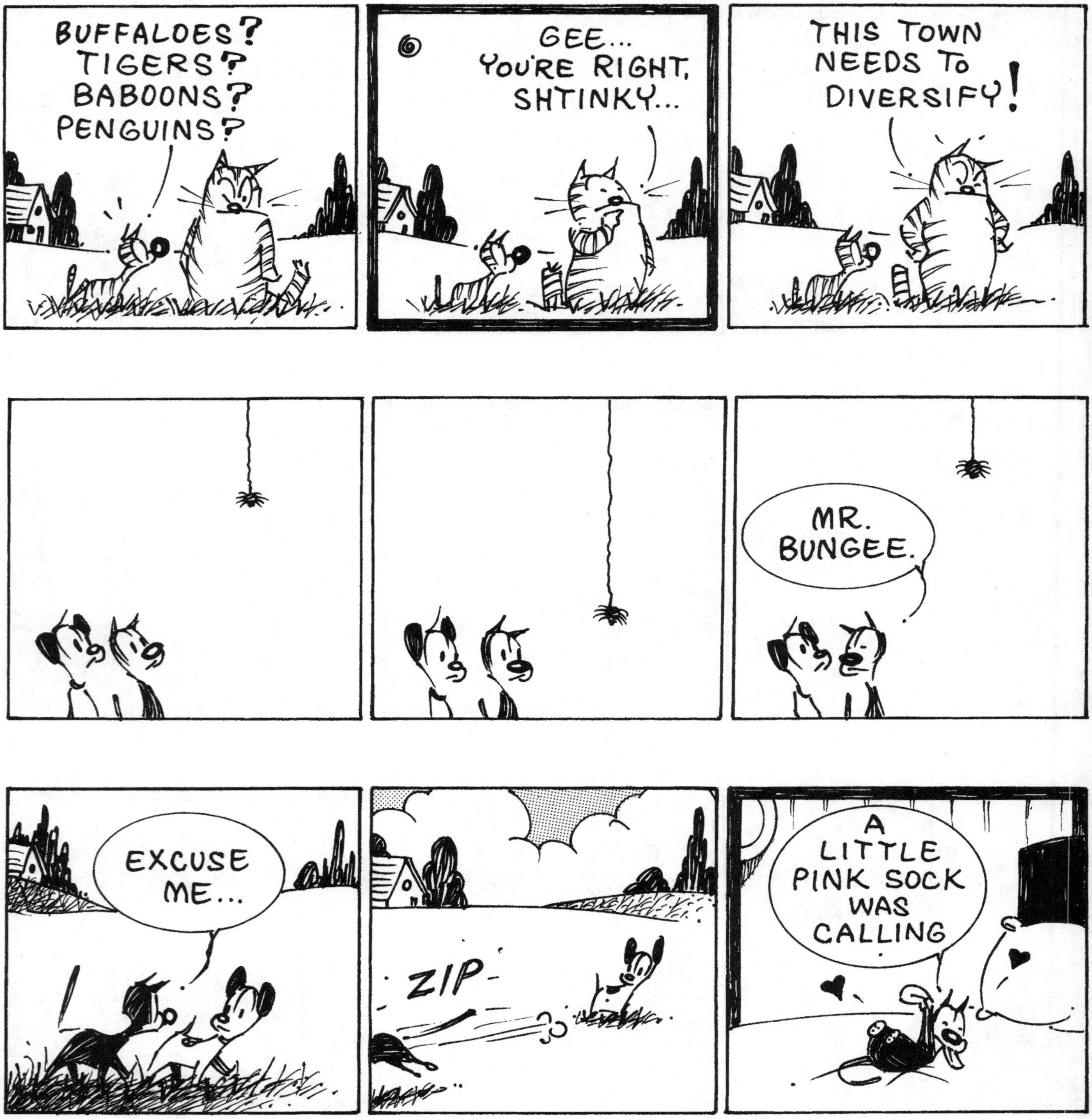
BUFFALOES? TIGERS? BABOONS? PENGUINS?
GEE... YOU'RE RIGHT, SHTINKY...
THIS TOWN NEEDS TO DIVERSIFY!
MR. BUNGEE.
EXCUSE ME...
ZIP
A LITTLE PINK SOCK WAS CALLING

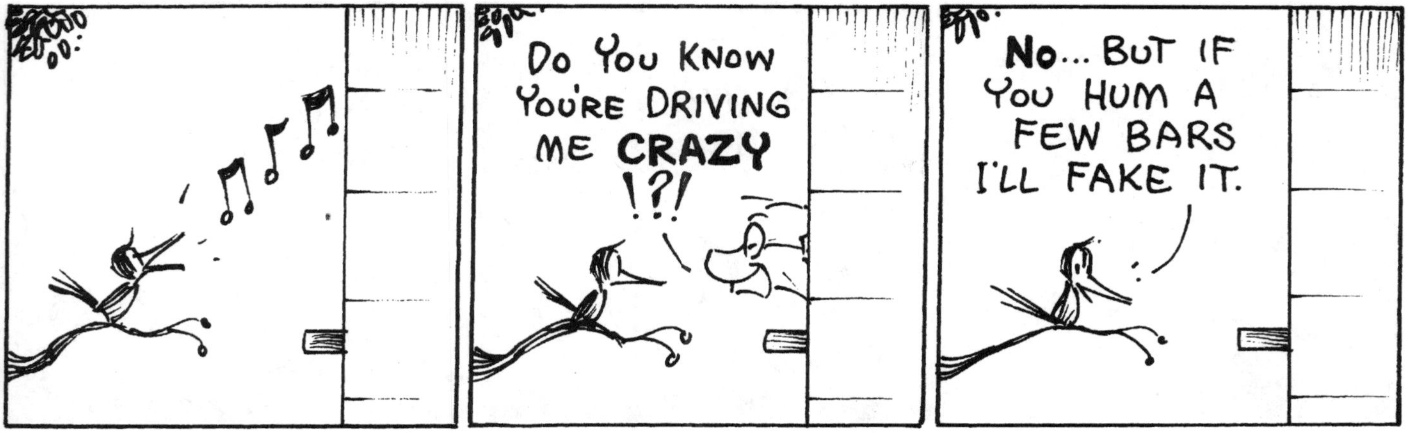
DO YOU KNOW YOU'RE DRIVING ME CRAZY !?!
NO... BUT IF YOU HUM A FEW BARS I'LL FAKE IT.

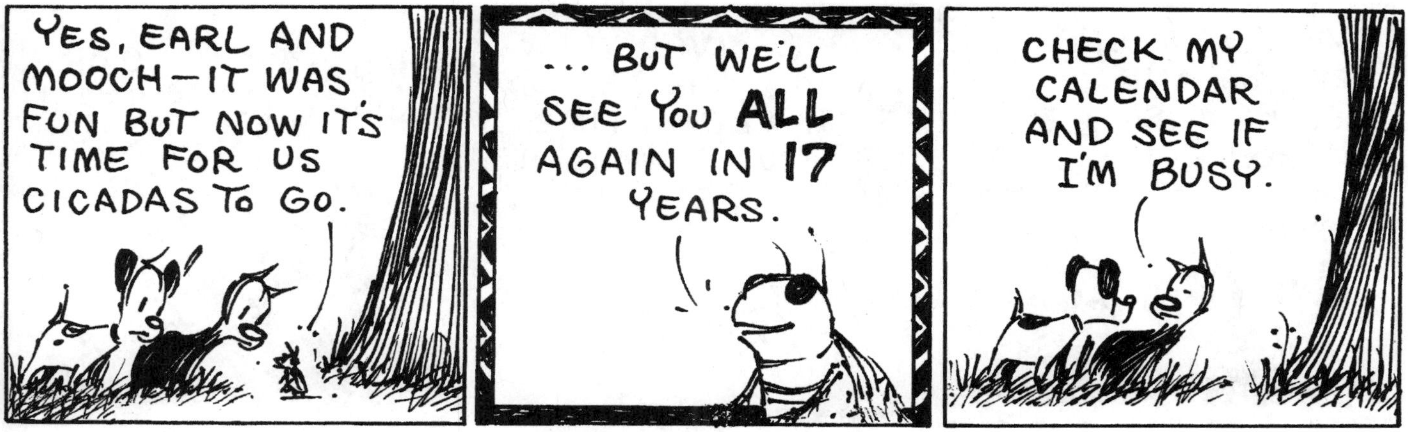
YES, EARL AND MOOCH — IT WAS FUN BUT NOW IT'S TIME FOR US CICADAS TO GO.
... BUT WE'LL SEE YOU ALL AGAIN IN 17 YEARS.
CHECK MY CALENDAR AND SEE IF I'M BUSY.

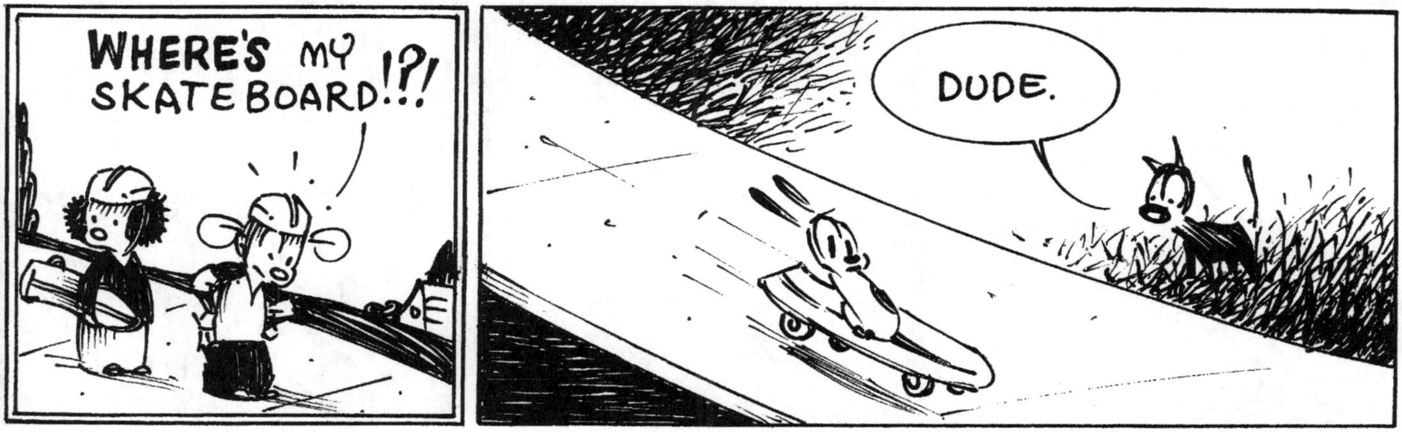
WHERE'S MY SKATEBOARD!?!
DUDE.

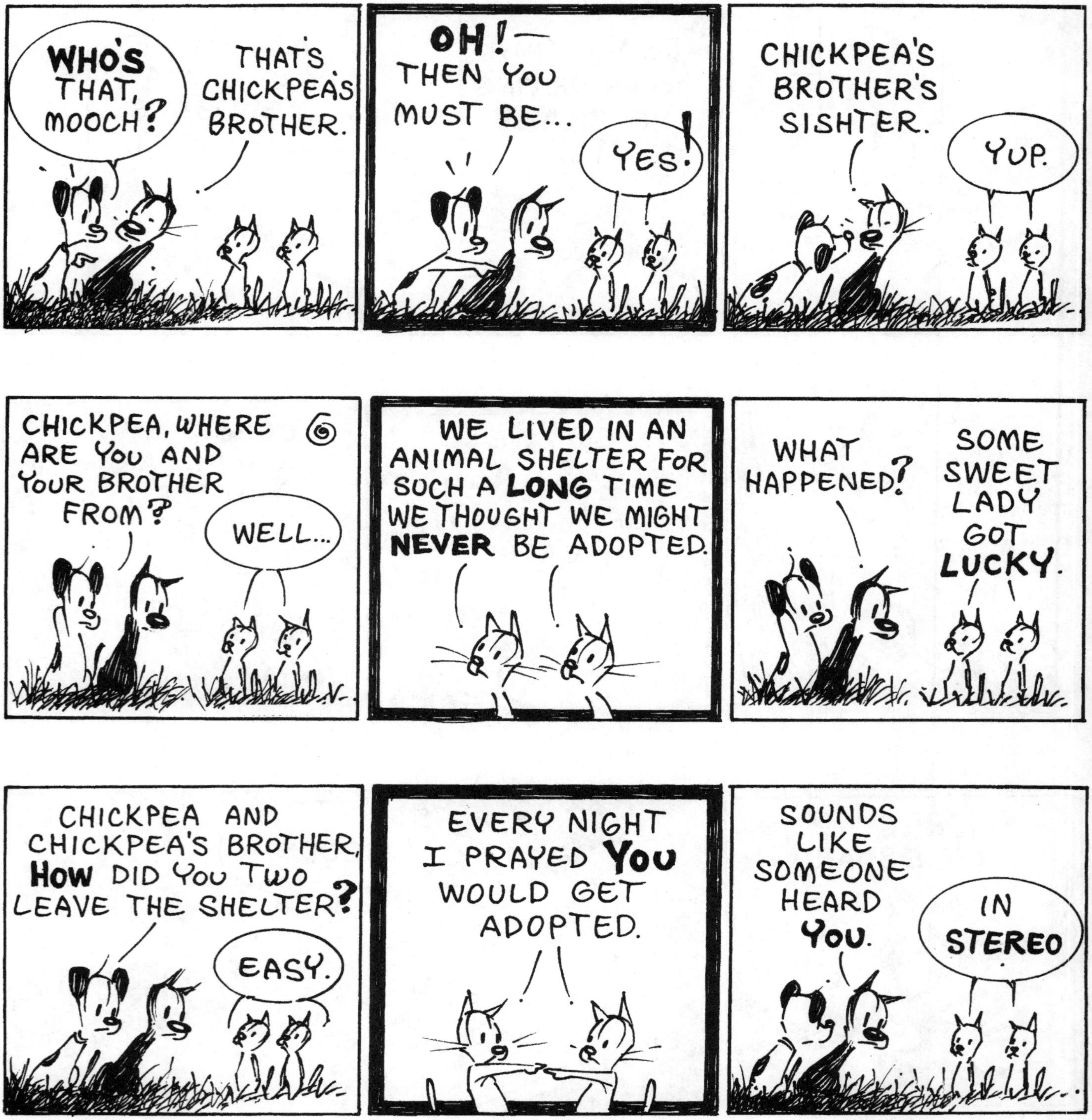
WHO'S THAT, MOOCH?
THAT'S CHICKPEA'S BROTHER.
OH!— THEN YOU MUST BE...
YES!
CHICKPEA'S BROTHER'S SISHTER.
YUP.
CHICKPEA, WHERE ARE YOU AND YOUR BROTHER FROM?
WELL...
WE LIVED IN AN ANIMAL SHELTER FOR SUCH A LONG TIME WE THOUGHT WE MIGHT NEVER BE ADOPTED.
WHAT HAPPENED?
SOME SWEET LADY GOT LUCKY.
CHICKPEA AND CHICKPEA'S BROTHER, HOW DID YOU TWO LEAVE THE SHELTER?
EASY.
EVERY NIGHT I PRAYED YOU WOULD GET ADOPTED.
SOUNDS LIKE SOMEONE HEARD YOU.
IN STEREO

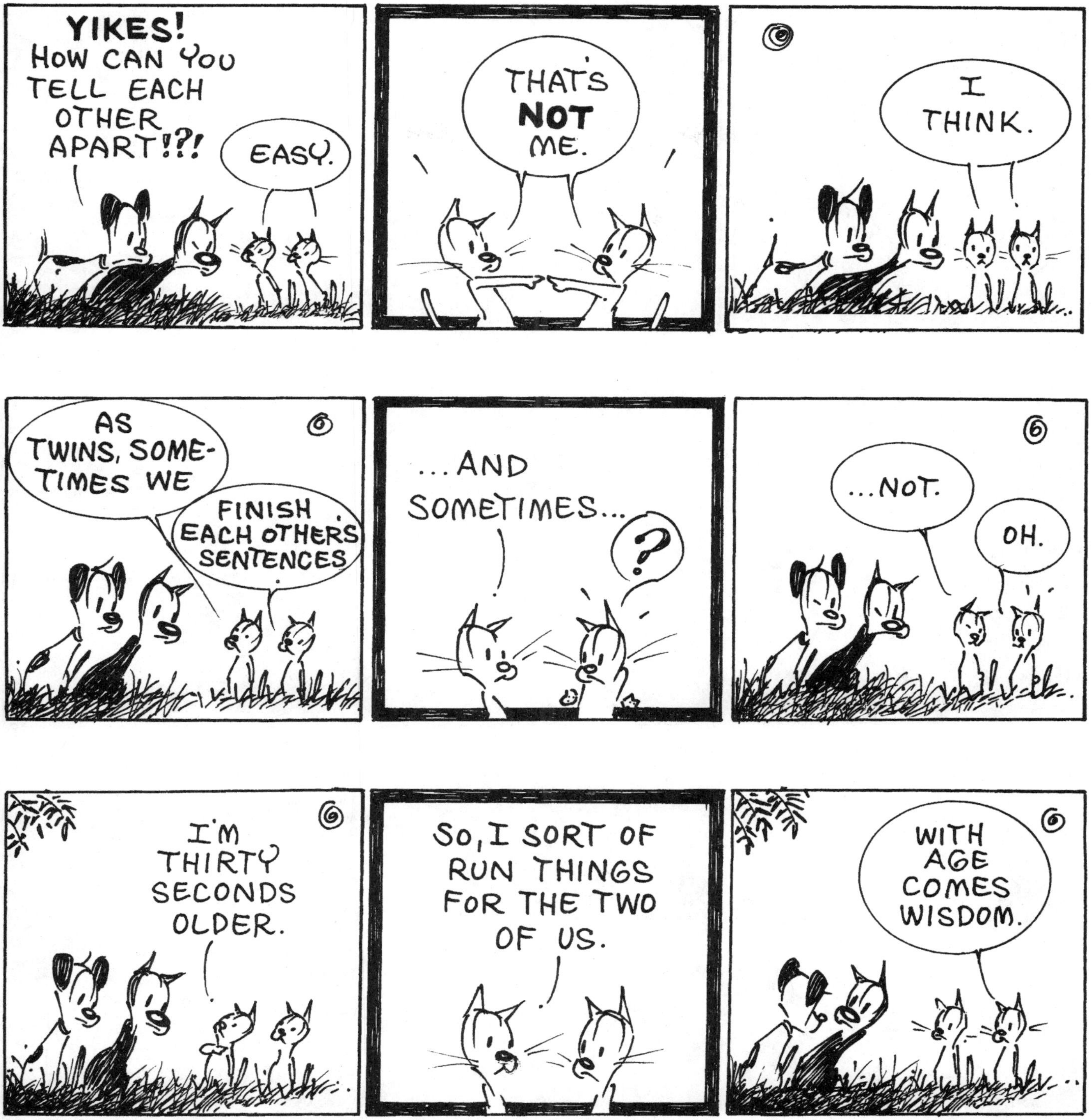
YIKES! HOW CAN YOU TELL EACH OTHER APART!?!
EASY.
THAT'S NOT ME.
I THINK.
AS TWINS, SOME-TIMES WE
FINISH EACH OTHER'S SENTENCES
...AND SOMETIMES...
?
...NOT.
OH.
I'M THIRTY SECONDS OLDER.
SO, I SORT OF RUN THINGS FOR THE TWO OF US.
WITH AGE COMES WISDOM.

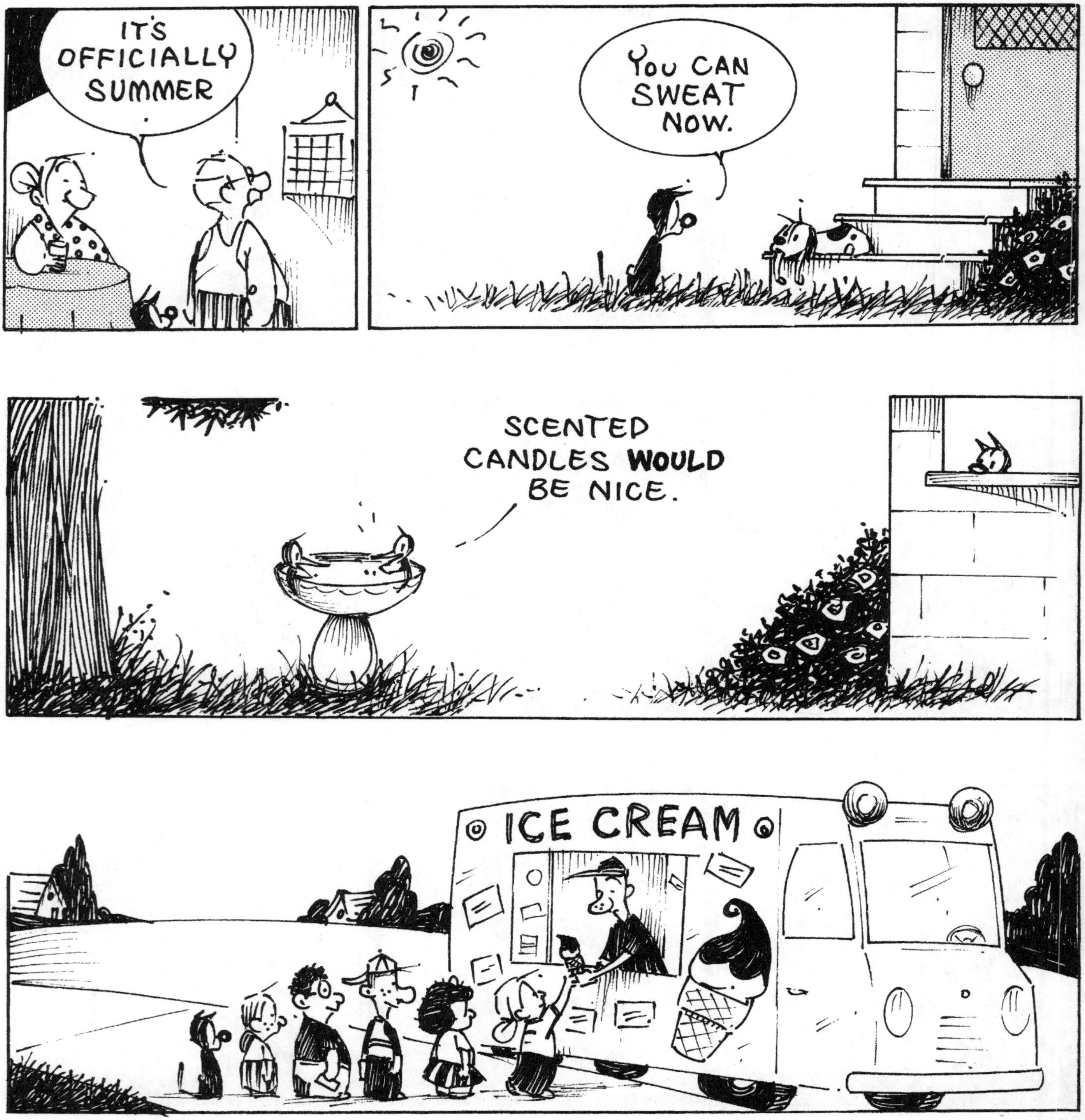
IT'S OFFICIALLY SUMMER
YOU CAN SWEAT NOW.
SCENTED CANDLES WOULD BE NICE.
ICE CREAM

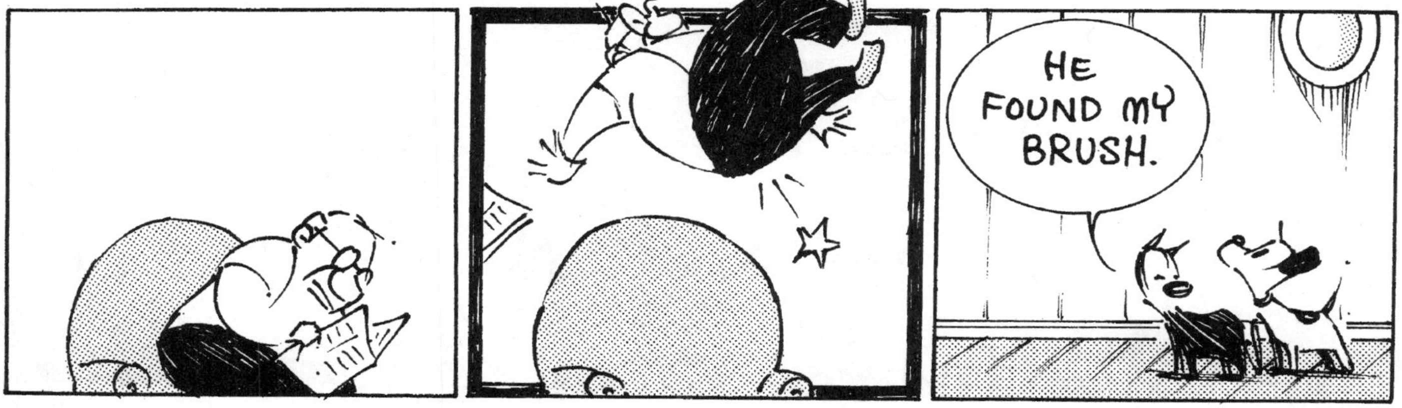
HE FOUND MY BRUSH.

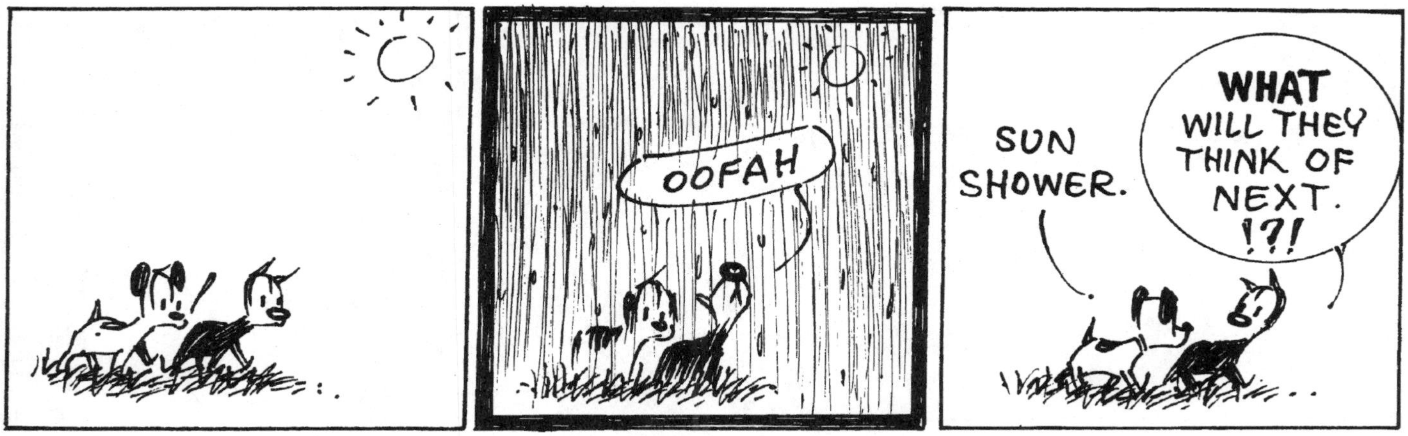
OOFAH
SUN SHOWER.
WHAT WILL THEY THINK OF NEXT. !?!

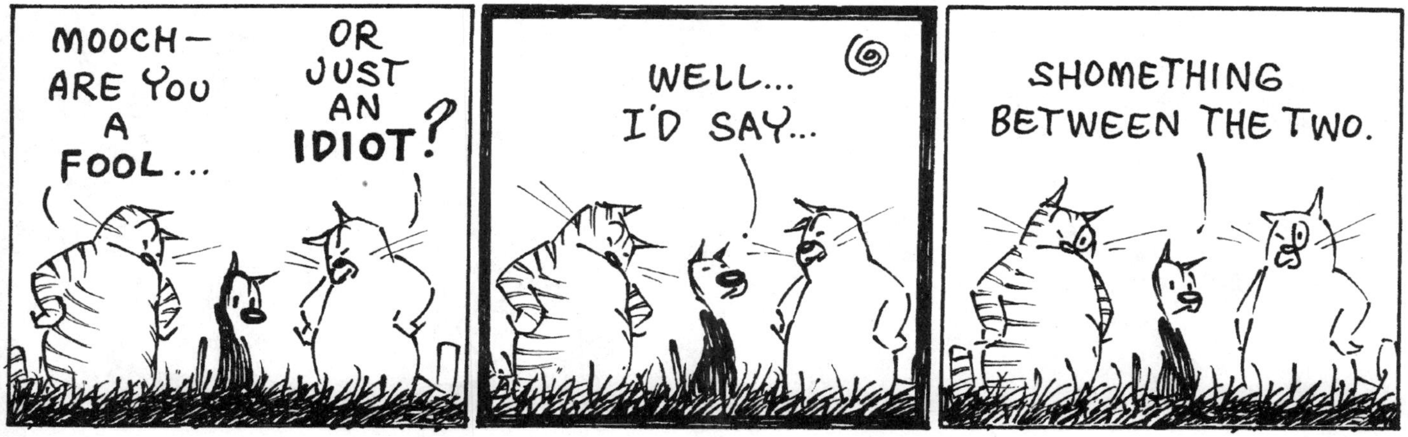
MOOCH- ARE YOU A FOOL...
OR JUST AN IDIOT?
WELL... I'D SAY...
SHOMETHING BETWEEN THE TWO.

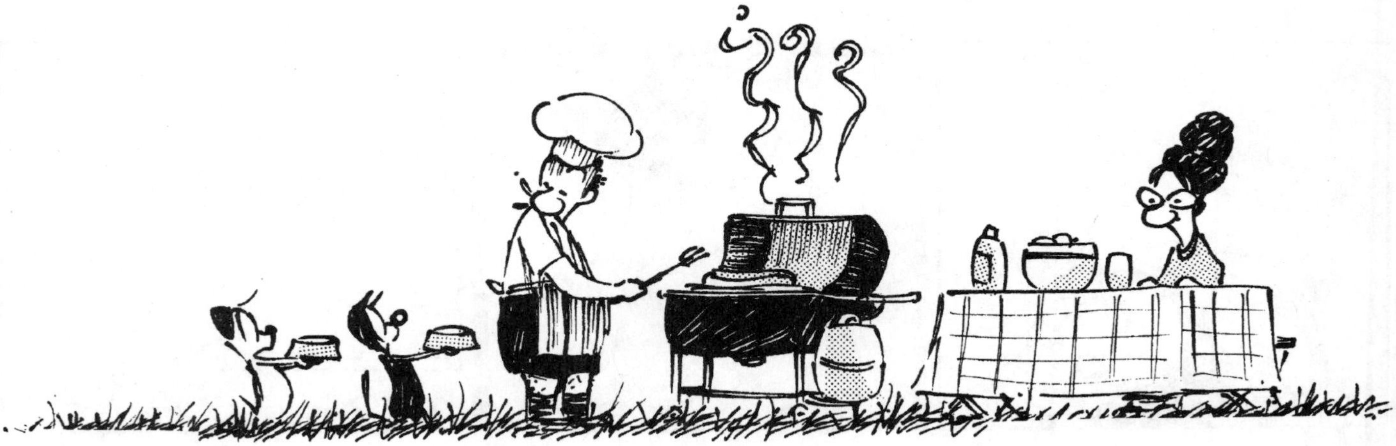

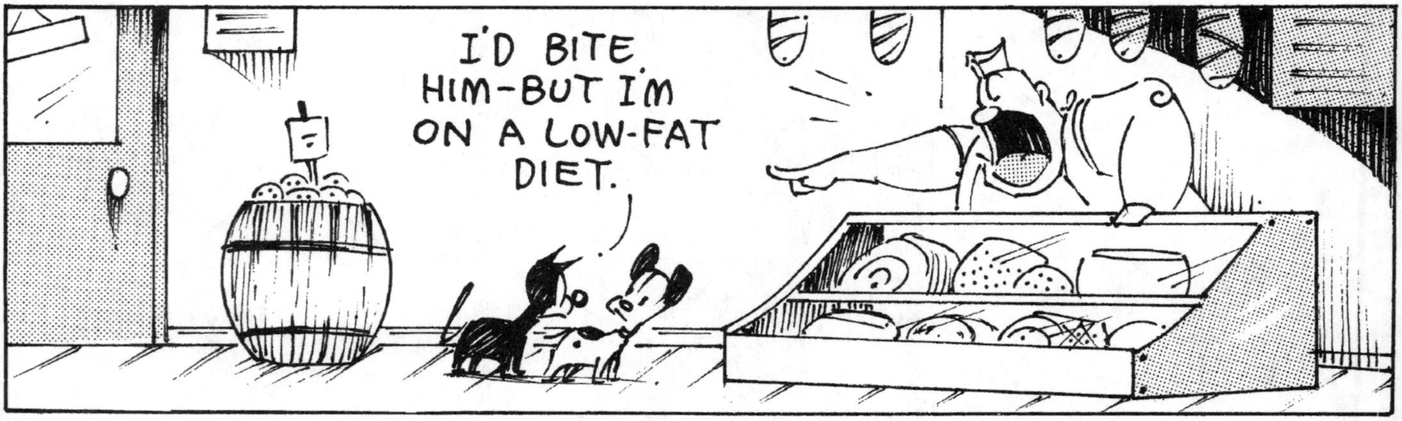
I'D BITE HIM-BUT I'M ON A LOW-FAT DIET.

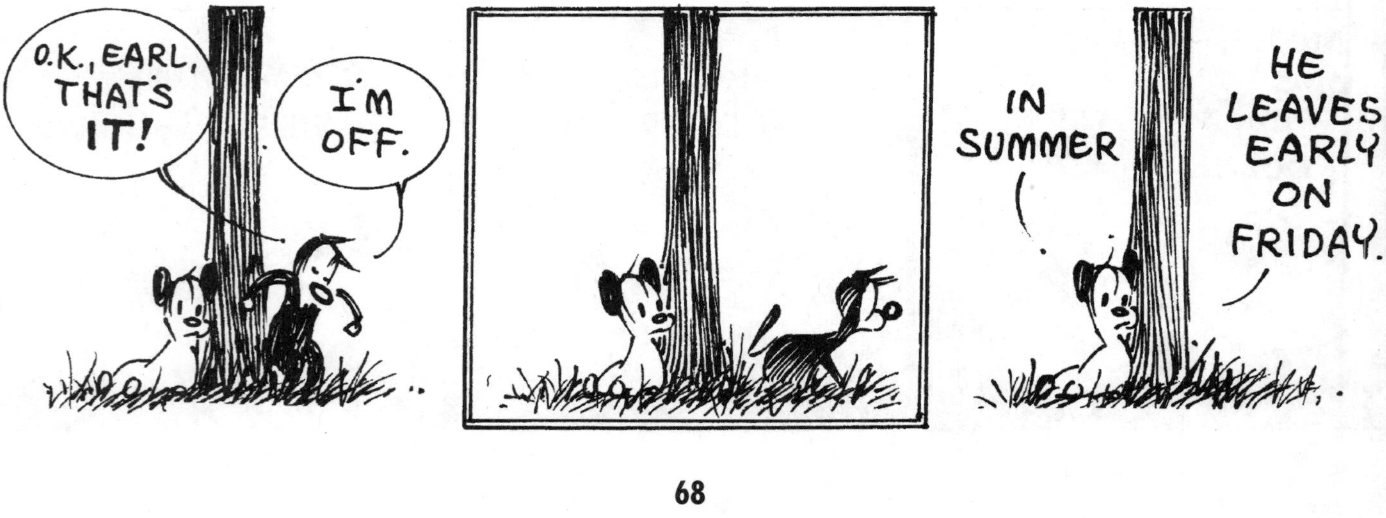
O.K., EARL, THAT'S IT!
I'M OFF.
IN SUMMER
HE LEAVES EARLY ON FRIDAY.

MUTTS

PATRICK McDONNELL

ACK! THE SUN IS TOO HOT!!! PHOOEY!

THE SAND IS ALL OVER AND THE OCEAN'S NOT BLUE ENOUGH! FAA!

AND THE PAPAYA AT BRUNCH WAS MUSHY! AUGH!

BLAH BLAH BLAH ·

⊙☆✳⚡!

KING CRAB

YOUR HIGHNESS!

YES?

I HAVE FOUND YOUR QUEEN.

⊙☆✳⚡!

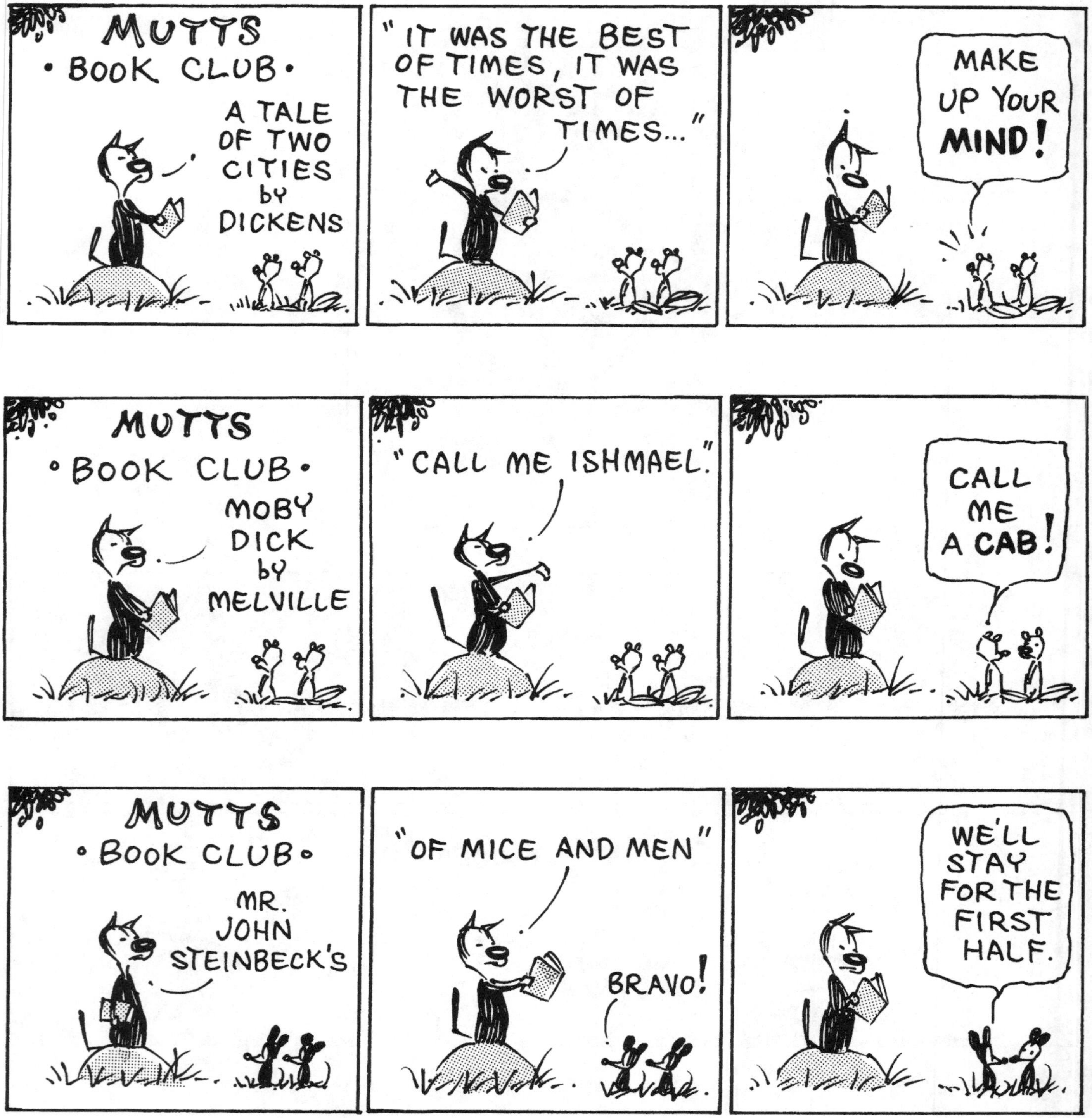
MUTTS
• BOOK CLUB •
A TALE OF TWO CITIES by DICKENS
"IT WAS THE BEST OF TIMES, IT WAS THE WORST OF TIMES..."
MAKE UP YOUR MIND!
MUTTS
• BOOK CLUB •
MOBY DICK by MELVILLE
"CALL ME ISHMAEL."
CALL ME A CAB!
MUTTS
• BOOK CLUB •
MR. JOHN STEINBECK'S
"OF MICE AND MEN"
BRAVO!
WE'LL STAY FOR THE FIRST HALF.

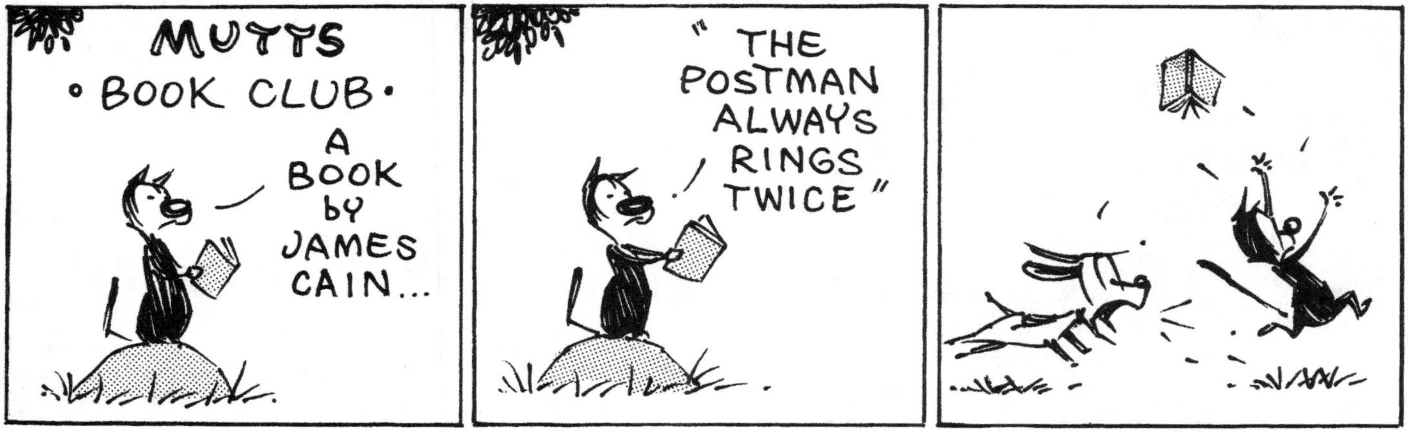
MUTTS
• BOOK CLUB •
A BOOK by JAMES CAIN...
" THE POSTMAN ALWAYS RINGS TWICE "

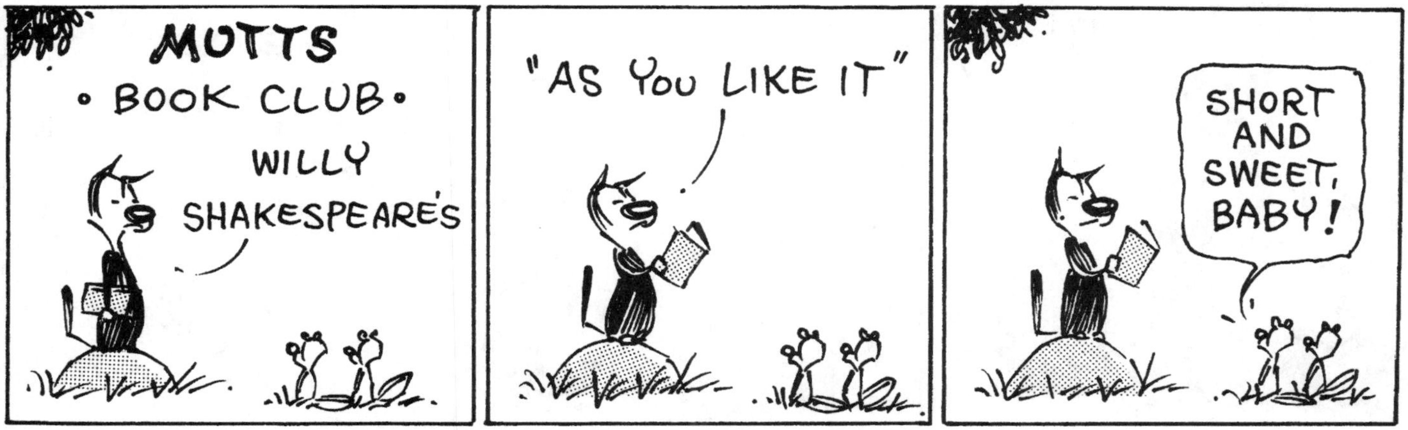
MUTTS
• BOOK CLUB •
WILLY SHAKESPEARE'S
"AS YOU LIKE IT"
SHORT AND SWEET, BABY!

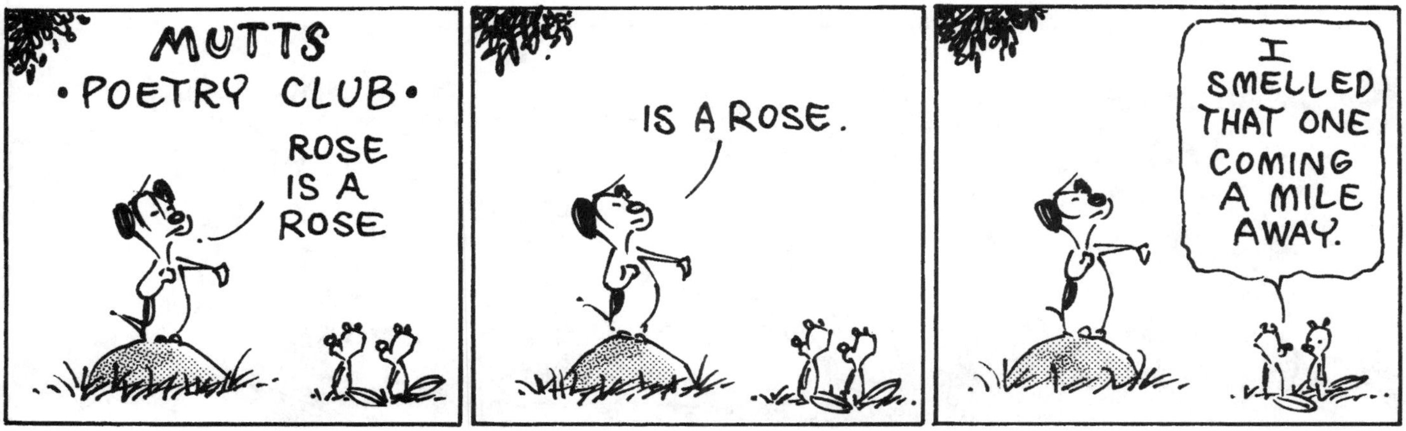
MUTTS
• POETRY CLUB •
ROSE IS A ROSE
IS A ROSE.
I SMELLED THAT ONE COMING A MILE AWAY.

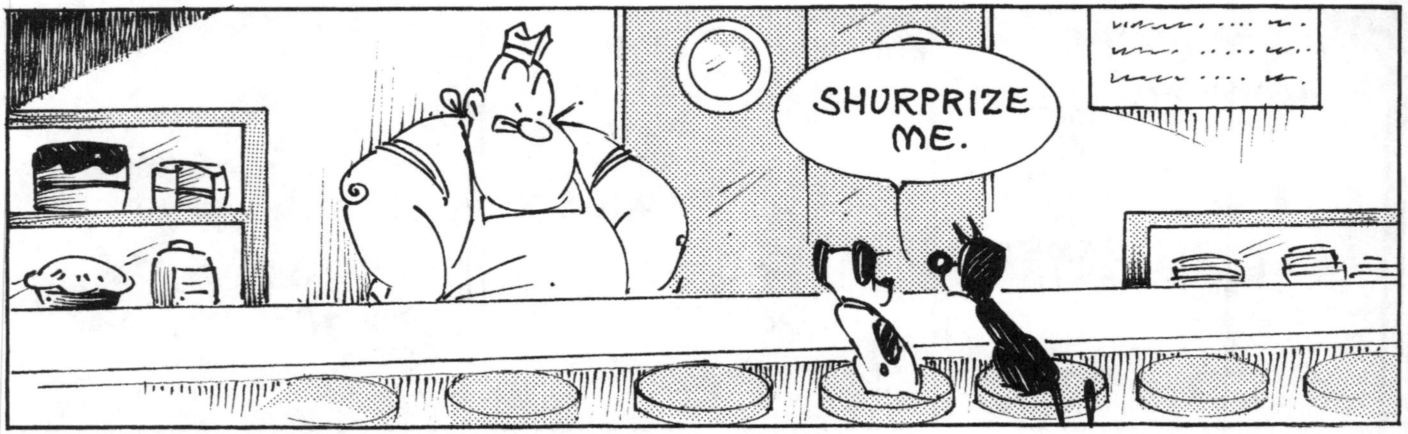
SHURPRIZE ME.

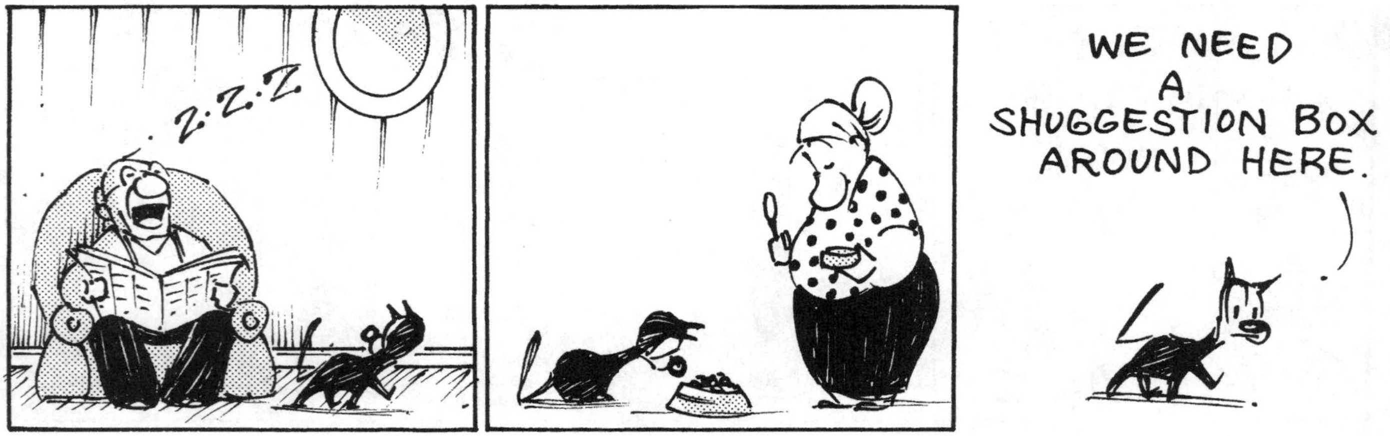
Z.Z.Z
WE NEED A SHUGGESTION BOX AROUND HERE.

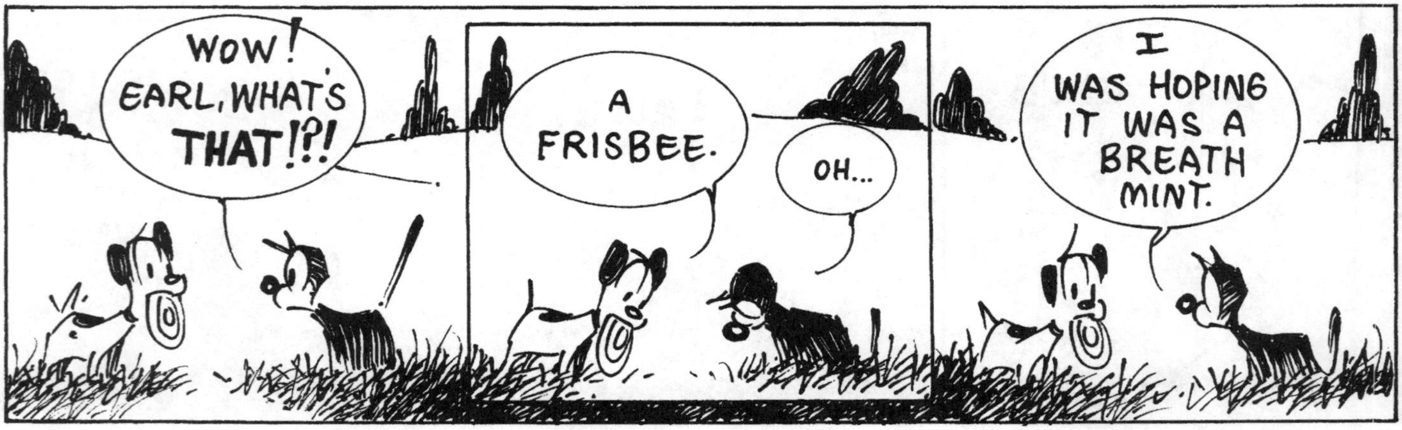
WOW! EARL, WHAT'S THAT!?!
A FRISBEE.
OH...
I WAS HOPING IT WAS A BREATH MINT.

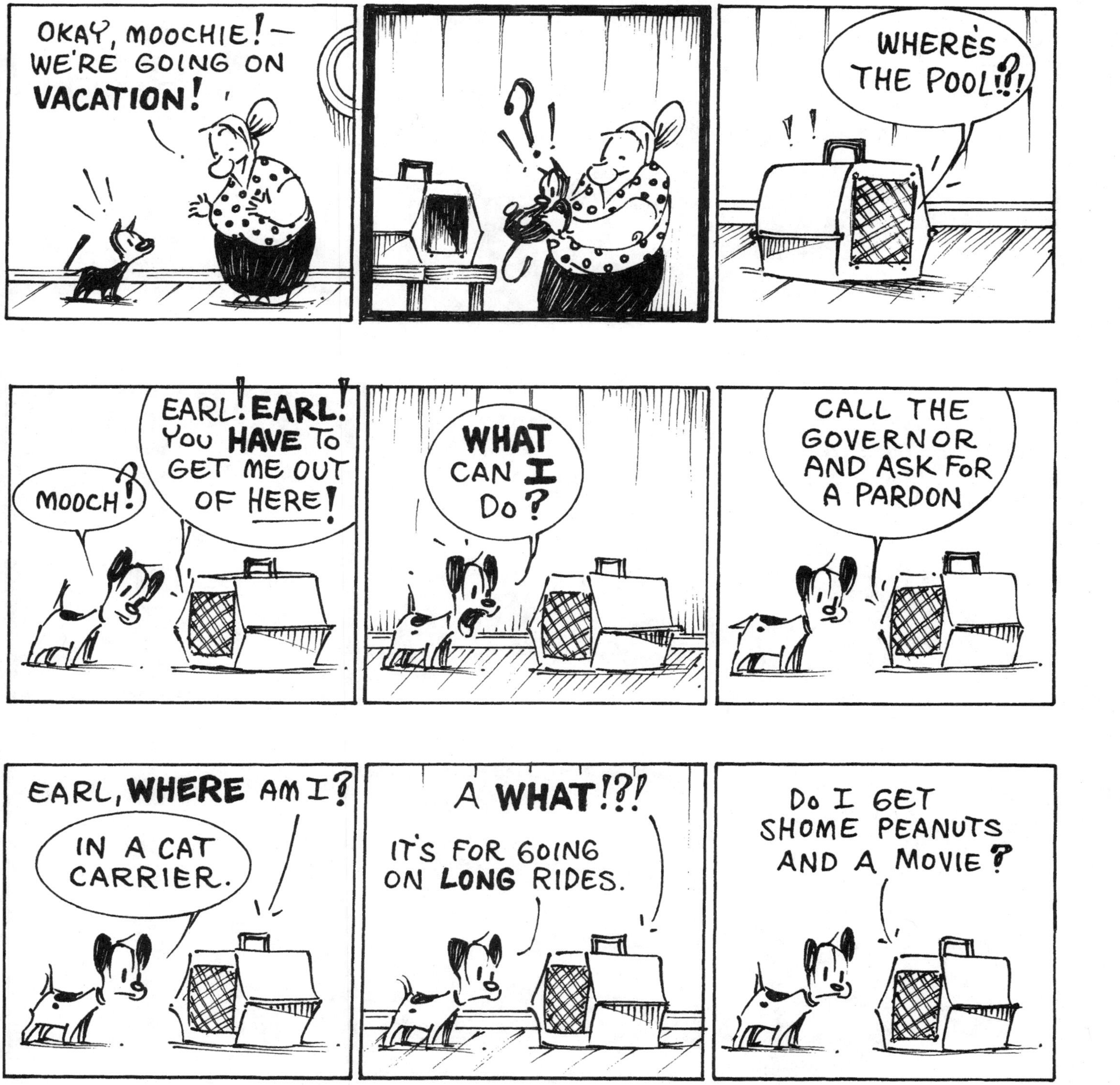
OKAY, MOOCHIE!— WE'RE GOING ON VACATION!
WHERE'S THE POOL!?!
MOOCH!?
EARL! EARL! YOU HAVE TO GET ME OUT OF HERE!
WHAT CAN I DO?
CALL THE GOVERNOR AND ASK FOR A PARDON
EARL, WHERE AM I?
IN A CAT CARRIER.
A WHAT!?!
IT'S FOR GOING ON LONG RIDES.
DO I GET SHOME PEANUTS AND A MOVIE?

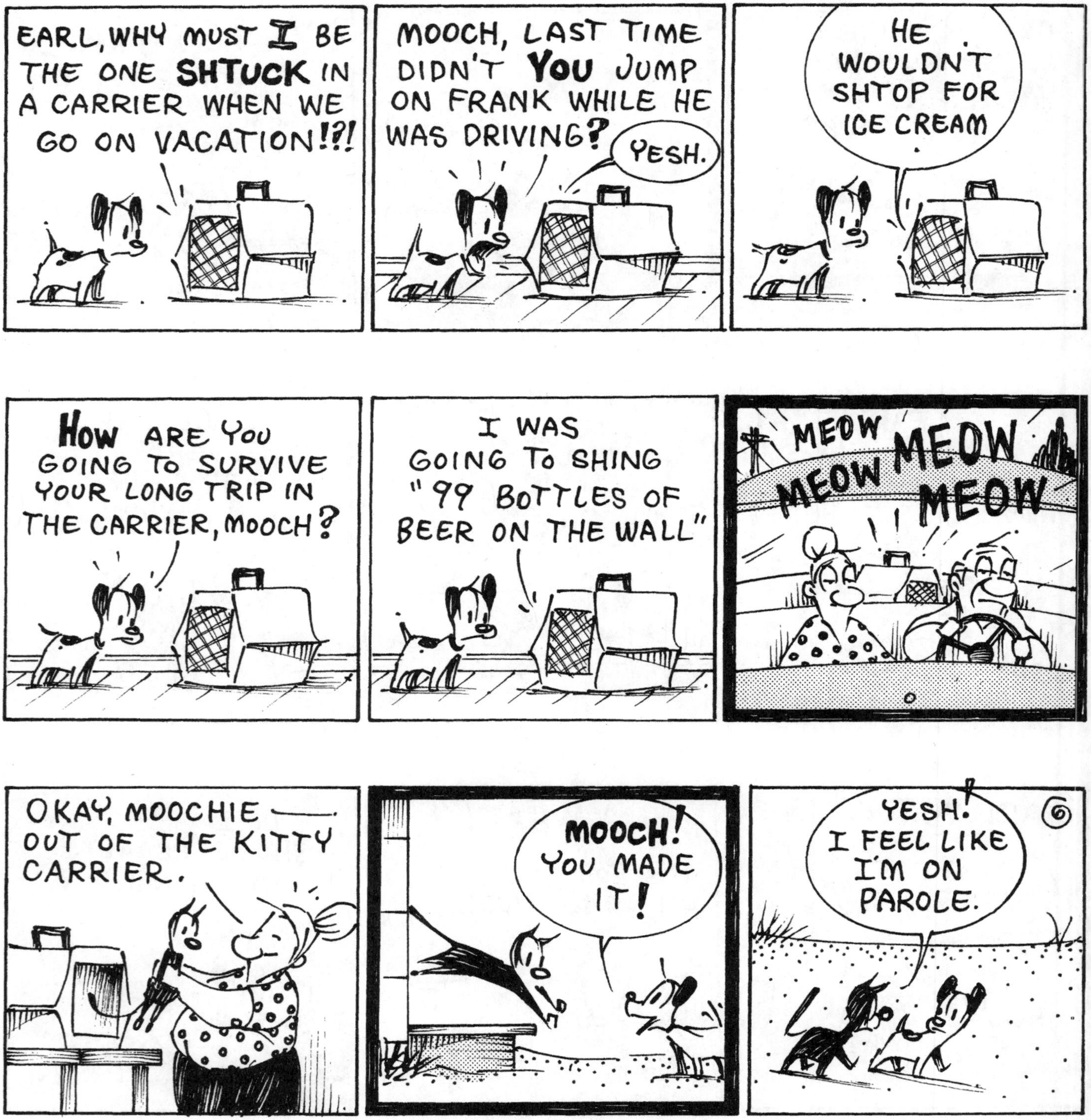
EARL, WHY MUST I BE THE ONE SHTUCK IN A CARRIER WHEN WE GO ON VACATION!?!
MOOCH, LAST TIME DIDN'T YOU JUMP ON FRANK WHILE HE WAS DRIVING?
YESH.
HE WOULDN'T SHTOP FOR ICE CREAM.
HOW ARE YOU GOING TO SURVIVE YOUR LONG TRIP IN THE CARRIER, MOOCH?
I WAS GOING TO SHING "99 BOTTLES OF BEER ON THE WALL"
MEOW MEOW MEOW MEOW MEOW
OKAY, MOOCHIE — OUT OF THE KITTY CARRIER.
MOOCH! YOU MADE IT!
YESH! I FEEL LIKE I'M ON PAROLE.

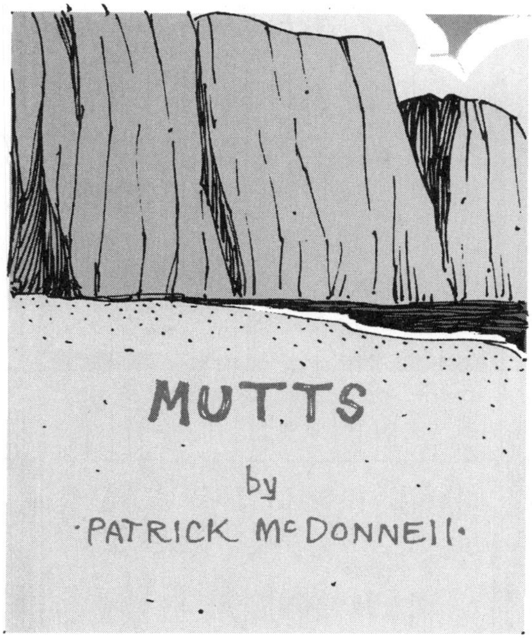
MUTTS
by
·PATRICK McDONNELL·

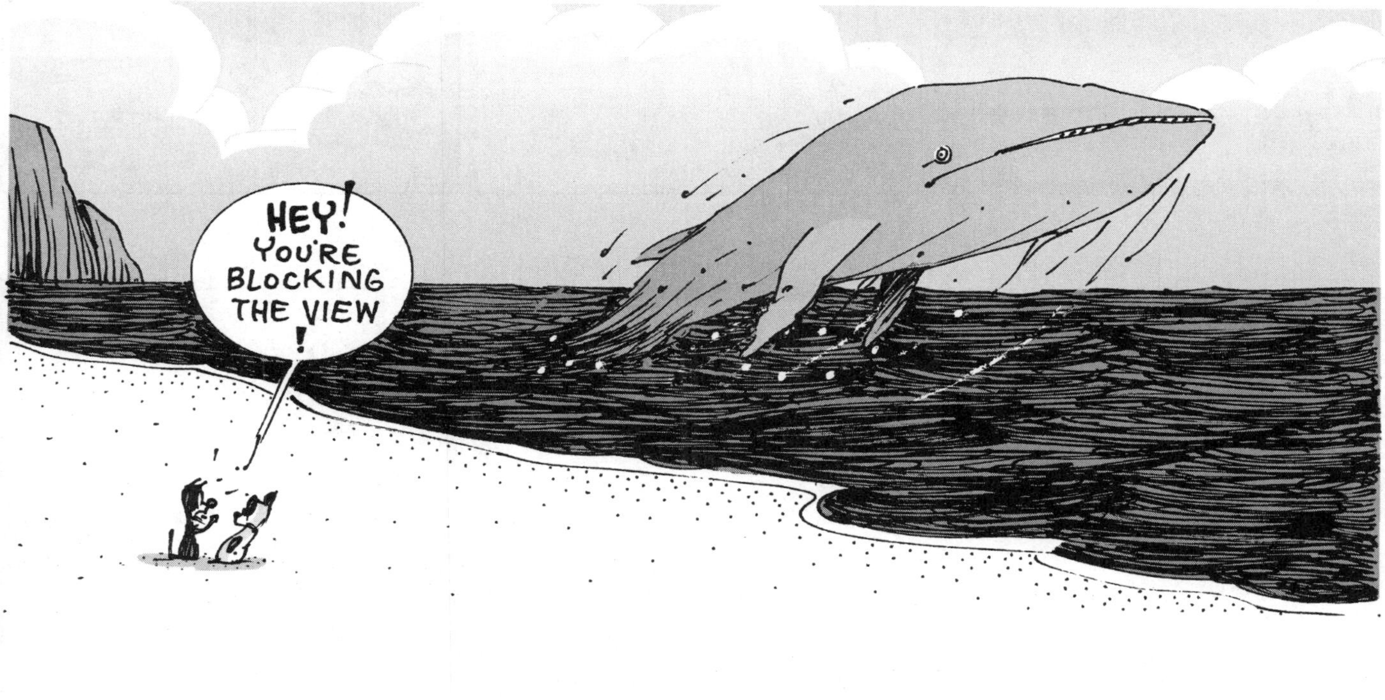
HEY! YOU'RE BLOCKING THE VIEW !

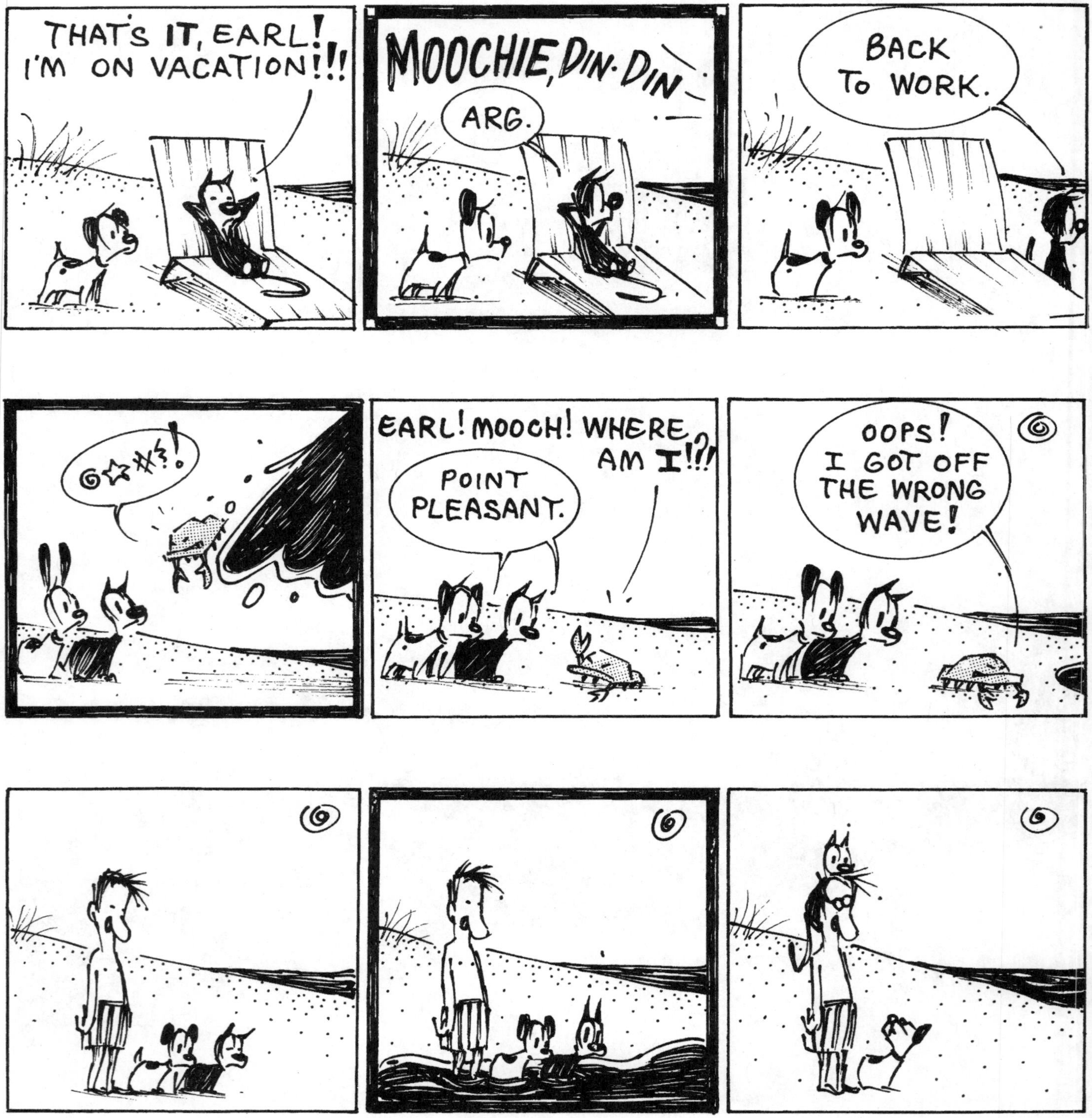
THAT'S IT, EARL! I'M ON VACATION!!!
MOOCHIE, DIN-DIN
ARG.
BACK TO WORK.
EARL! MOOCH! WHERE AM I!?!
POINT PLEASANT.
OOPS! I GOT OFF THE WRONG WAVE!

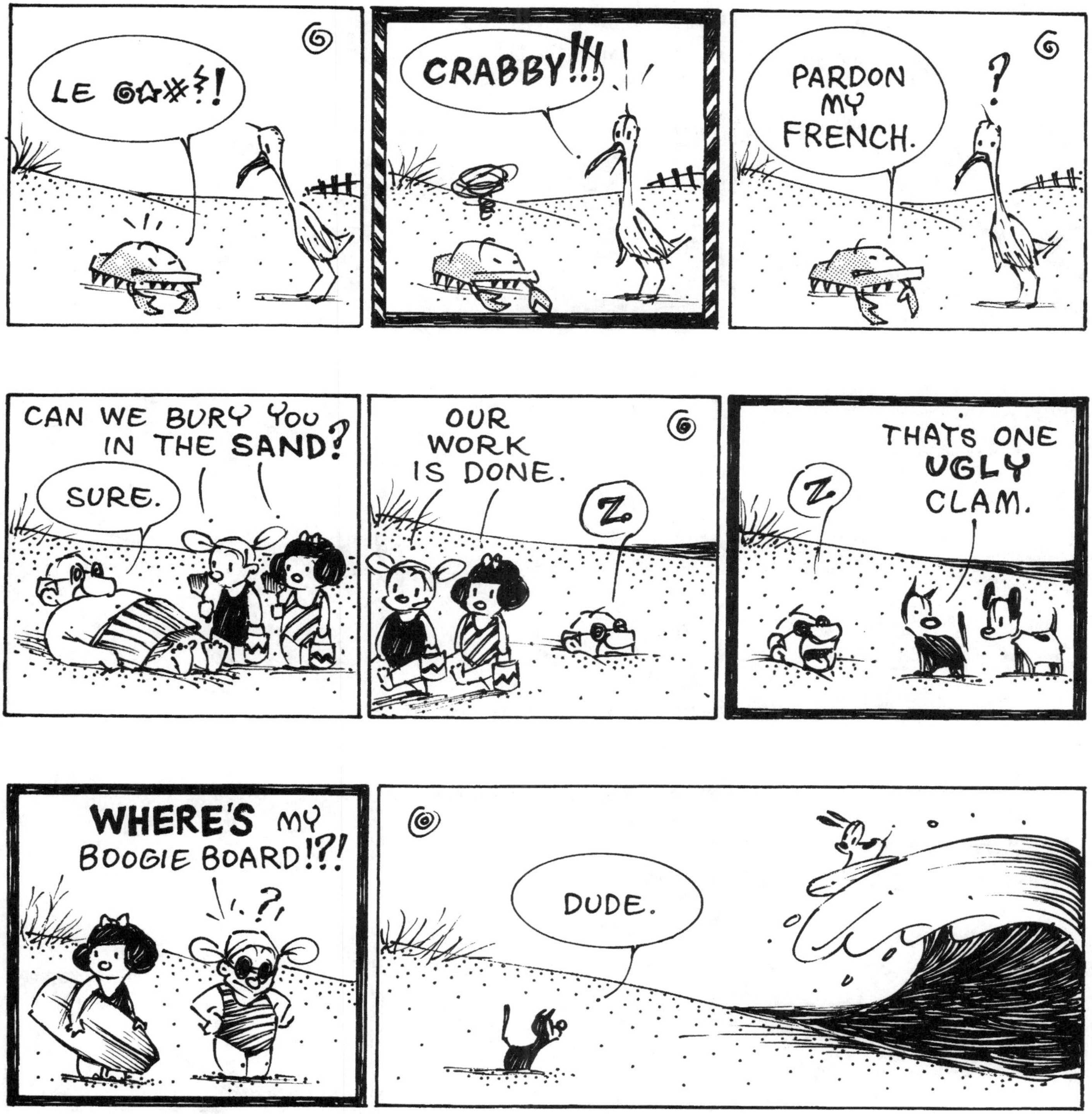
LE @☆*?!
CRABBY!!!
PARDON MY FRENCH.
CAN WE BURY YOU IN THE SAND?
SURE.
OUR WORK IS DONE.
Z
Z
THATS ONE UGLY CLAM.
WHERE'S MY BOOGIE BOARD!?!
DUDE.

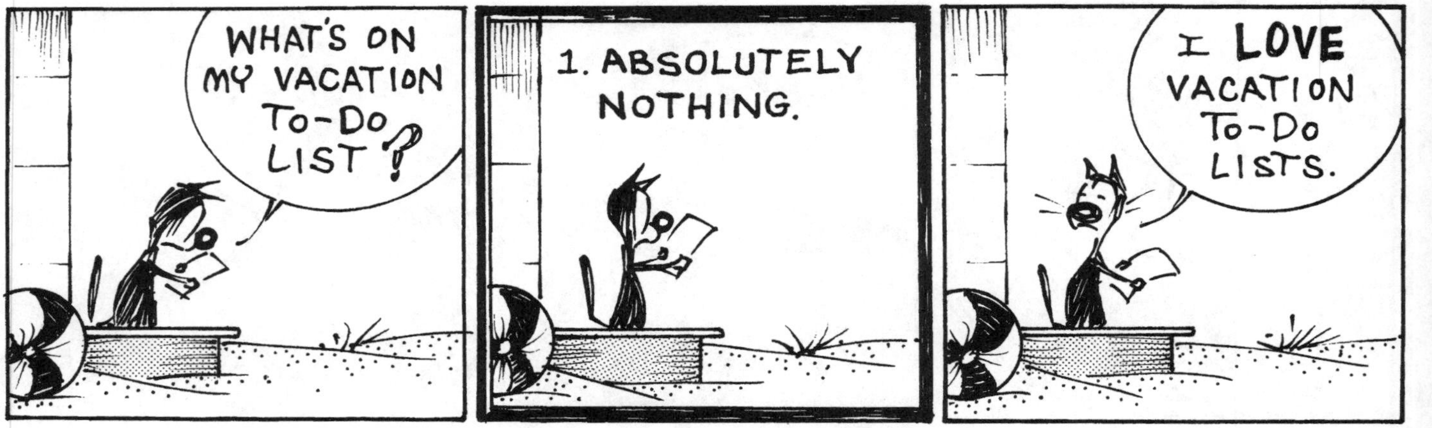
WHAT'S ON MY VACATION TO-DO LIST?
1. ABSOLUTELY NOTHING.
I LOVE VACATION TO-DO LISTS.

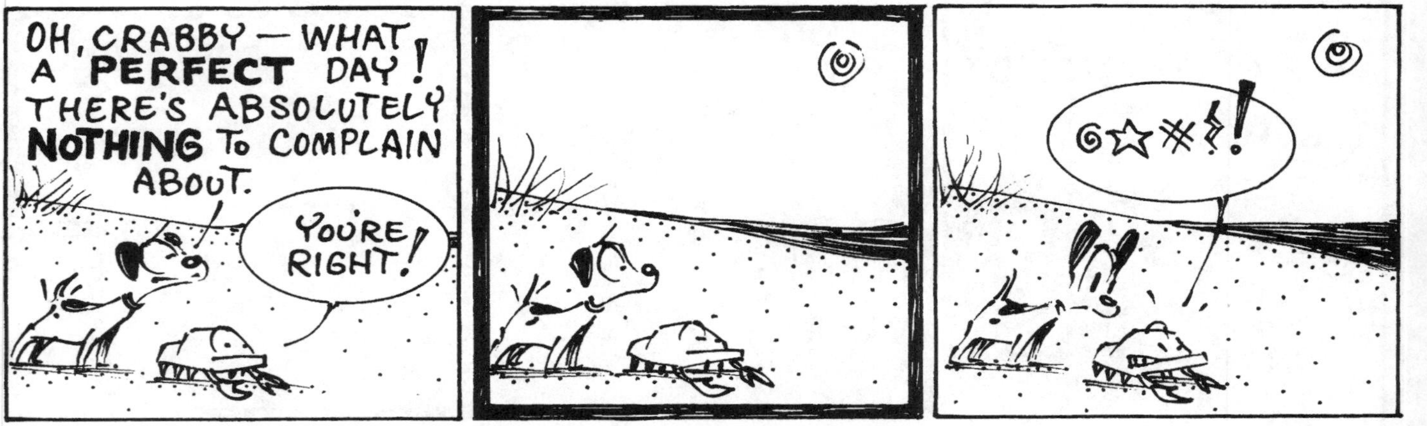
OH, CRABBY — WHAT A PERFECT DAY! THERE'S ABSOLUTELY NOTHING TO COMPLAIN ABOUT.
YOU'RE RIGHT!
@☆#ϟ!

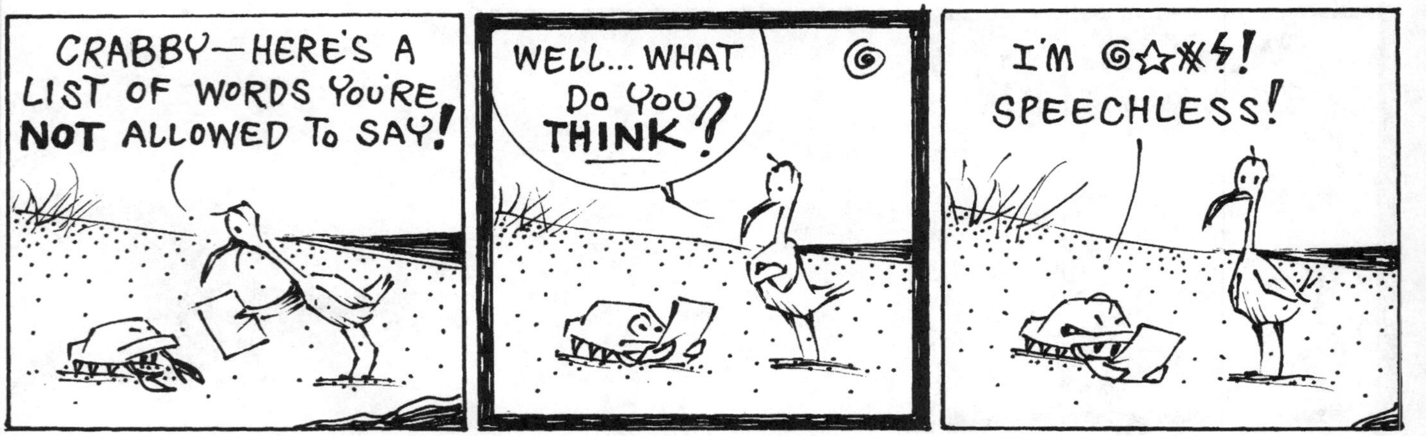
CRABBY — HERE'S A LIST OF WORDS YOU'RE NOT ALLOWED TO SAY!
WELL... WHAT DO YOU THINK?
I'M @☆#ϟ! SPEECHLESS!

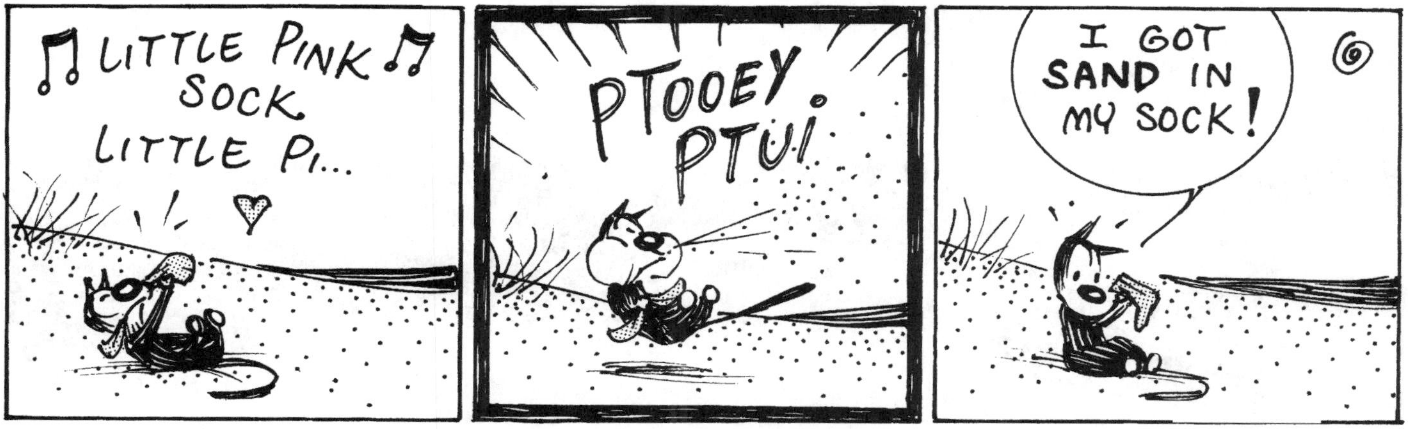
LITTLE PINK SOCK. LITTLE PI...
PTOOEY. PTUI
I GOT SAND IN MY SOCK!

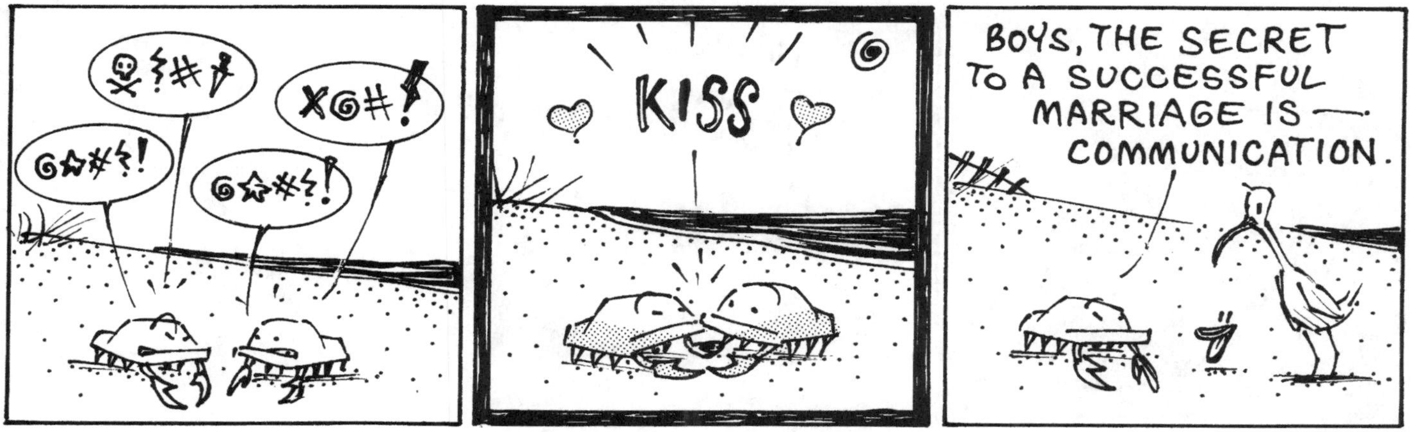
KISS
BOYS, THE SECRET TO A SUCCESSFUL MARRIAGE IS— COMMUNICATION.

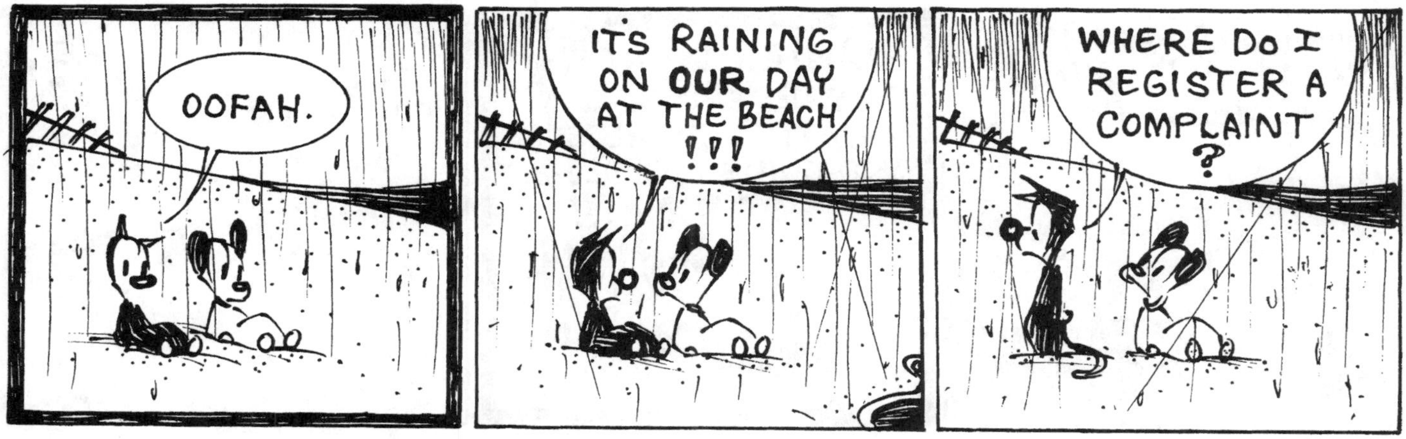
OOFAH.
ITS RAINING ON OUR DAY AT THE BEACH !!!
WHERE DO I REGISTER A COMPLAINT ?

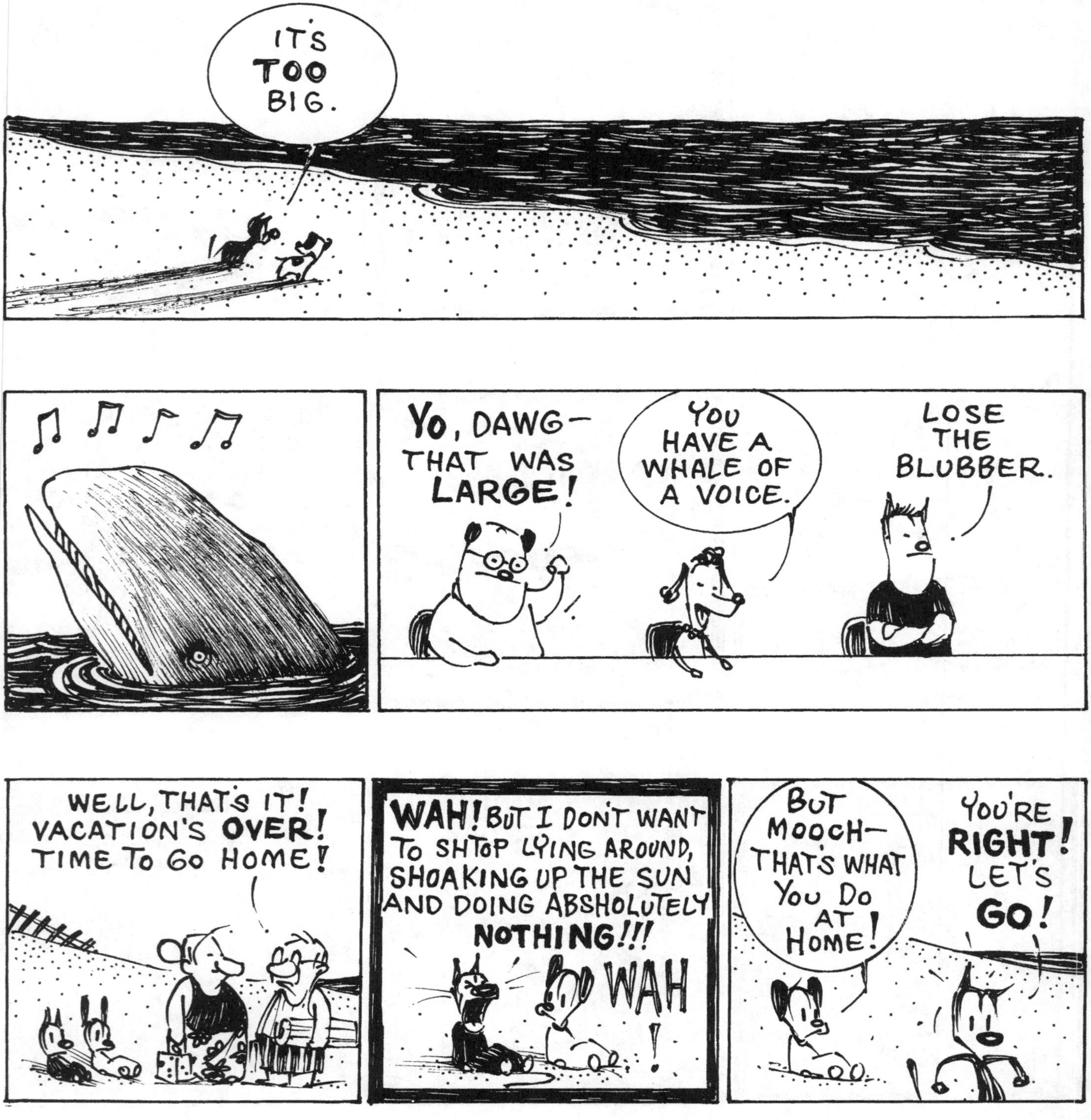
IT'S TOO BIG.
YO, DAWG— THAT WAS LARGE!
YOU HAVE A WHALE OF A VOICE.
LOSE THE BLUBBER.
WELL, THAT'S IT! VACATION'S OVER! TIME TO GO HOME!
WAH! BUT I DON'T WANT TO SHTOP LYING AROUND, SHOAKING UP THE SUN AND DOING ABSHOLUTELY NOTHING!!!
WAH!
BUT MOOCH— THAT'S WHAT YOU DO AT HOME!
YOU'RE RIGHT! LET'S GO!

MUTTS.
by PATRICK McDONNEL.

THE 400th TREAT

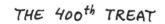

THE 2,500th WALK

THE 5,000th THROW

THE 8,000th BELLYRUB

THE 1,000,000th KISS

94-04

HAPPY ANNIVERSARY

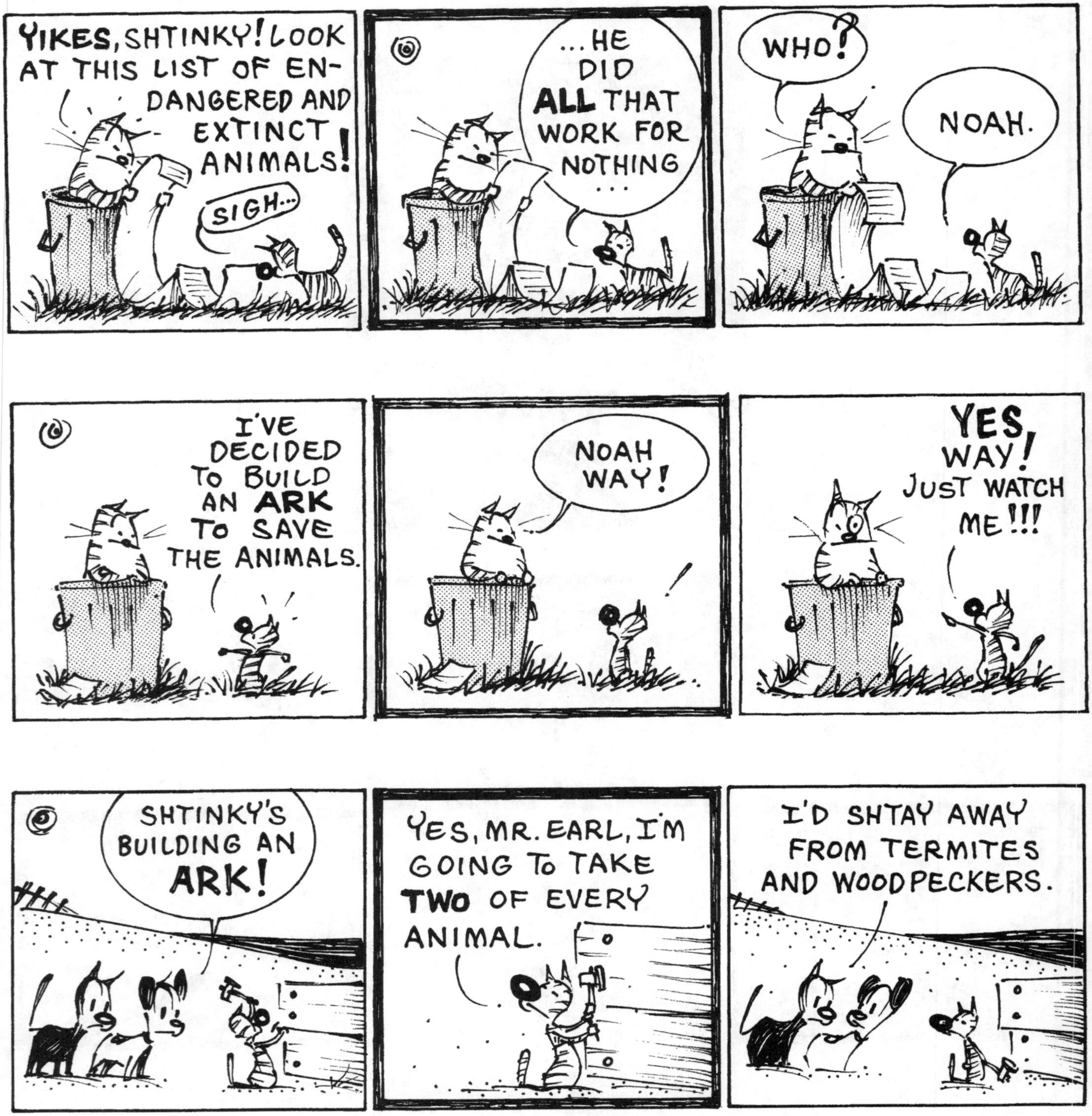
YIKES, SHTINKY! LOOK AT THIS LIST OF ENDANGERED AND EXTINCT ANIMALS!
SIGH...
...HE DID ALL THAT WORK FOR NOTHING...
WHO?
NOAH.
I'VE DECIDED TO BUILD AN ARK TO SAVE THE ANIMALS.
NOAH WAY!
YES, WAY! JUST WATCH ME!!!
SHTINKY'S BUILDING AN ARK!
YES, MR. EARL, I'M GOING TO TAKE TWO OF EVERY ANIMAL.
I'D SHTAY AWAY FROM TERMITES AND WOODPECKERS.

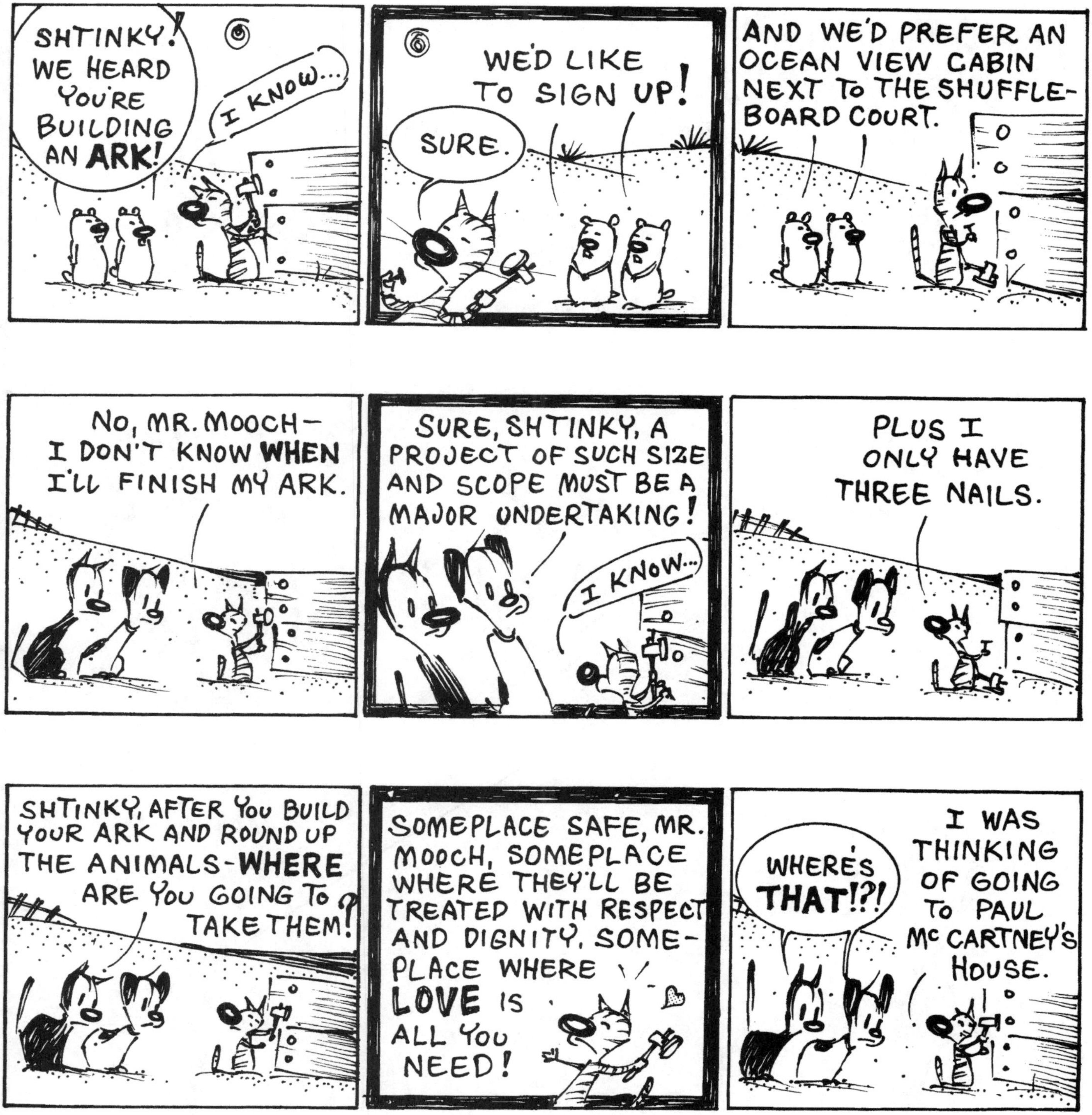
SHTINKY! WE HEARD YOU'RE BUILDING AN ARK!
I KNOW...
WE'D LIKE TO SIGN UP!
SURE.
AND WE'D PREFER AN OCEAN VIEW CABIN NEXT TO THE SHUFFLE-BOARD COURT.
NO, MR. MOOCH— I DON'T KNOW WHEN I'LL FINISH MY ARK.
SURE, SHTINKY, A PROJECT OF SUCH SIZE AND SCOPE MUST BE A MAJOR UNDERTAKING!
I KNOW...
PLUS I ONLY HAVE THREE NAILS.
SHTINKY, AFTER YOU BUILD YOUR ARK AND ROUND UP THE ANIMALS-WHERE ARE YOU GOING TO TAKE THEM?
SOMEPLACE SAFE, MR. MOOCH, SOMEPLACE WHERE THEY'LL BE TREATED WITH RESPECT AND DIGNITY. SOME-PLACE WHERE LOVE IS ALL YOU NEED!
WHERE'S THAT!?!
I WAS THINKING OF GOING TO PAUL McCARTNEY'S HOUSE.

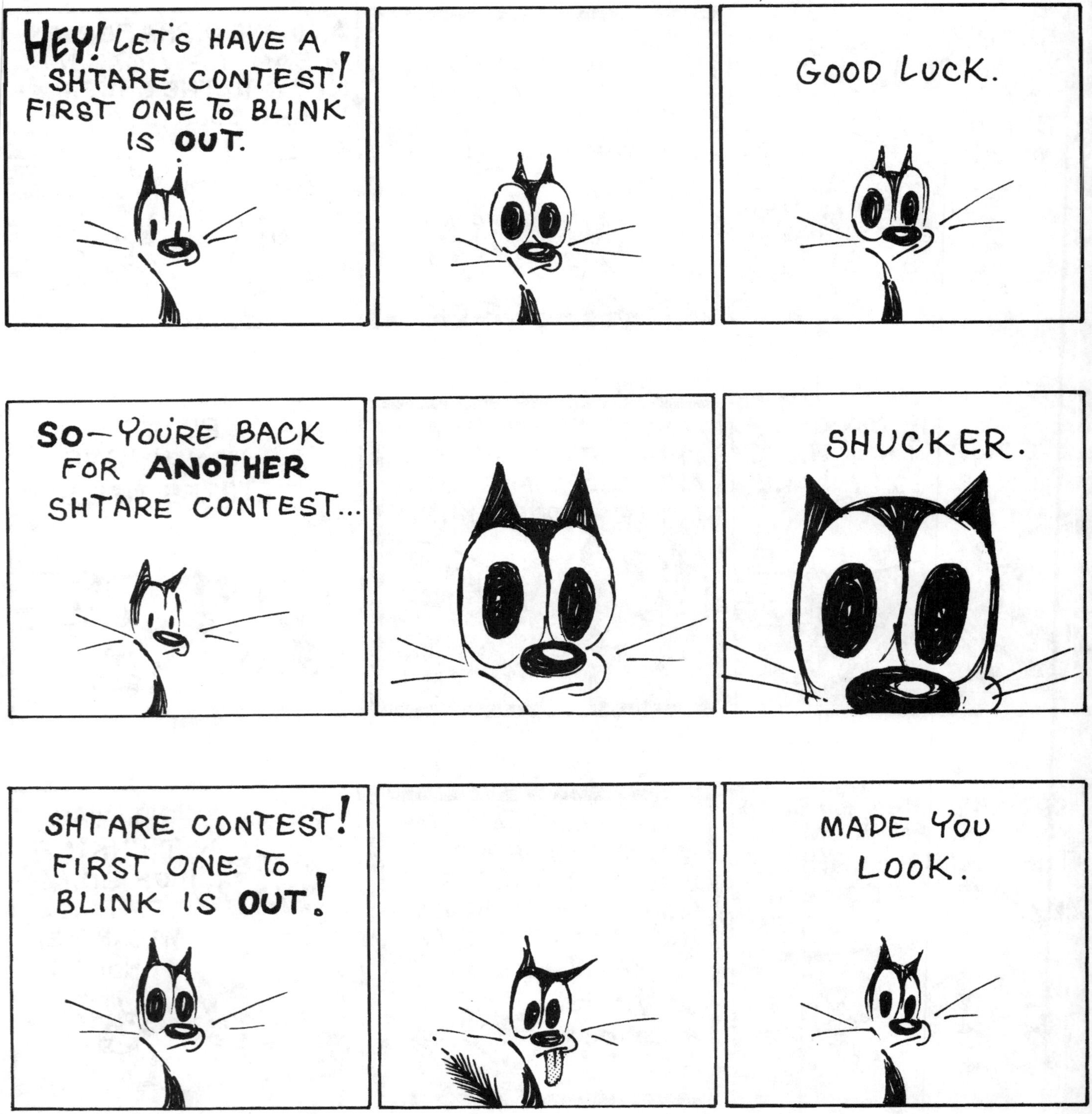
HEY! LET'S HAVE A SHTARE CONTEST! FIRST ONE TO BLINK IS OUT.
GOOD LUCK.
SO—YOU'RE BACK FOR ANOTHER SHTARE CONTEST...
SHUCKER.
SHTARE CONTEST! FIRST ONE TO BLINK IS OUT!
MADE YOU LOOK.

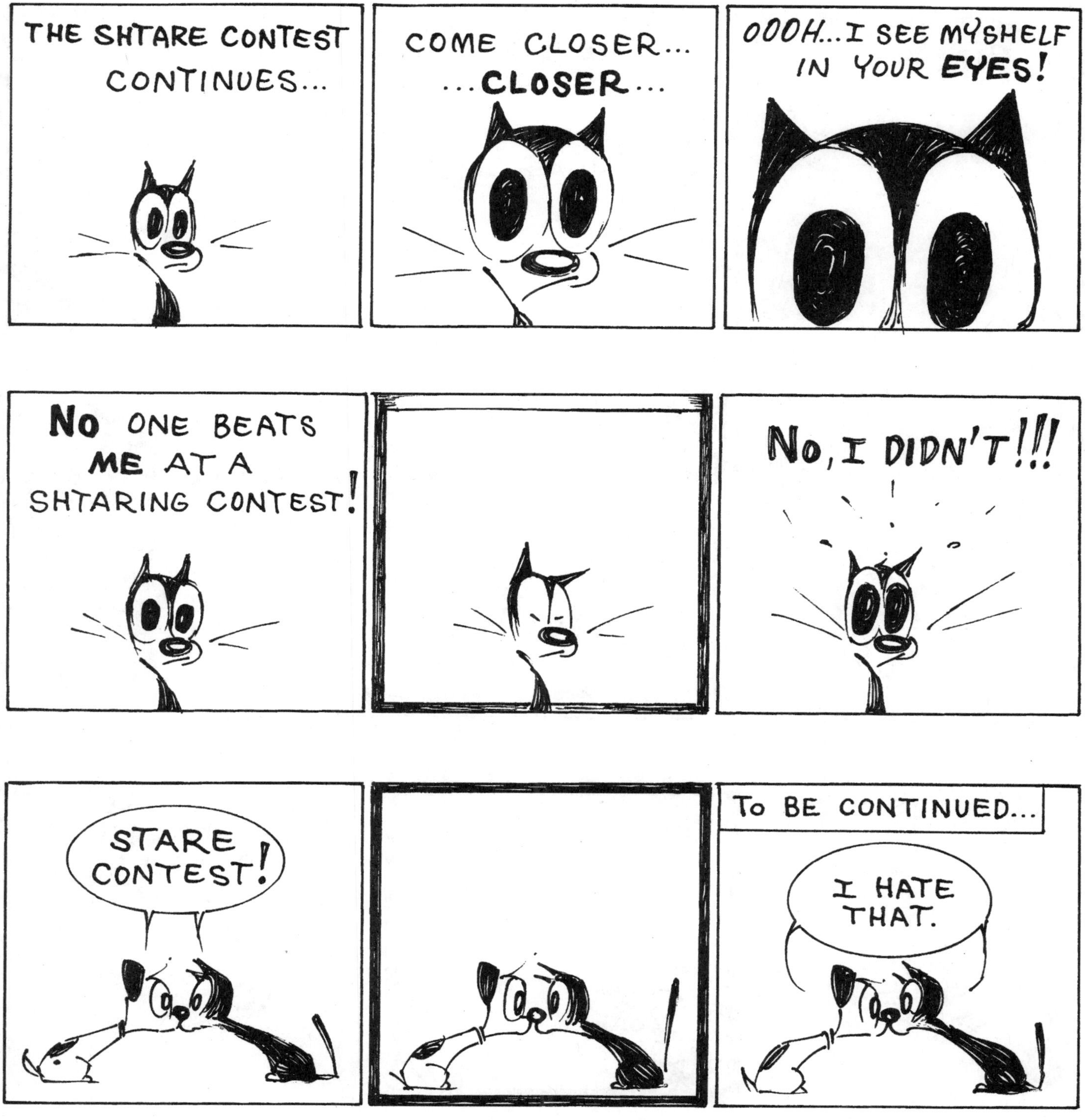
THE SHTARE CONTEST CONTINUES...
COME CLOSER... ...CLOSER...
OOOH...I SEE MYSHELF IN YOUR EYES!
NO ONE BEATS ME AT A SHTARING CONTEST!
NO, I DIDN'T!!!
STARE CONTEST!
TO BE CONTINUED...
I HATE THAT.

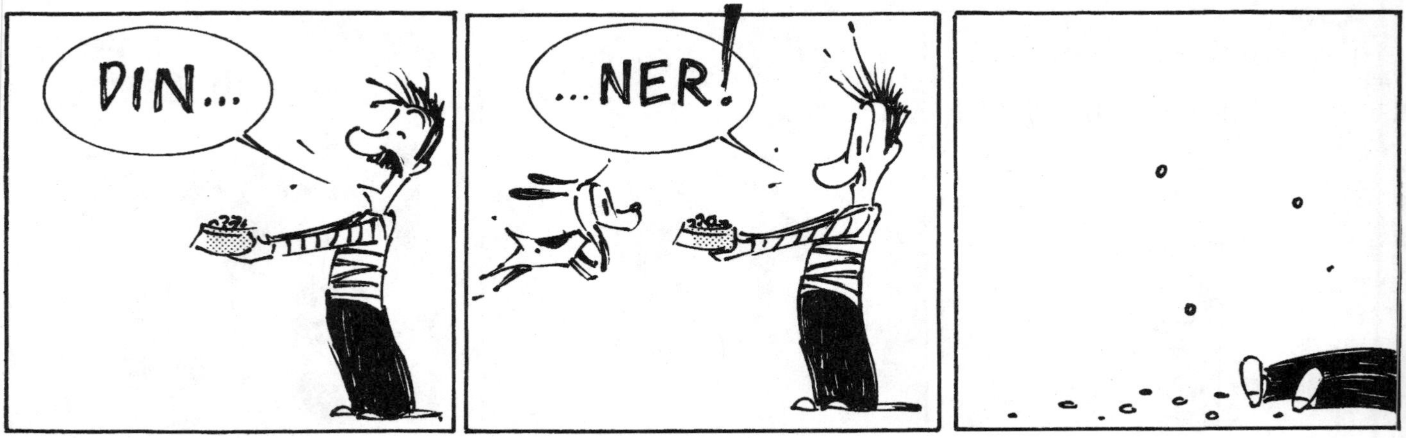
DIN...
...NER!

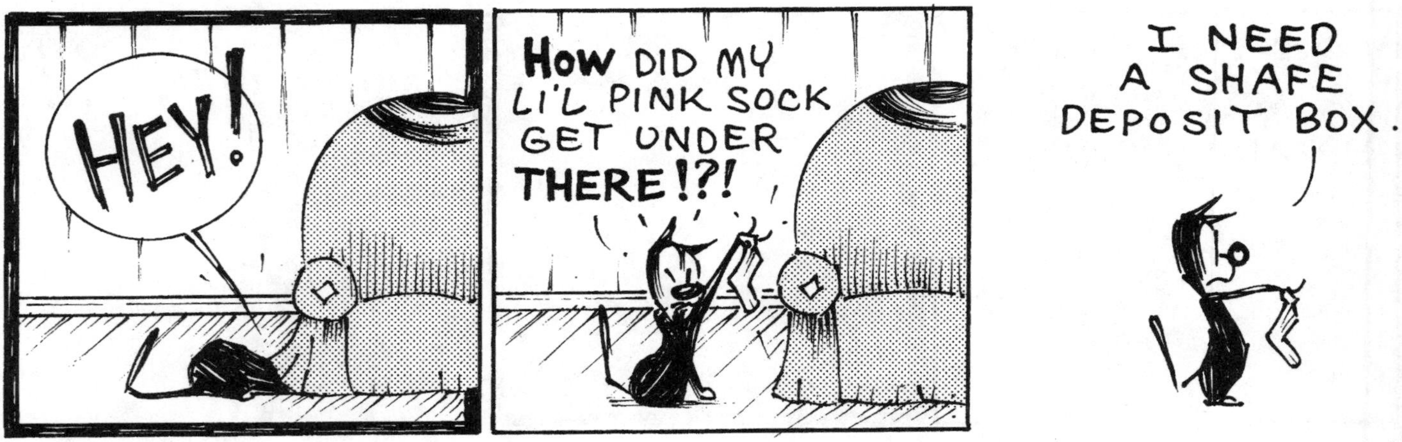
HEY!
HOW DID MY LI'L PINK SOCK GET UNDER THERE!?!
I NEED A SHAFE DEPOSIT BOX.

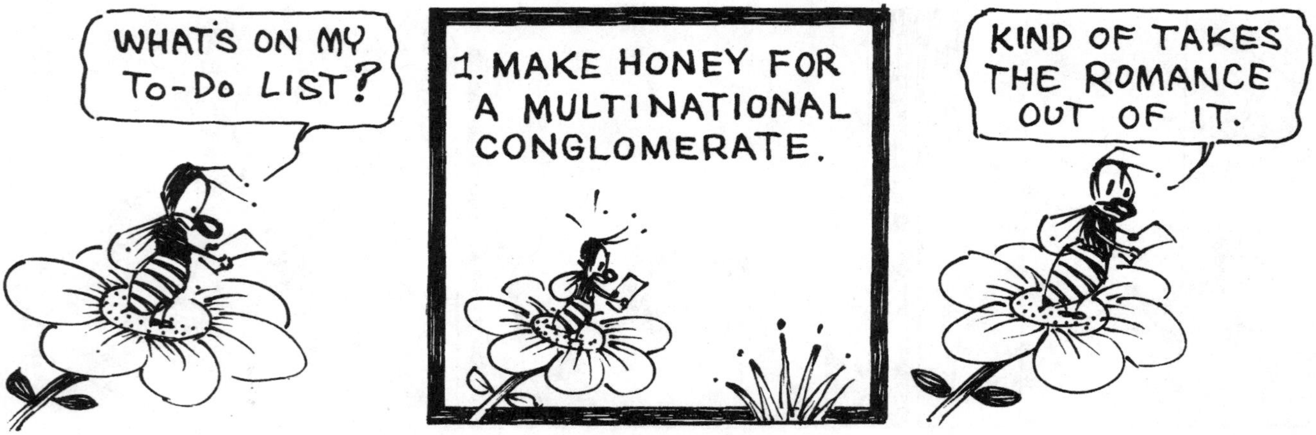
WHAT'S ON MY TO-DO LIST?
1. MAKE HONEY FOR A MULTINATIONAL CONGLOMERATE.
KIND OF TAKES THE ROMANCE OUT OF IT.

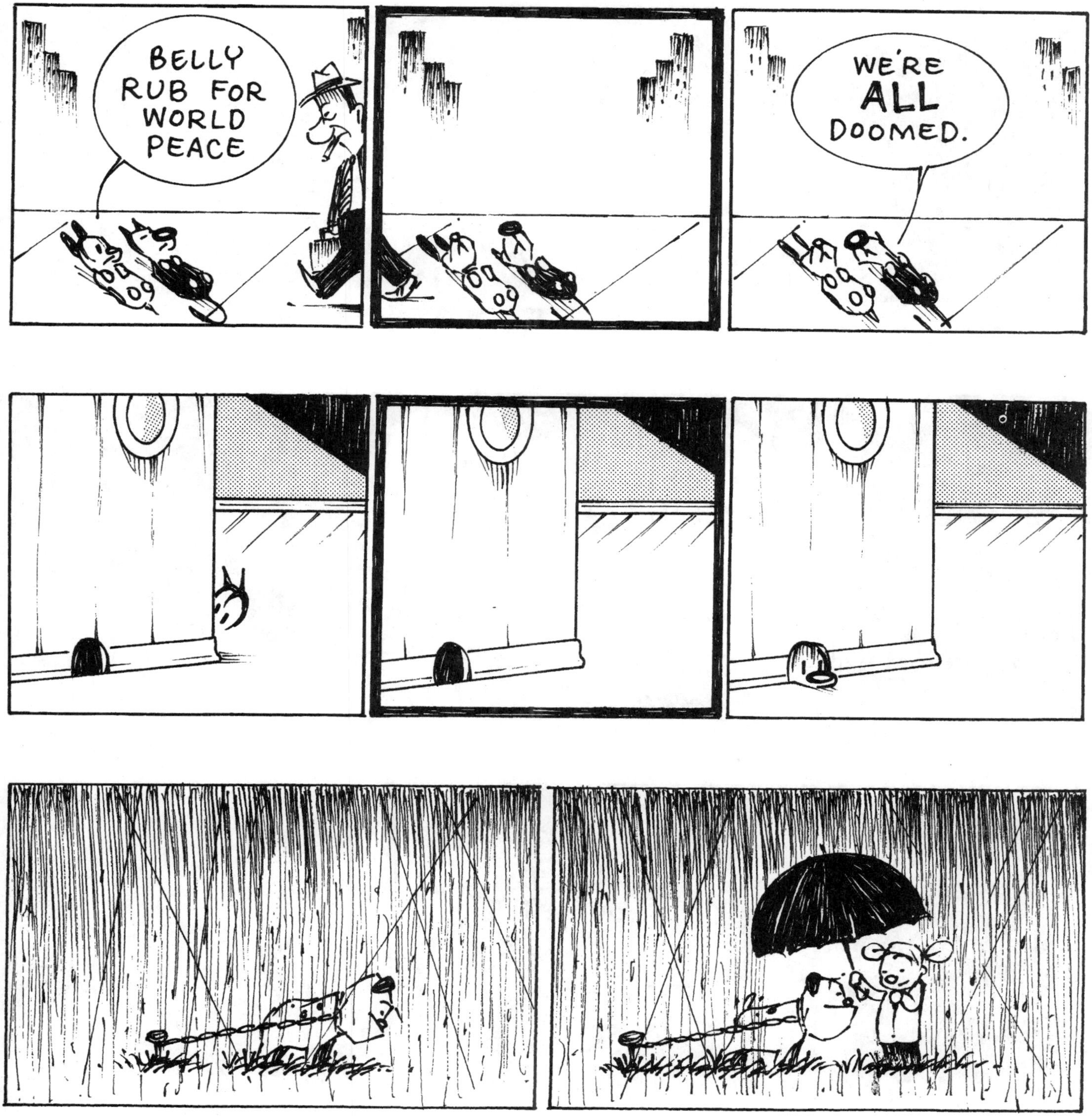
BELLY RUB FOR WORLD PEACE
WE'RE ALL DOOMED.

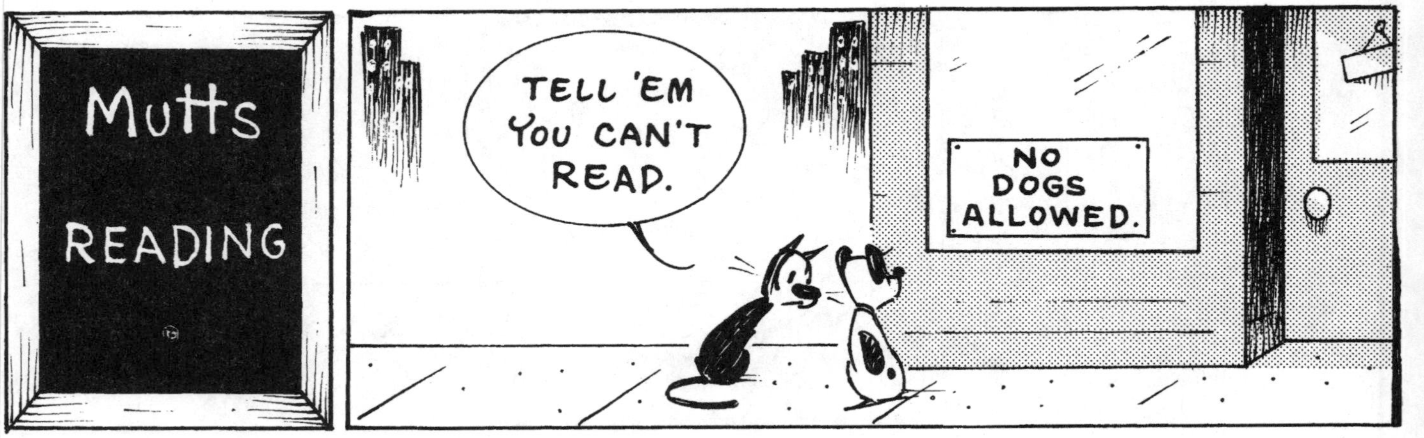
Mutts
READING
TELL 'EM YOU CAN'T READ.
NO DOGS ALLOWED.

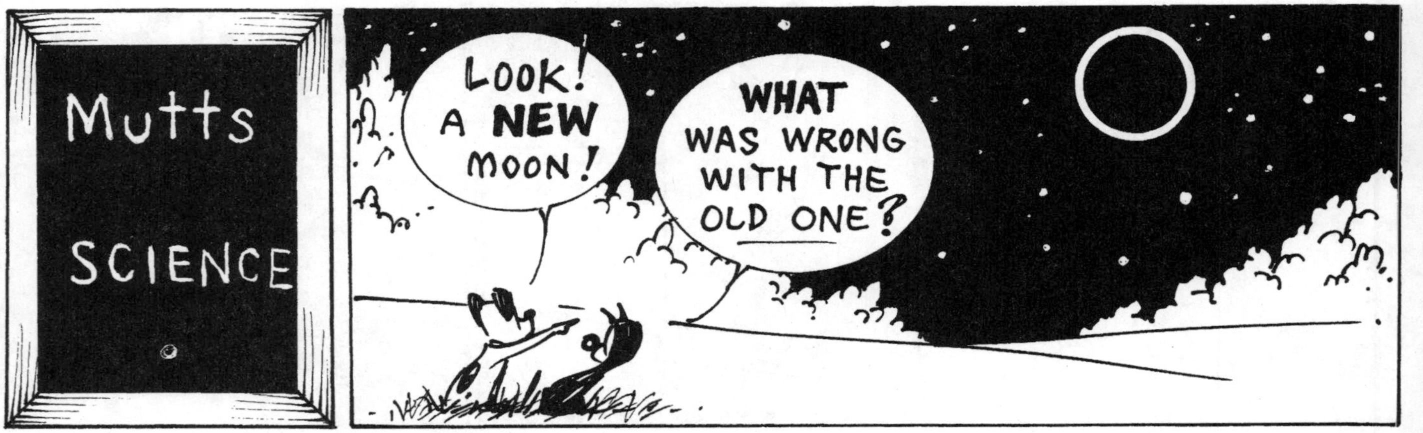
Mutts
SCIENCE
LOOK! A NEW MOON!
WHAT WAS WRONG WITH THE OLD ONE?

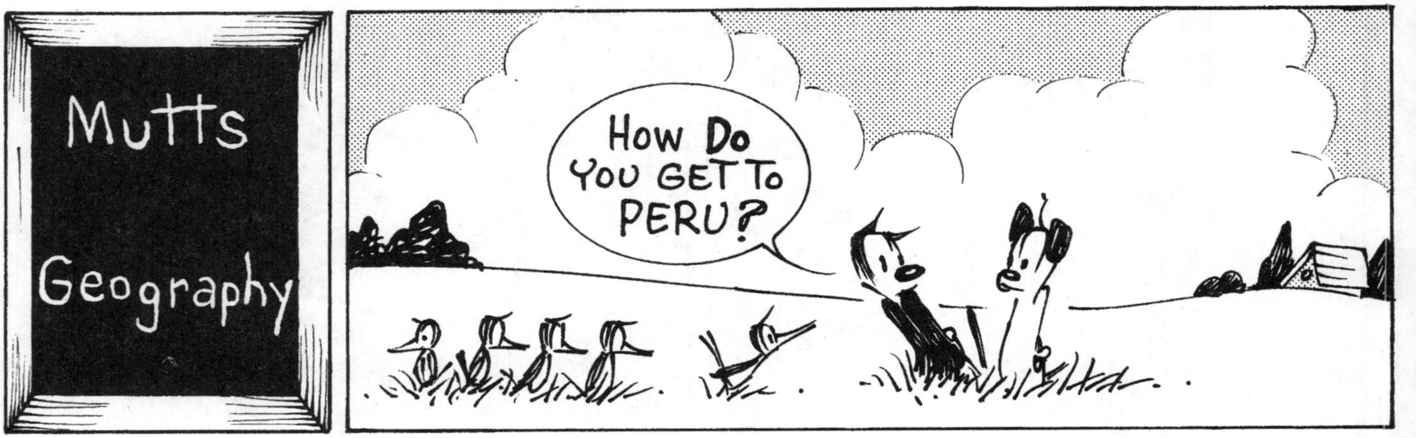
Mutts
Geography
HOW DO YOU GET TO PERU?

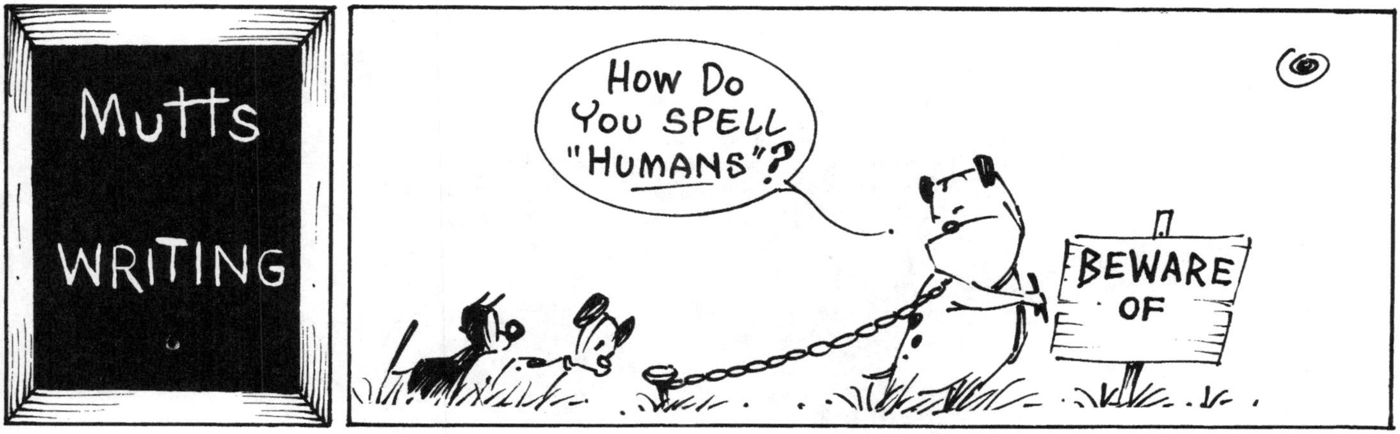
Mutts WRITING
HOW DO YOU SPELL "HUMANS"?
BEWARE OF

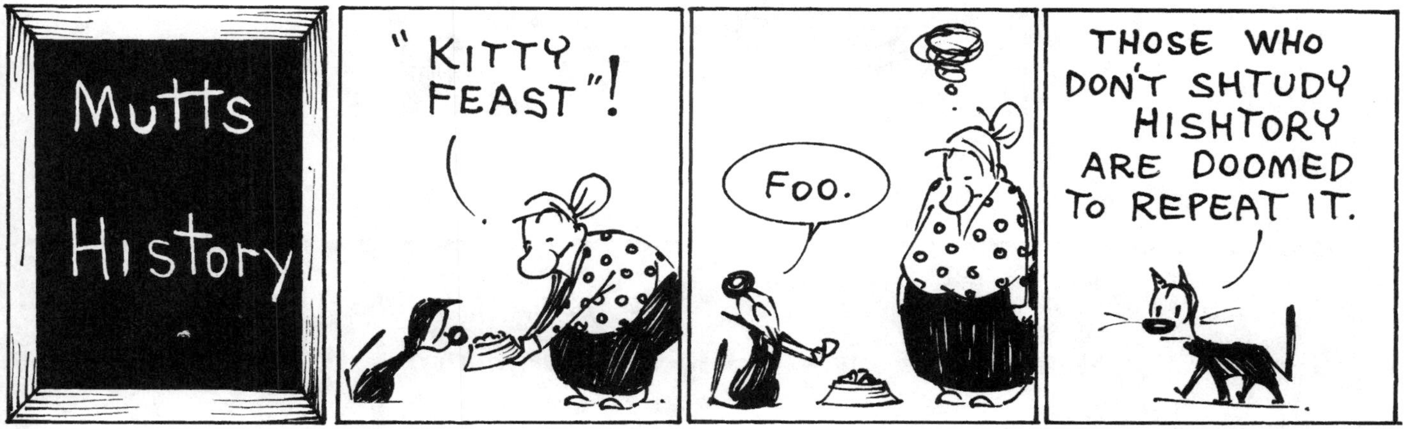
Mutts History
"KITTY FEAST"!
FOO.
THOSE WHO DON'T SHTUDY HISHTORY ARE DOOMED TO REPEAT IT.

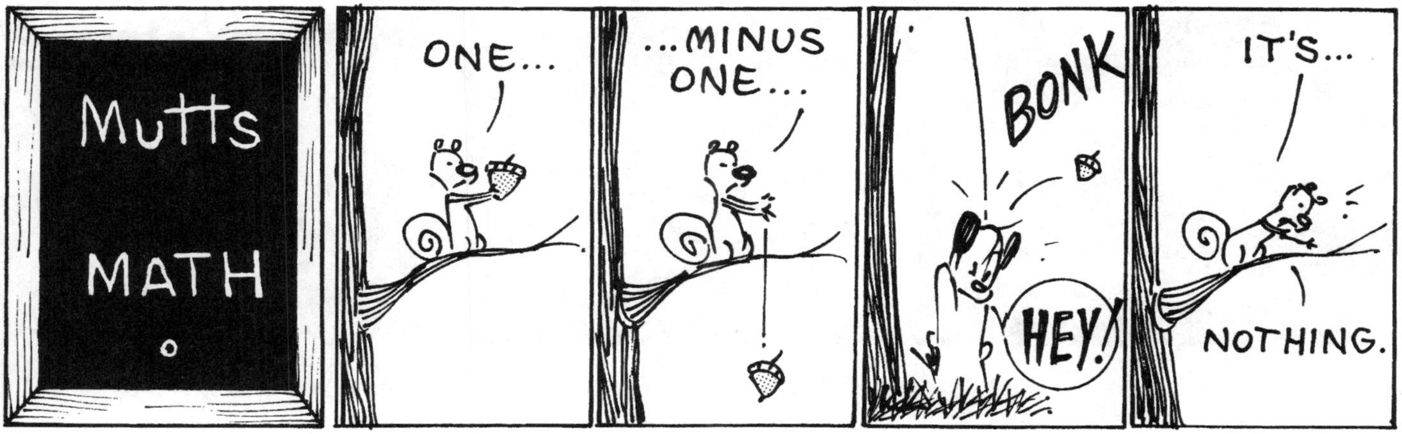
Mutts MATH
ONE...
...MINUS ONE...
BONK
HEY!
IT'S...
NOTHING.

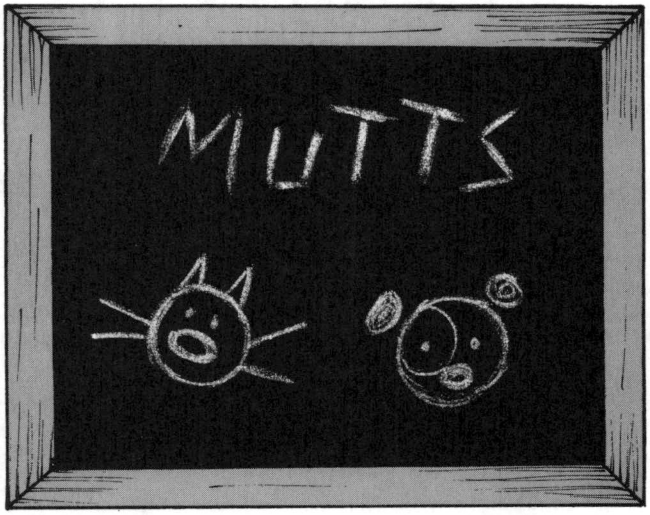
MUTTS

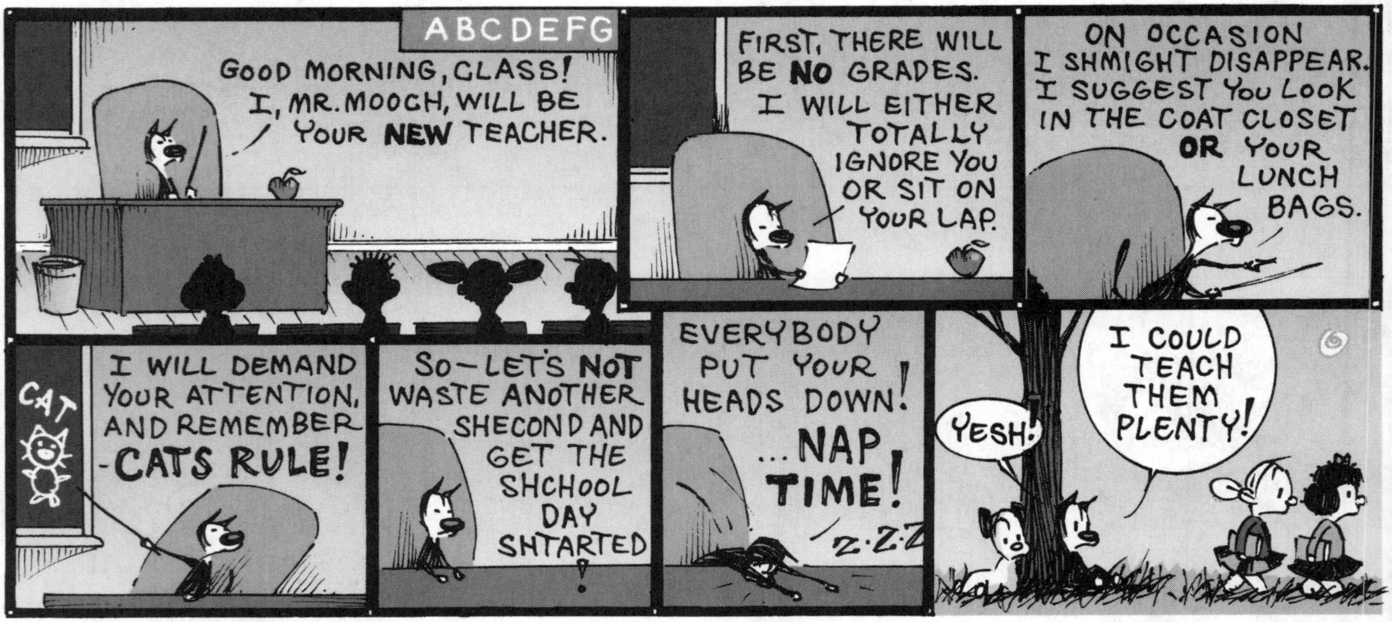
ABCDEFG
GOOD MORNING, CLASS! I, MR. MOOCH, WILL BE YOUR NEW TEACHER.
FIRST, THERE WILL BE NO GRADES.
I WILL EITHER TOTALLY IGNORE YOU OR SIT ON YOUR LAP.
ON OCCASION I SHMIGHT DISAPPEAR. I SUGGEST YOU LOOK IN THE COAT CLOSET OR YOUR LUNCH BAGS.
CAT
I WILL DEMAND YOUR ATTENTION, AND REMEMBER -CATS RULE!
SO—LET'S NOT WASTE ANOTHER SHECOND AND GET THE SHCHOOL DAY SHTARTED!
EVERYBODY PUT YOUR HEADS DOWN!
...NAP TIME!
Z·Z·Z
YESH!
I COULD TEACH THEM PLENTY!

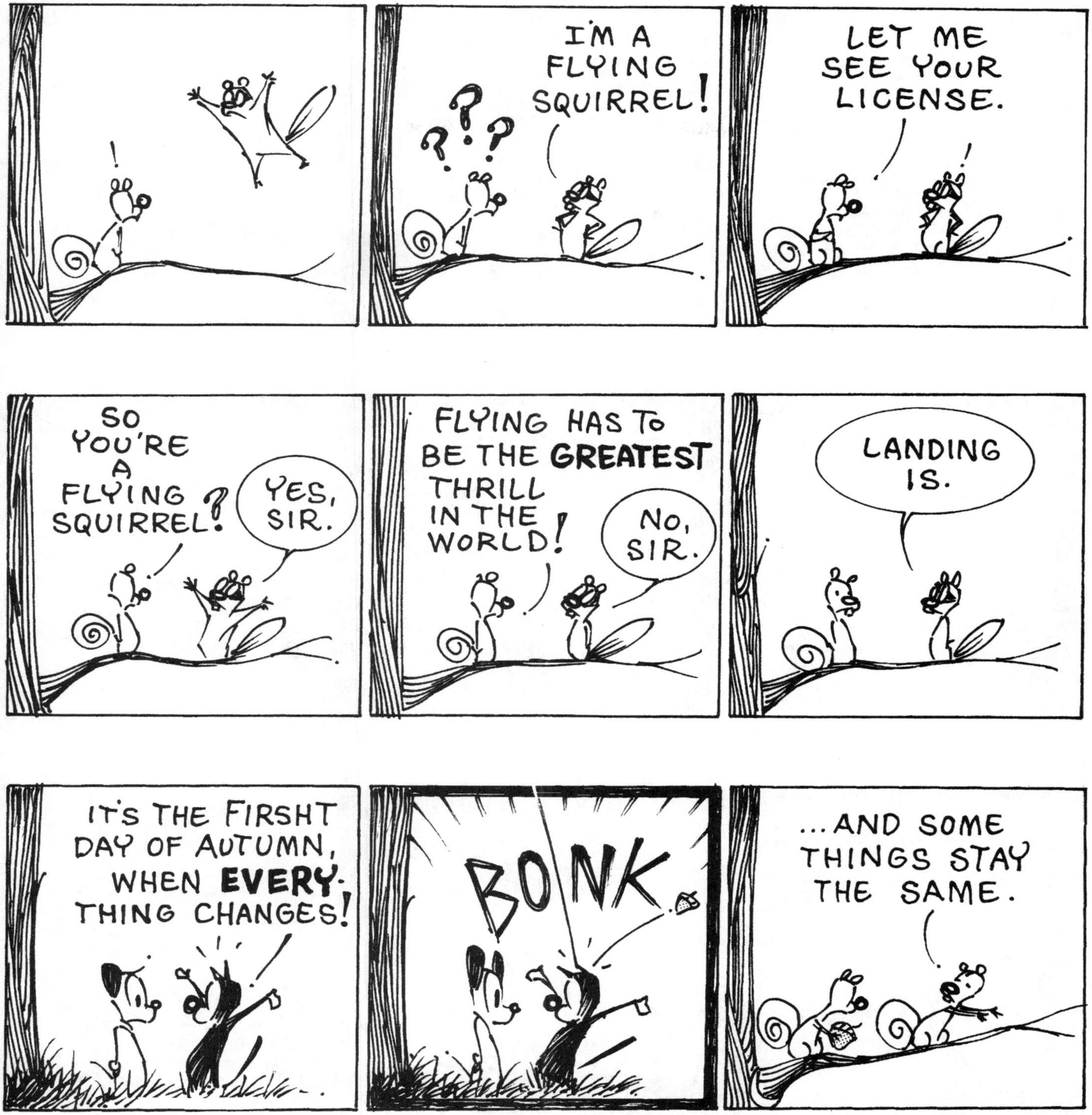
!
I'M A FLYING SQUIRREL!
???
LET ME SEE YOUR LICENSE.
!
SO YOU'RE A FLYING SQUIRREL?
YES, SIR.
FLYING HAS TO BE THE GREATEST THRILL IN THE WORLD!
NO, SIR.
LANDING IS.
IT'S THE FIRSHT DAY OF AUTUMN, WHEN EVERYTHING CHANGES!
BONK
...AND SOME THINGS STAY THE SAME.

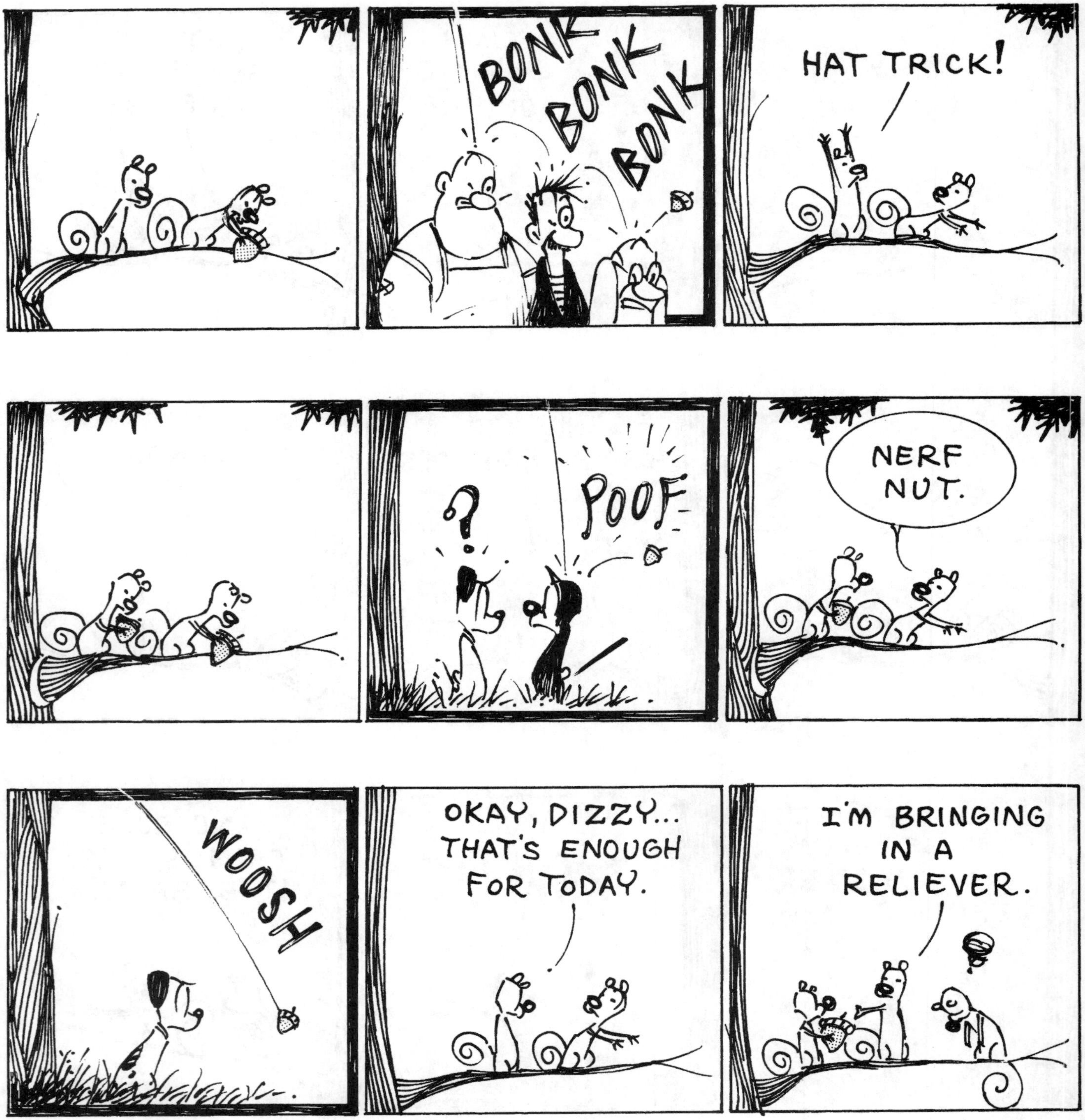
BONK
BONK
BONK
HAT TRICK!
POOF
NERF NUT.
WOOSH
OKAY, DIZZY... THAT'S ENOUGH FOR TODAY.
I'M BRINGING IN A RELIEVER.

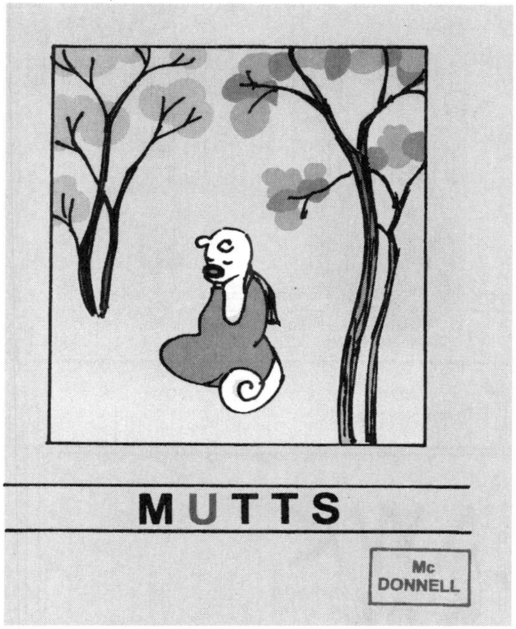
MUTTS
Mc DONNELL

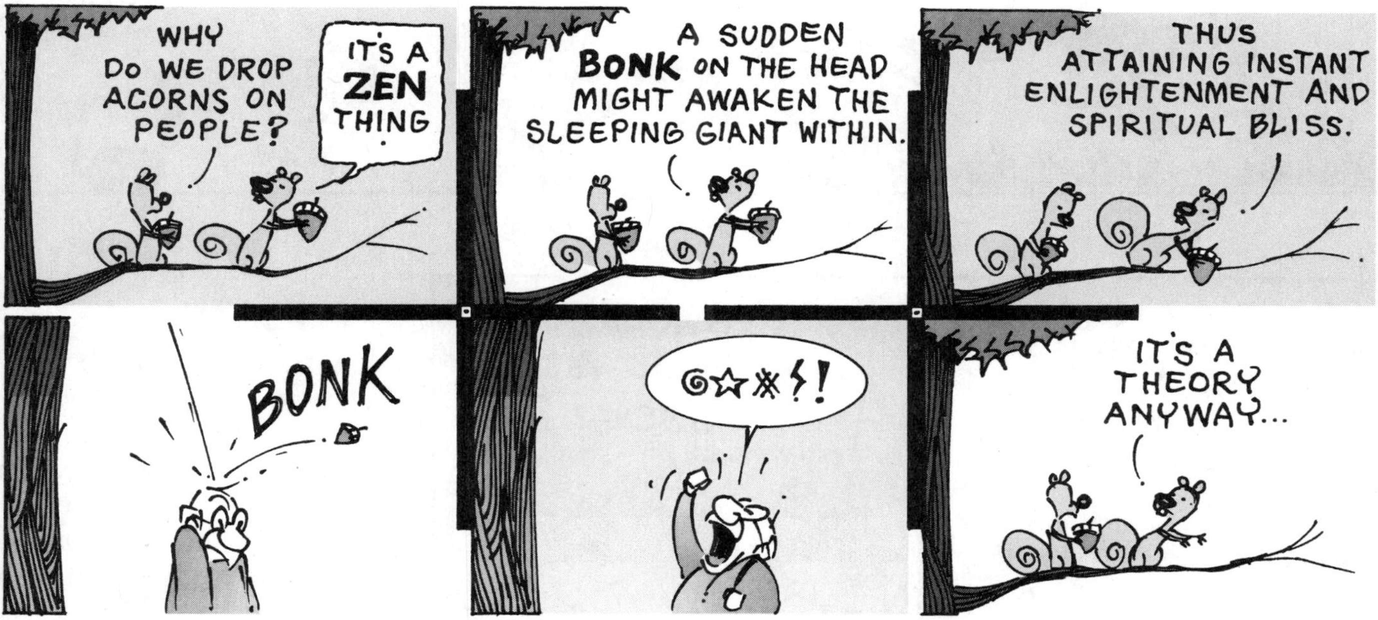
WHY DO WE DROP ACORNS ON PEOPLE?
IT'S A ZEN THING
A SUDDEN BONK ON THE HEAD MIGHT AWAKEN THE SLEEPING GIANT WITHIN.
THUS ATTAINING INSTANT ENLIGHTENMENT AND SPIRITUAL BLISS.
BONK
IT'S A THEORY ANYWAY...

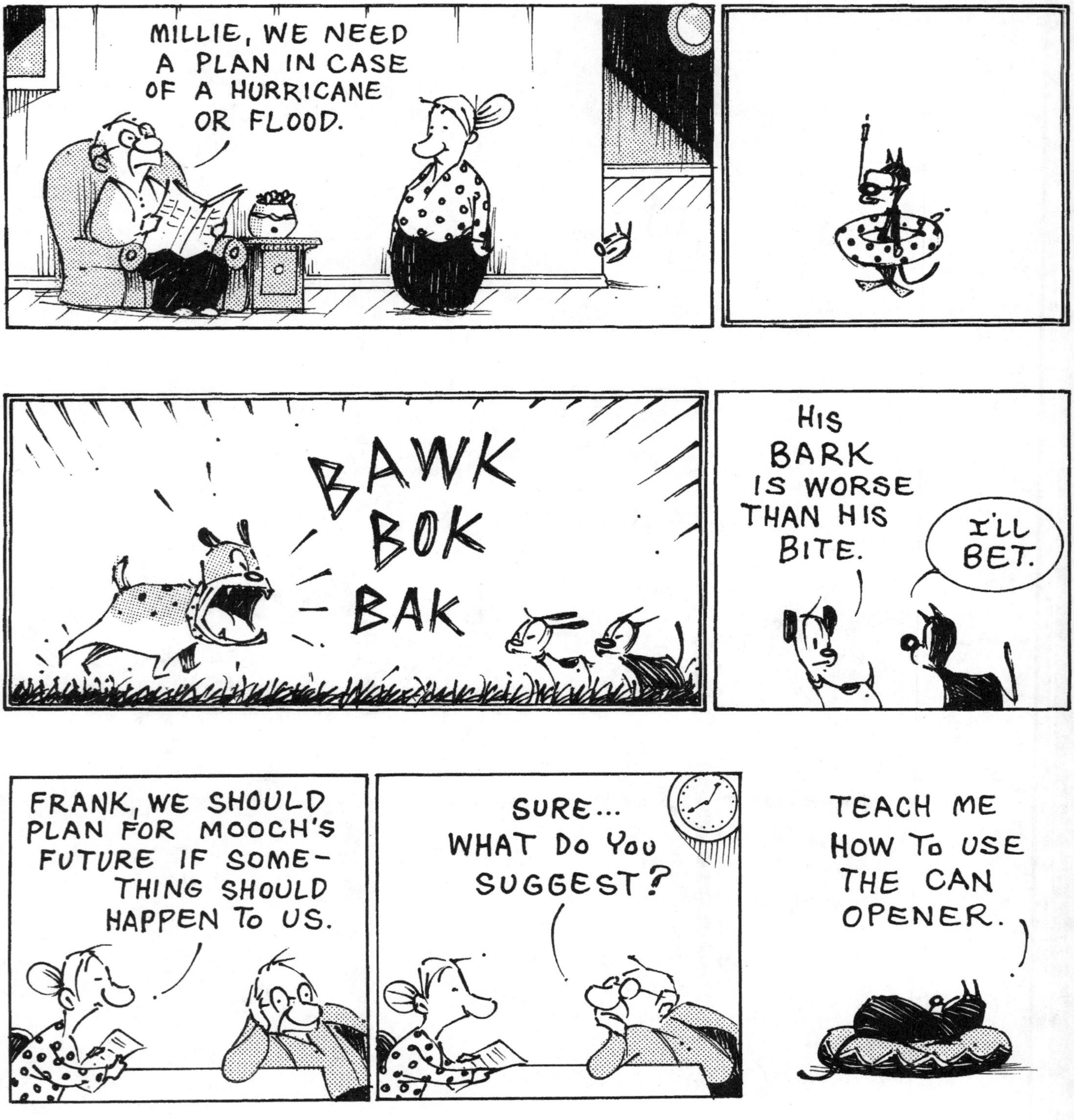
MILLIE, WE NEED A PLAN IN CASE OF A HURRICANE OR FLOOD.
BAWK
BOK
BAK
HIS BARK IS WORSE THAN HIS BITE.
I'LL BET.
FRANK, WE SHOULD PLAN FOR MOOCH'S FUTURE IF SOMETHING SHOULD HAPPEN TO US.
SURE... WHAT DO YOU SUGGEST?
TEACH ME HOW TO USE THE CAN OPENER.

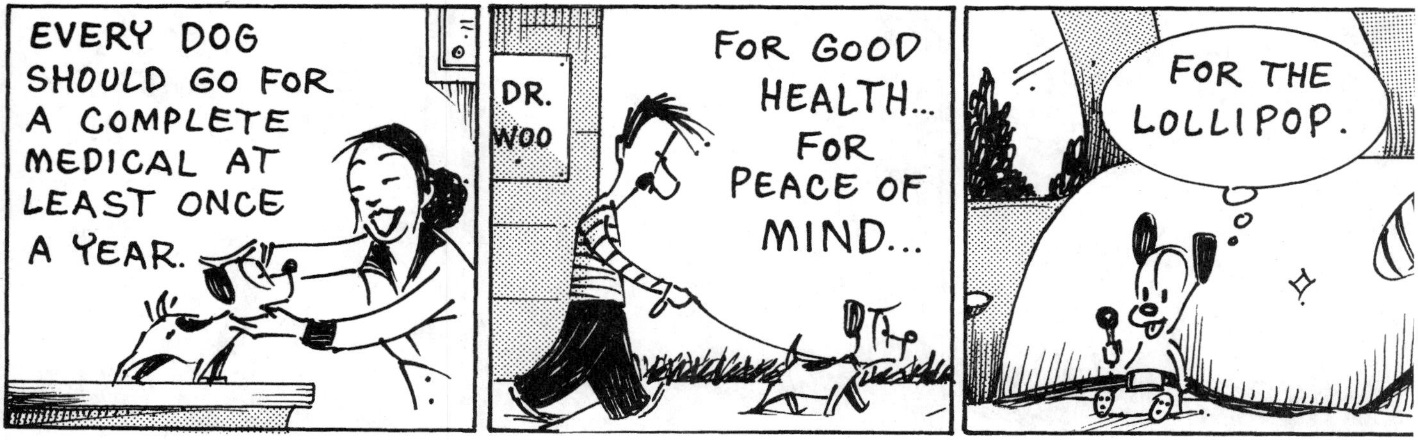
EVERY DOG SHOULD GO FOR A COMPLETE MEDICAL AT LEAST ONCE A YEAR.
DR. WOO
FOR GOOD HEALTH... FOR PEACE OF MIND...
FOR THE LOLLIPOP.

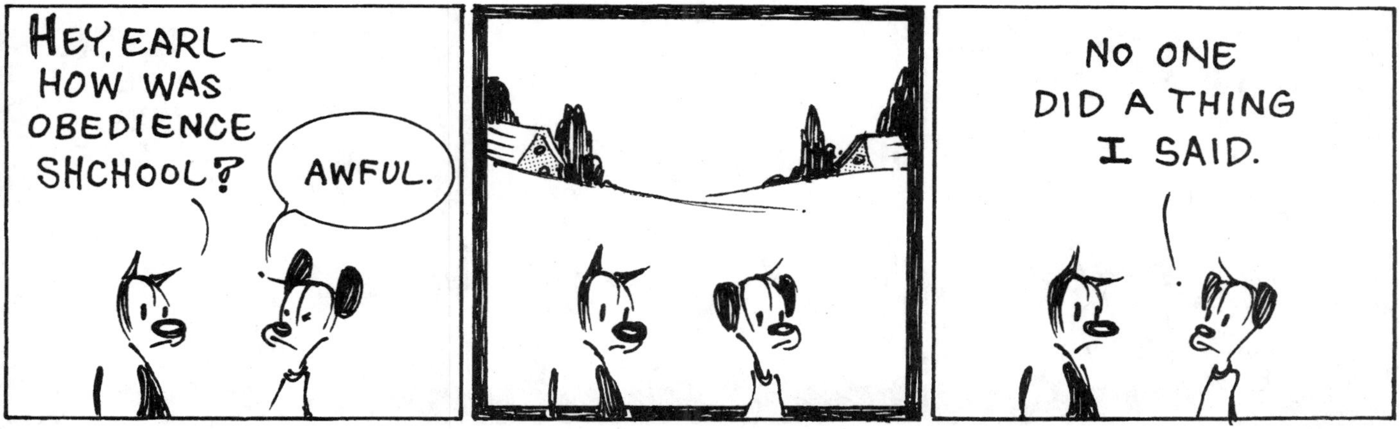
HEY, EARL— HOW WAS OBEDIENCE SHCHOOL?
AWFUL.
NO ONE DID A THING I SAID.

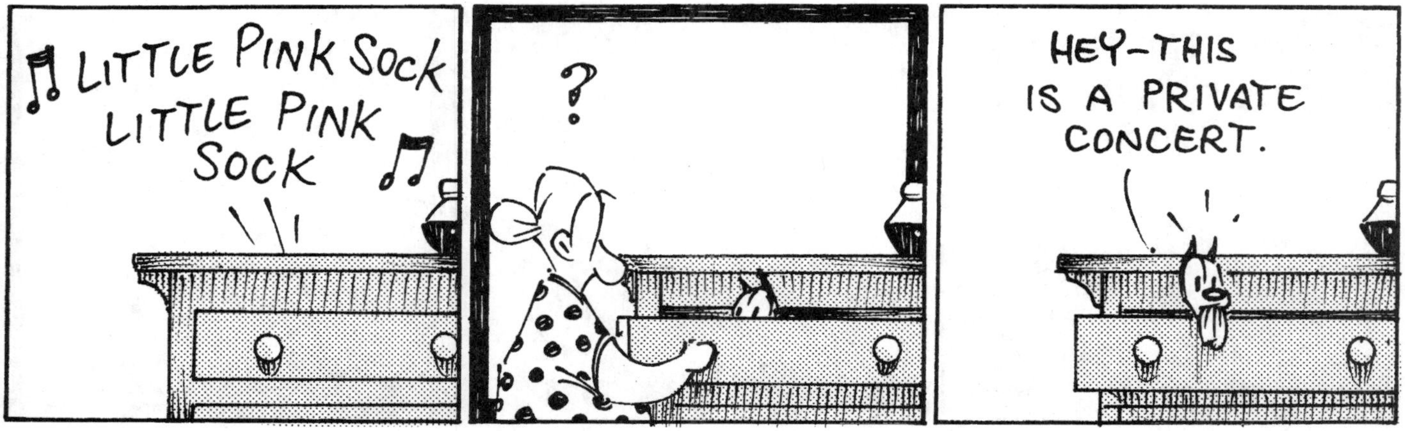
LITTLE PINK SOCK LITTLE PINK SOCK
?
HEY—THIS IS A PRIVATE CONCERT.

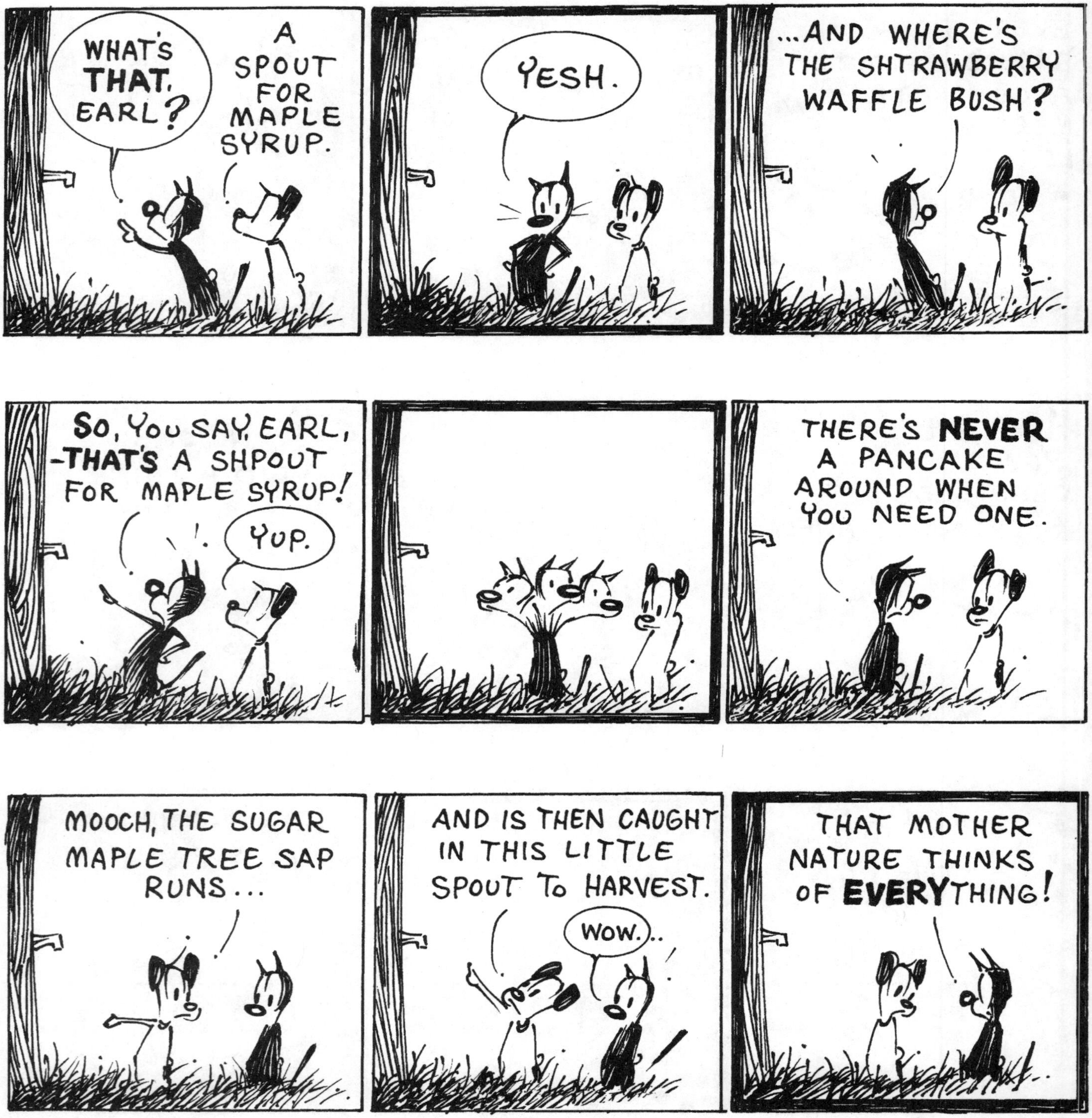
WHAT'S THAT, EARL?
A SPOUT FOR MAPLE SYRUP.
YESH.
...AND WHERE'S THE SHTRAWBERRY WAFFLE BUSH?
SO, YOU SAY, EARL, -THAT'S A SHPOUT FOR MAPLE SYRUP!
YUP.
THERE'S NEVER A PANCAKE AROUND WHEN YOU NEED ONE.
MOOCH, THE SUGAR MAPLE TREE SAP RUNS...
AND IS THEN CAUGHT IN THIS LITTLE SPOUT TO HARVEST.
WOW.
THAT MOTHER NATURE THINKS OF EVERYTHING!

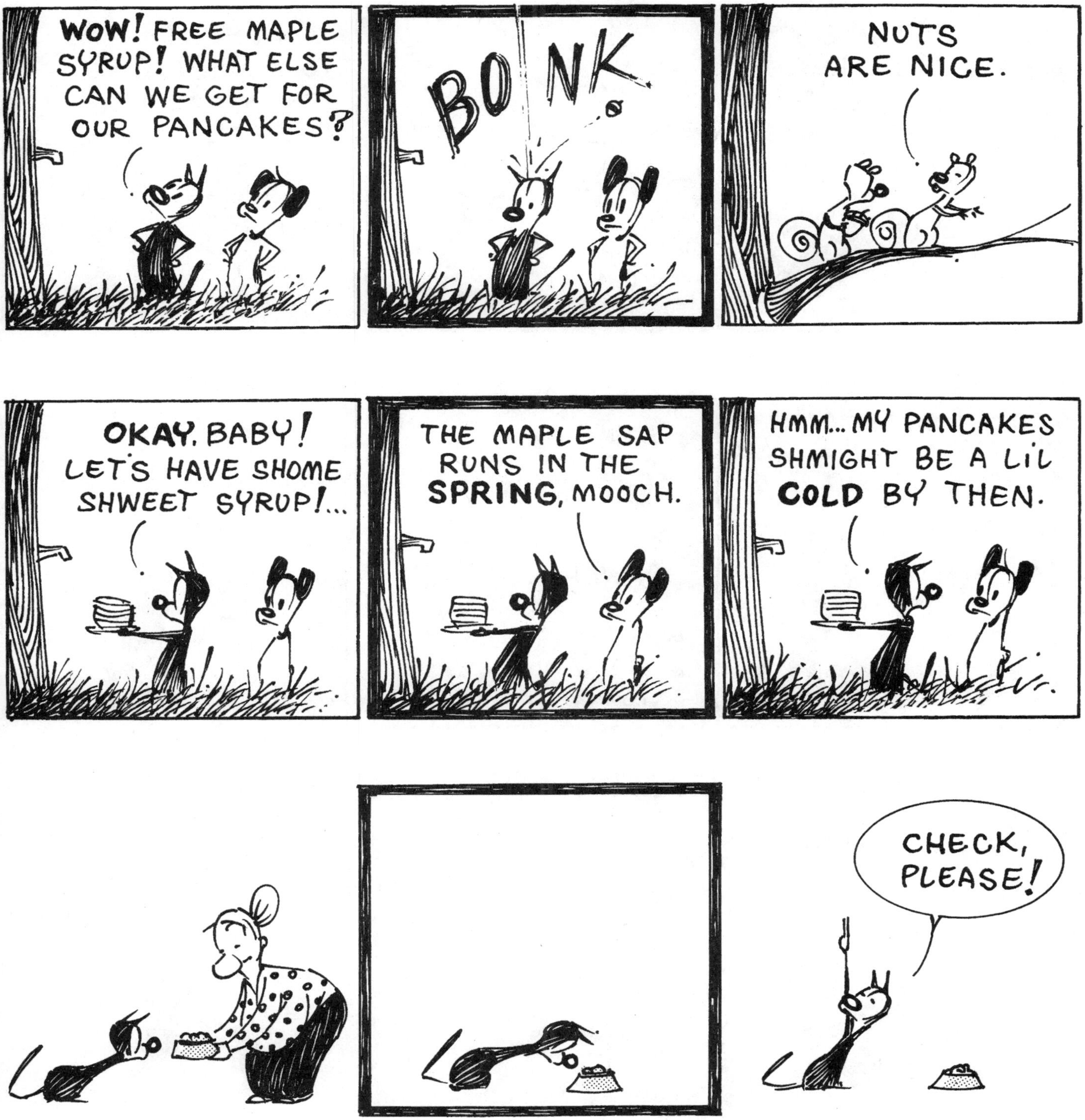
WOW! FREE MAPLE SYRUP! WHAT ELSE CAN WE GET FOR OUR PANCAKES?
BONK
NUTS ARE NICE.
OKAY, BABY! LET'S HAVE SHOME SHWEET SYRUP!...
THE MAPLE SAP RUNS IN THE SPRING, MOOCH.
HMM... MY PANCAKES SHMIGHT BE A LIL COLD BY THEN.
CHECK, PLEASE!

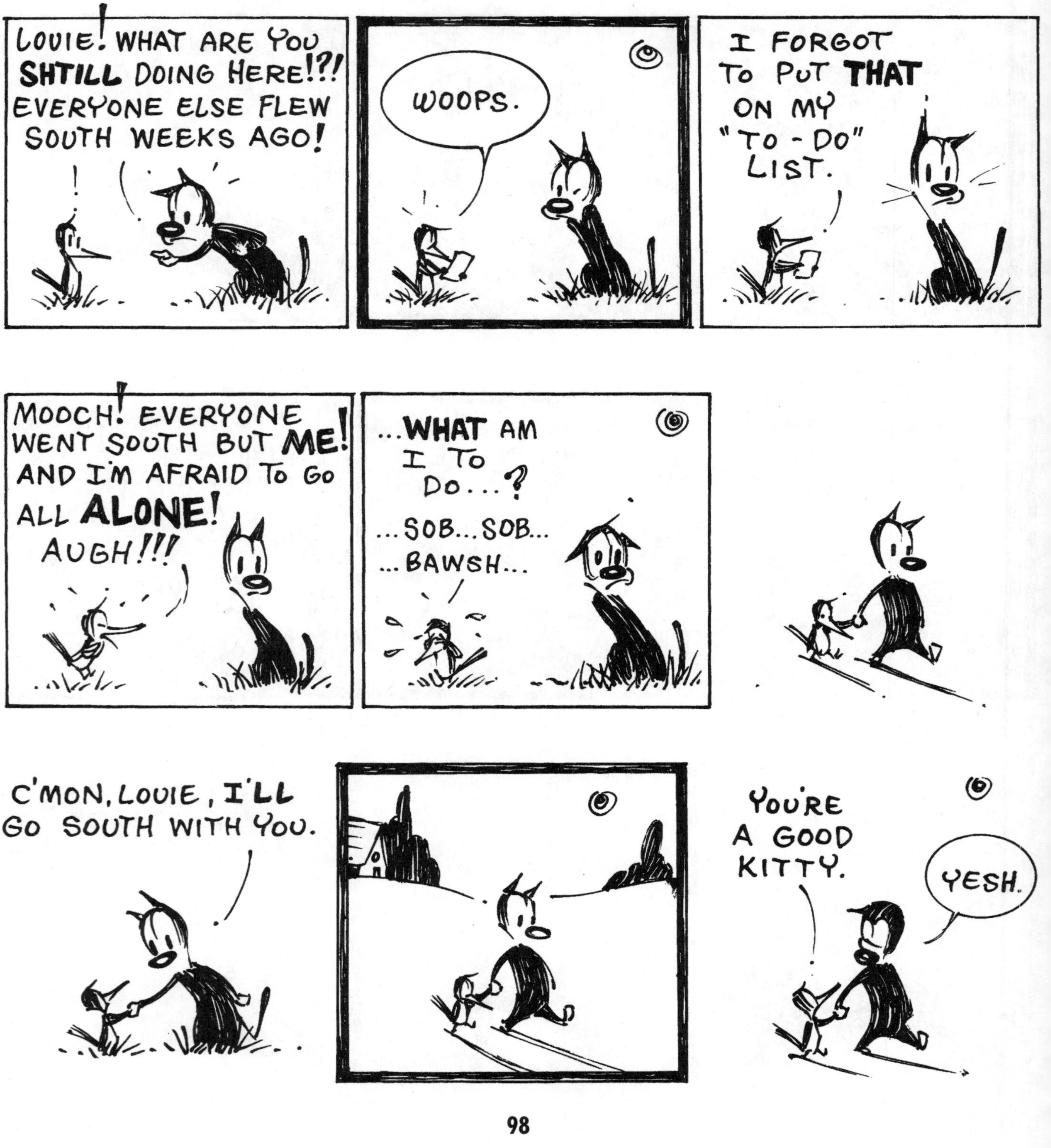
LOUIE! WHAT ARE YOU SHTILL DOING HERE!?! EVERYONE ELSE FLEW SOUTH WEEKS AGO!
WOOPS.
I FORGOT TO PUT THAT ON MY "TO-DO" LIST.
MOOCH! EVERYONE WENT SOUTH BUT ME! AND I'M AFRAID TO GO ALL ALONE! AUGH!!!
...WHAT AM I TO DO...?
...SOB...SOB... ...BAWSH...
C'MON, LOUIE, I'LL GO SOUTH WITH YOU.
YOU'RE A GOOD KITTY.
YESH.

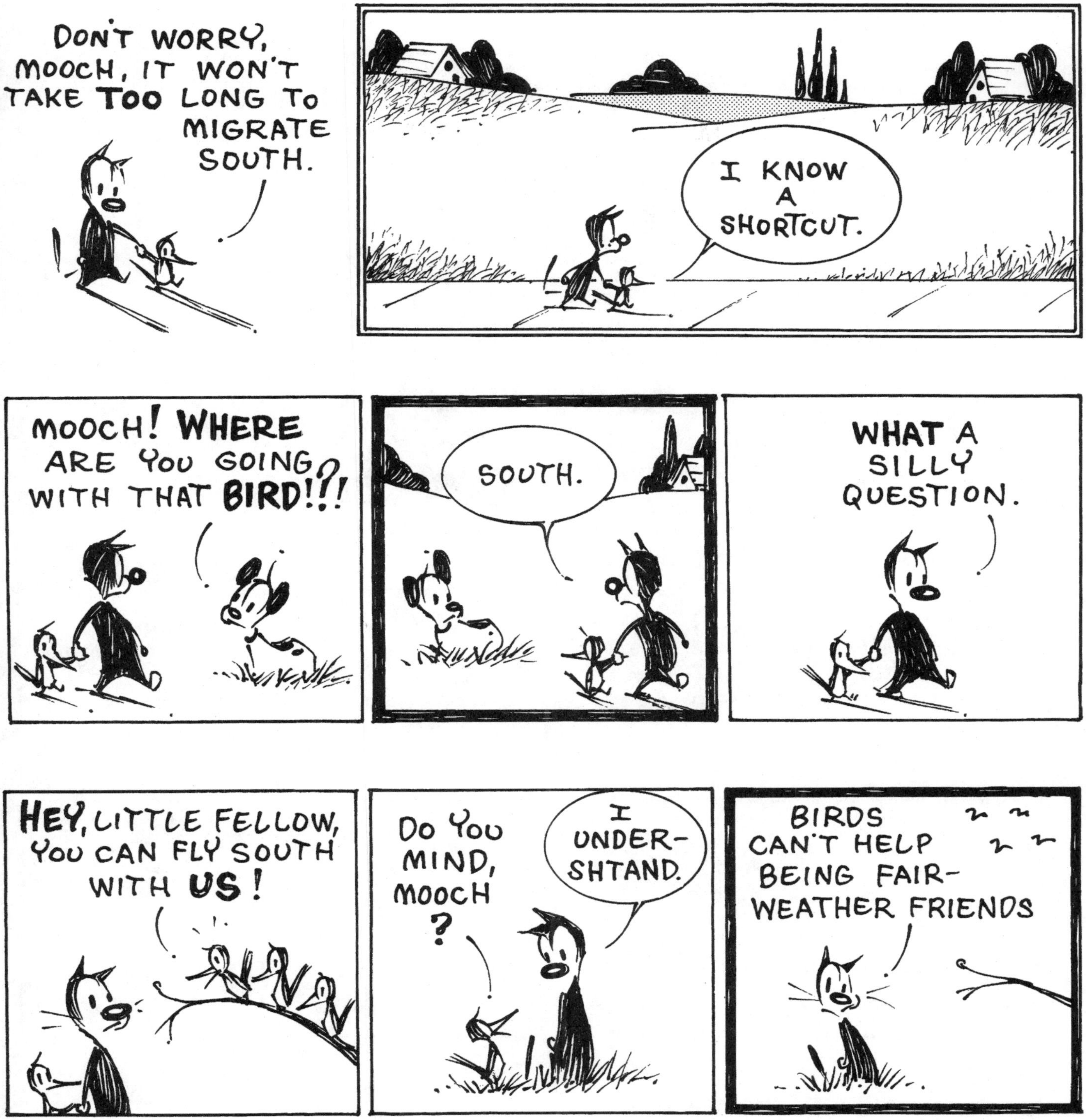

DON'T WORRY, MOOCH, IT WON'T TAKE TOO LONG TO MIGRATE SOUTH.
I KNOW A SHORTCUT.
MOOCH! WHERE ARE YOU GOING WITH THAT BIRD!?!
SOUTH.
WHAT A SILLY QUESTION.
HEY, LITTLE FELLOW, YOU CAN FLY SOUTH WITH US!
DO YOU MIND, MOOCH?
I UNDER-SHTAND.
BIRDS CAN'T HELP BEING FAIR-WEATHER FRIENDS

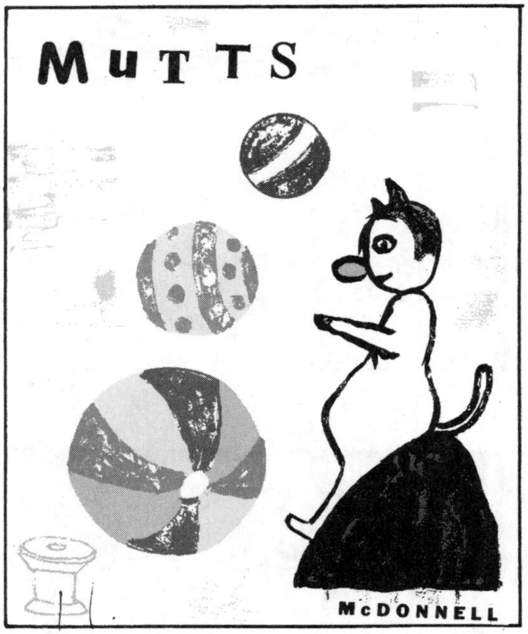
MUTTS
McDONNELL

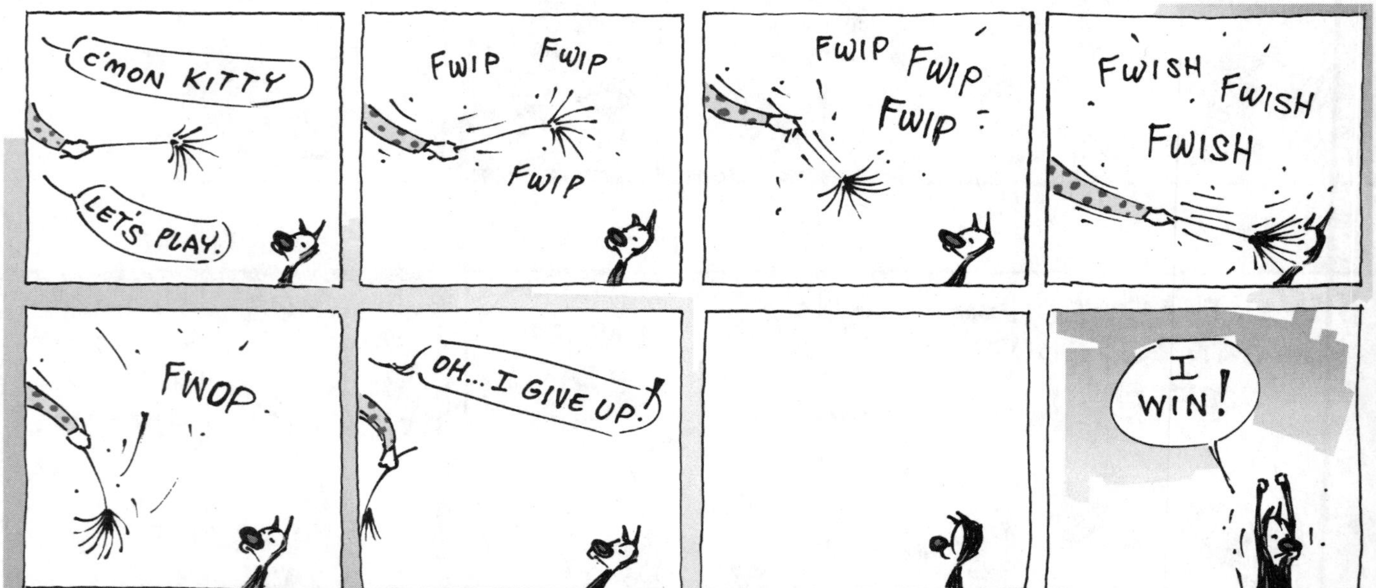
C'MON KITTY
LET'S PLAY.
FWIP FWIP
FWIP
FWIP FWIP
FWIP
FWISH FWISH
FWISH
FWOP
OH... I GIVE UP.
I WIN!

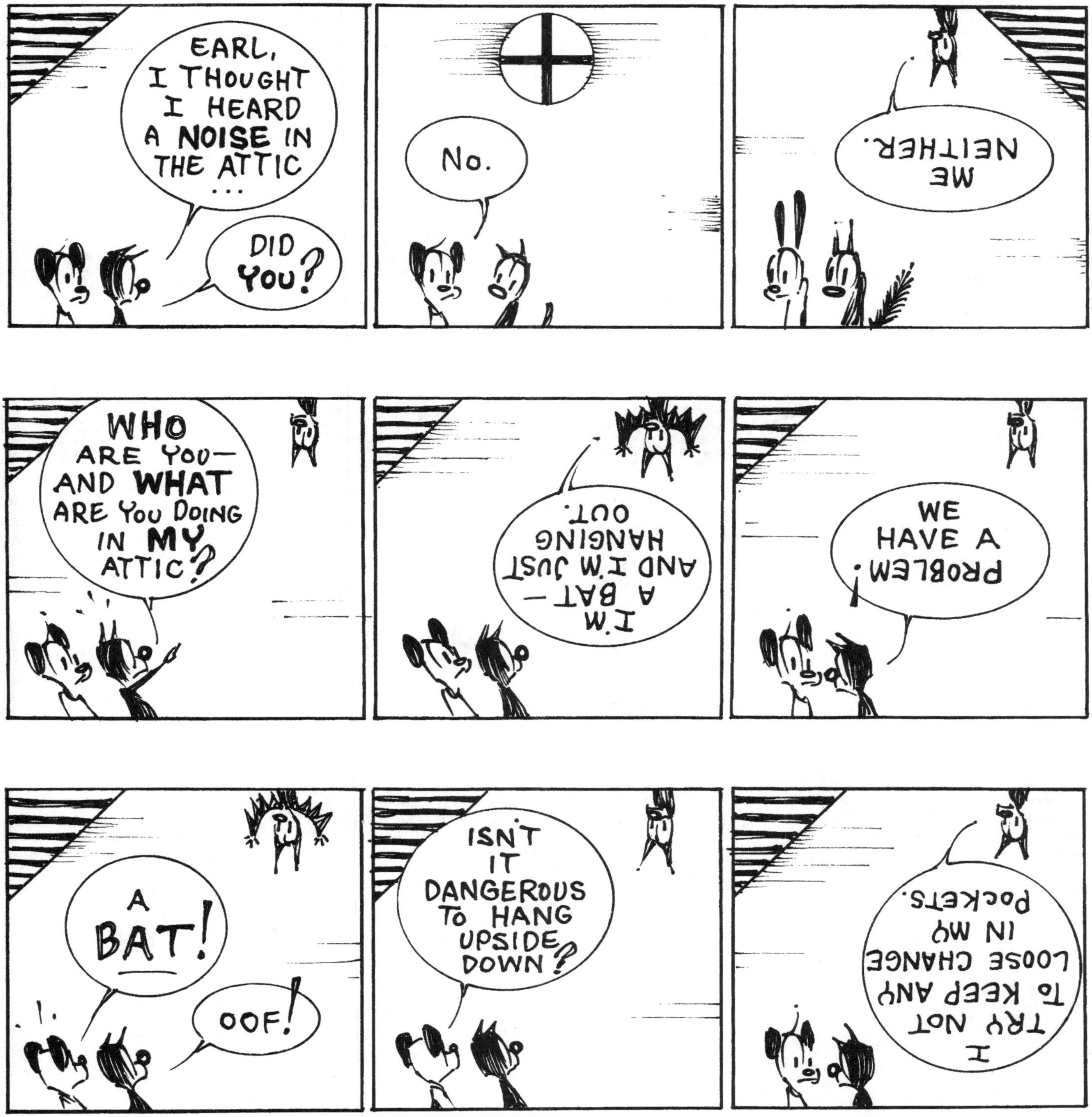
EARL, I THOUGHT I HEARD A NOISE IN THE ATTIC...
DID YOU?
No.
ME NEITHER.
WHO ARE YOU— AND WHAT ARE YOU DOING IN MY ATTIC?
I'M A BAT— AND I'M JUST HANGING OUT.
WE HAVE A PROBLEM!
A BAT!
OOF!
ISN'T IT DANGEROUS TO HANG UPSIDE DOWN?
I TRY NOT TO KEEP ANY LOOSE CHANGE IN MY POCKETS.

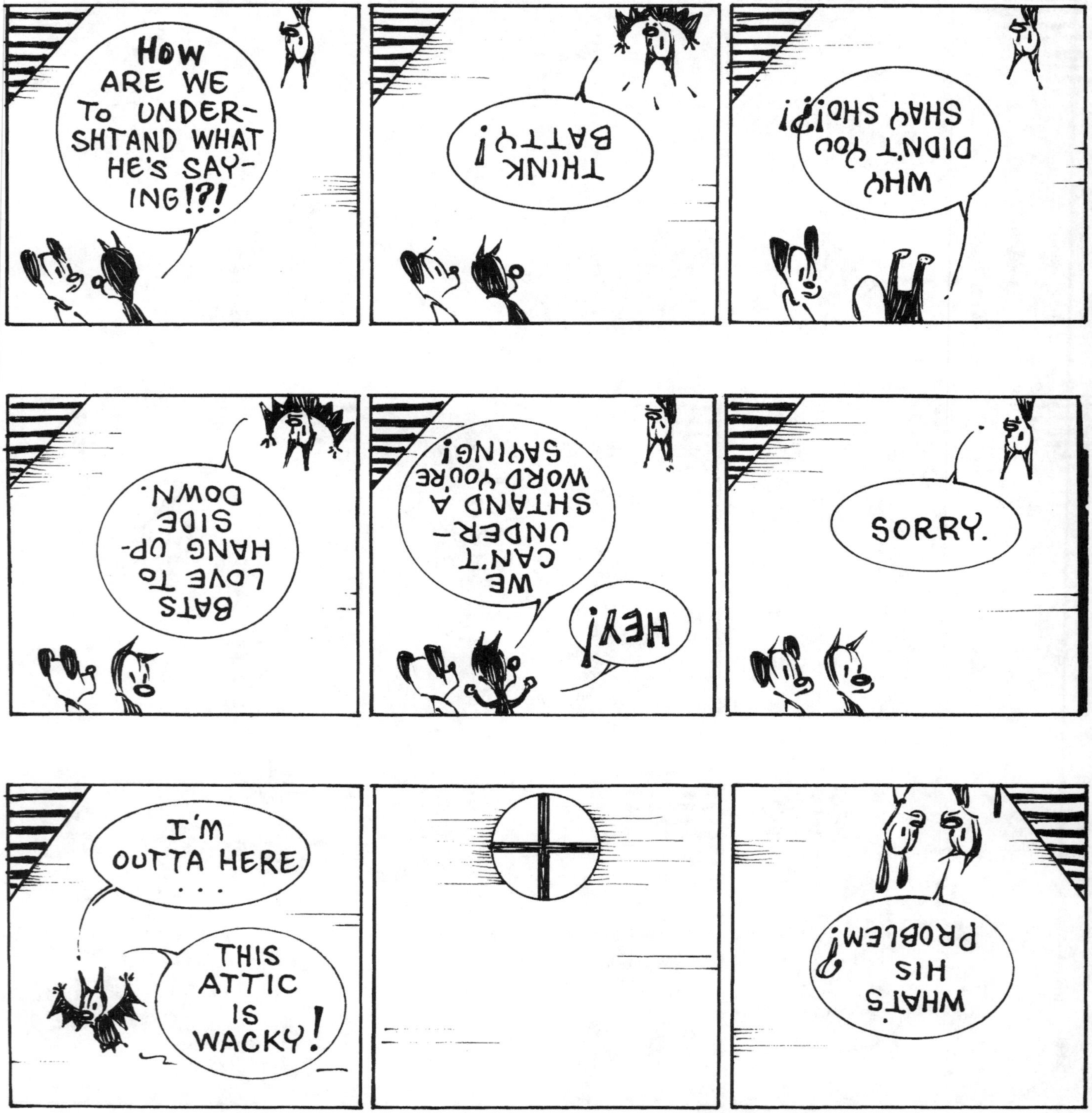
HOW ARE WE TO UNDER-SHTAND WHAT HE'S SAY-ING!?!
THINK BATTY!
WHY DIDN'T YOU SHAY SHO!?!
BATS LOVE TO HANG UP-SIDE DOWN.
WE CAN'T UNDER-SHTAND A WORD YOU'RE SAYING!
HEY!
SORRY.
I'M OUTTA HERE . . .
THIS ATTIC IS WACKY!
WHAT'S HIS PROBLEM?

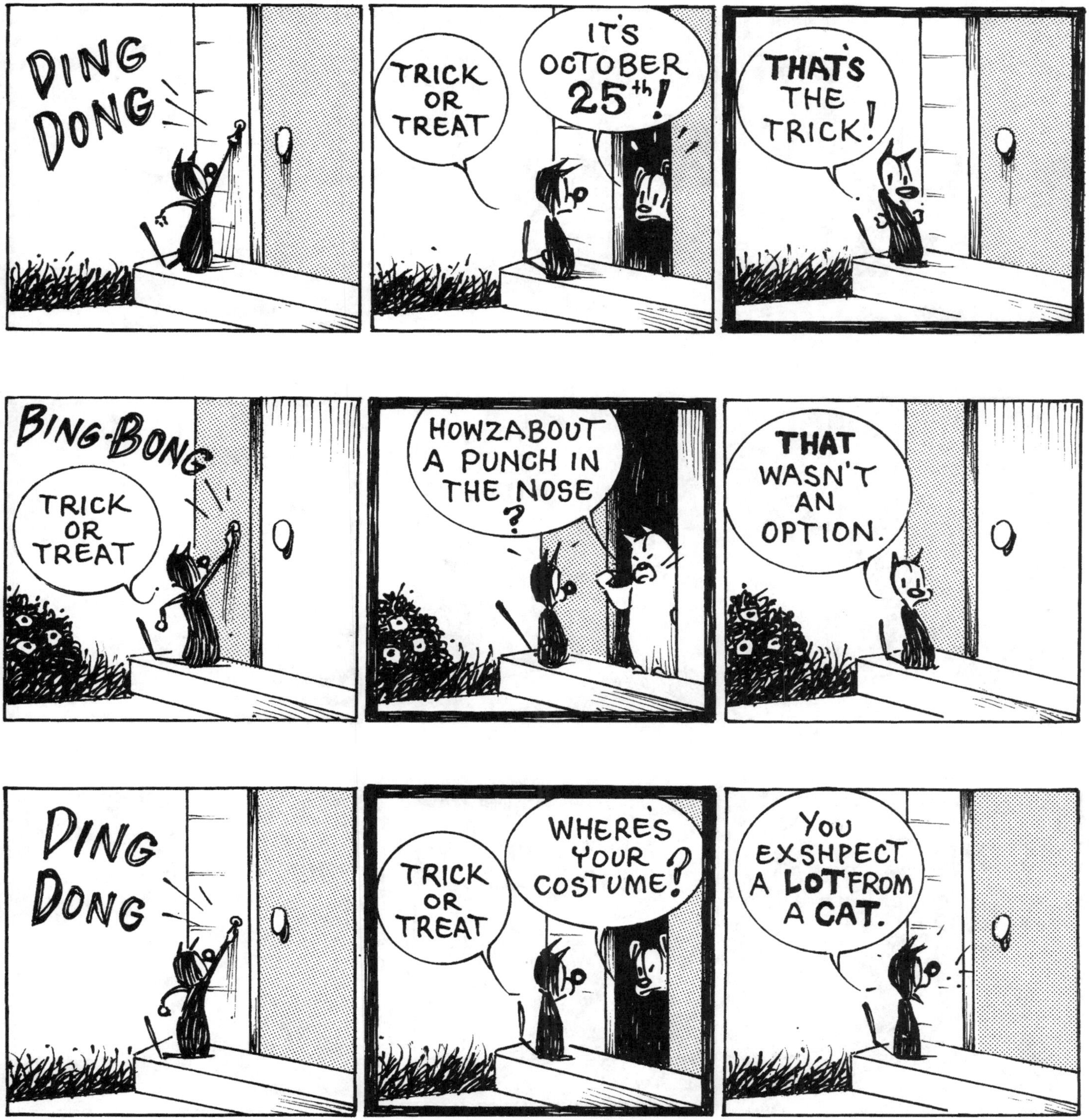
DING DONG
TRICK OR TREAT
IT'S OCTOBER 25th!
THAT'S THE TRICK!
BING-BONG
TRICK OR TREAT
HOWZABOUT A PUNCH IN THE NOSE?
THAT WASN'T AN OPTION.
DING DONG
TRICK OR TREAT
WHERE'S YOUR COSTUME?
YOU EXSHPECT A LOT FROM A CAT.

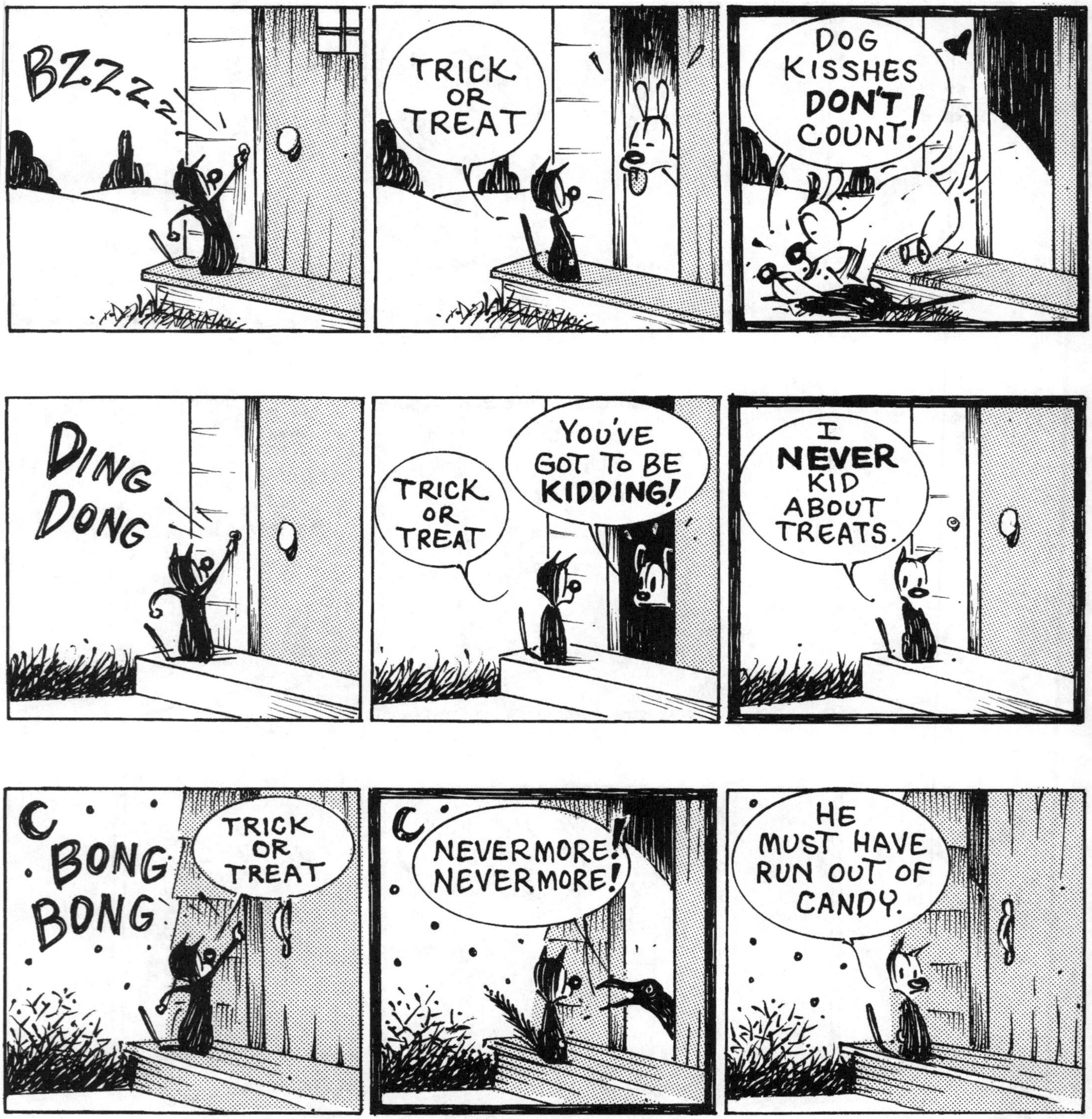
BZZZZZ
TRICK OR TREAT
DOG KISSHES DON'T COUNT!
DING DONG
TRICK OR TREAT
YOU'VE GOT TO BE KIDDING!
I NEVER KID ABOUT TREATS.
BONG BONG
TRICK OR TREAT
NEVERMORE! NEVERMORE!
HE MUST HAVE RUN OUT OF CANDY.

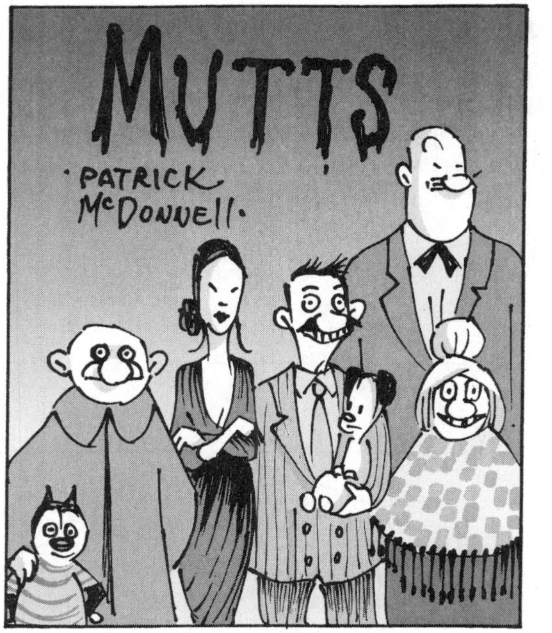
MUTTS
PATRICK McDONNELL

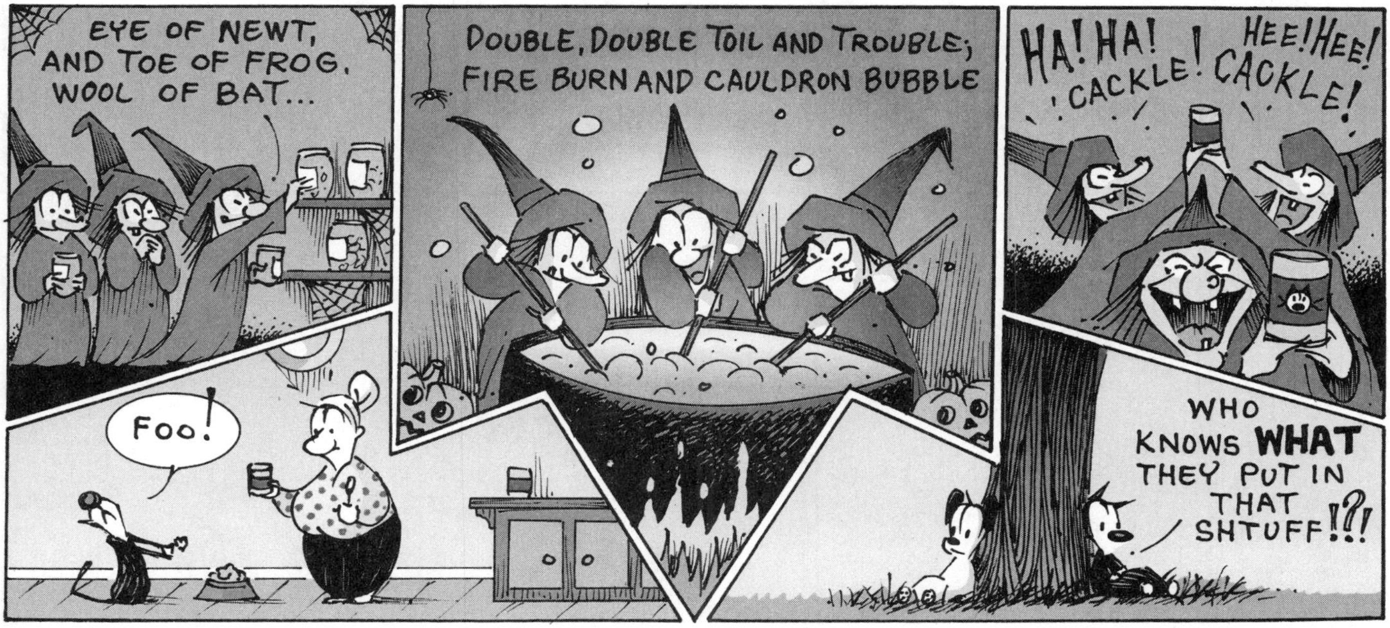
EYE OF NEWT, AND TOE OF FROG, WOOL OF BAT...
DOUBLE, DOUBLE TOIL AND TROUBLE; FIRE BURN AND CAULDRON BUBBLE
HA! HA! CACKLE!
HEE! HEE! CACKLE!
FOO!
WHO KNOWS WHAT THEY PUT IN THAT SHTUFF!?!

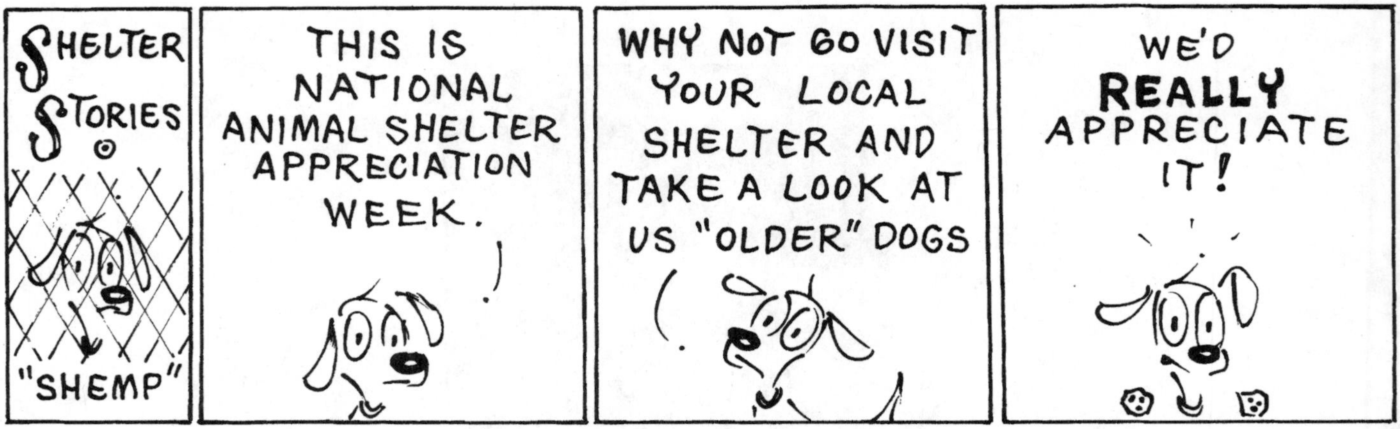
SHELTER STORIES
"SHEMP"
THIS IS NATIONAL ANIMAL SHELTER APPRECIATION WEEK.
WHY NOT GO VISIT YOUR LOCAL SHELTER AND TAKE A LOOK AT US "OLDER" DOGS
WE'D REALLY APPRECIATE IT!

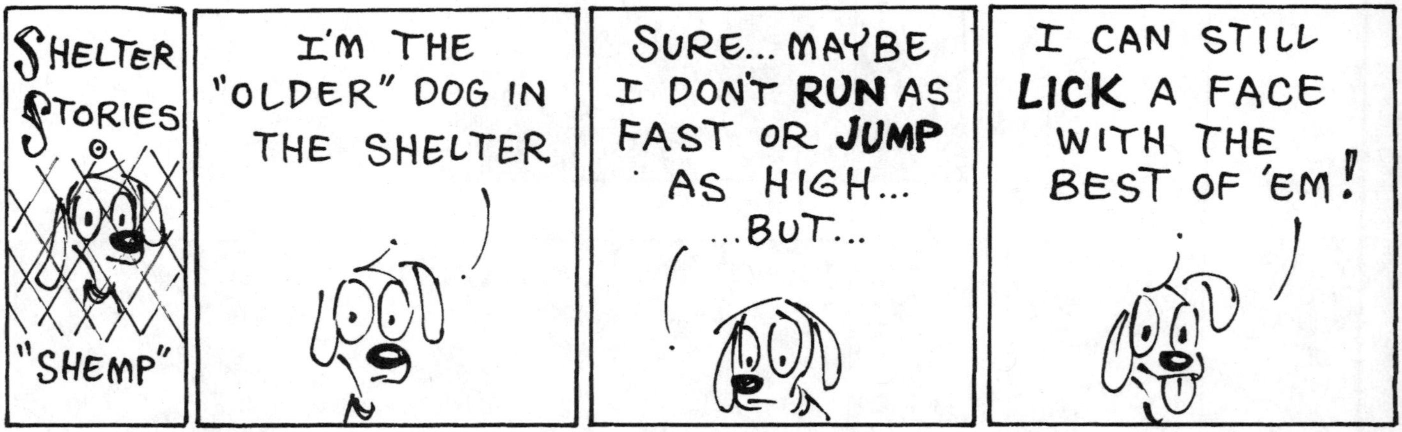
SHELTER STORIES
"SHEMP"
I'M THE "OLDER" DOG IN THE SHELTER
SURE... MAYBE I DON'T RUN AS FAST OR JUMP AS HIGH... ...BUT...
I CAN STILL LICK A FACE WITH THE BEST OF 'EM!

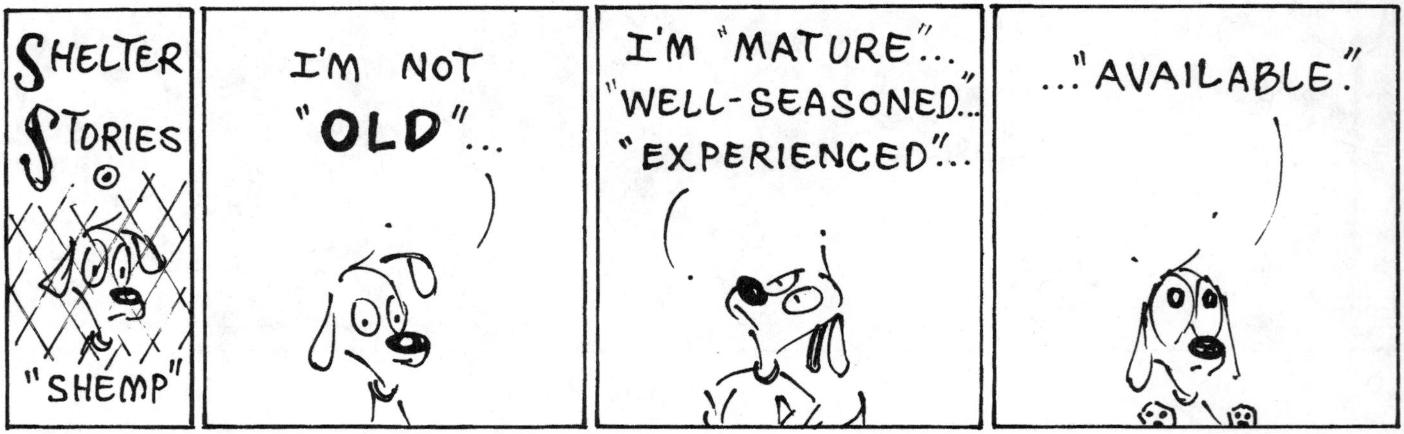
SHELTER STORIES
"SHEMP"
I'M NOT "OLD"...
I'M "MATURE"... "WELL-SEASONED"... "EXPERIENCED"...
..."AVAILABLE."

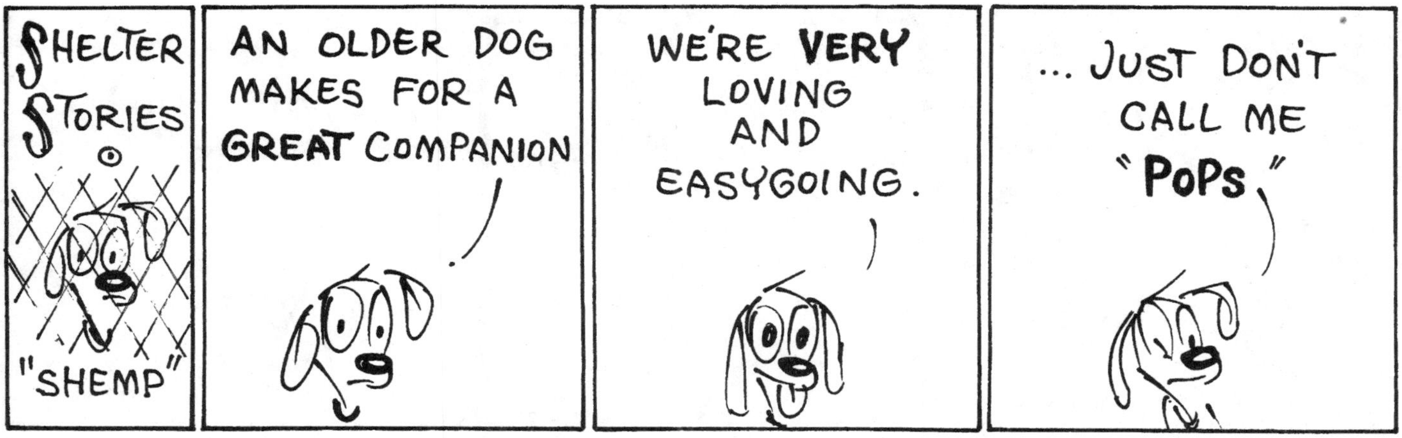
SHELTER STORIES
"SHEMP"
AN OLDER DOG MAKES FOR A GREAT COMPANION
WE'RE VERY LOVING AND EASYGOING.
... JUST DON'T CALL ME "POPS."

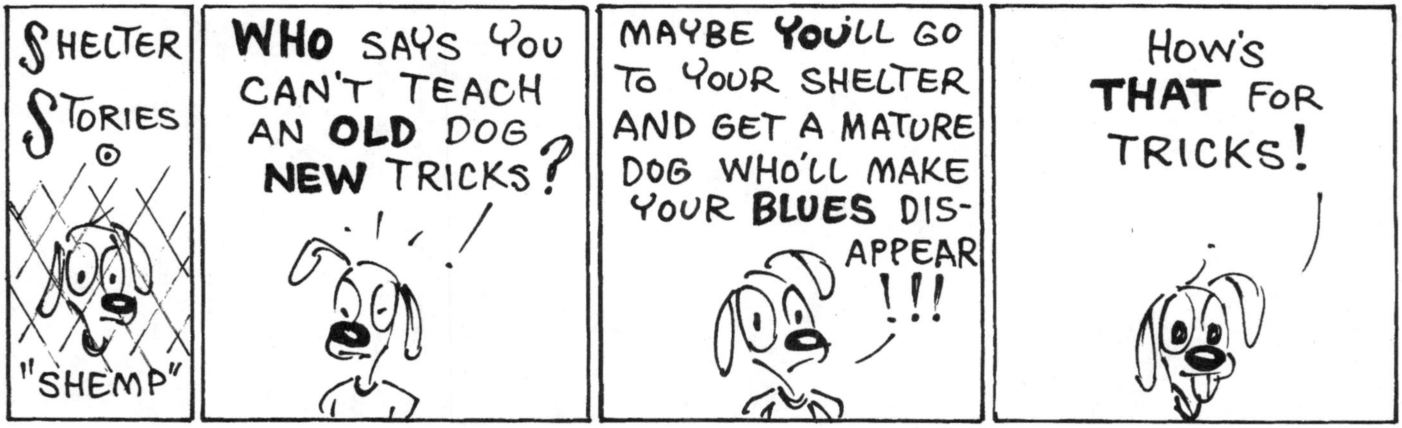
SHELTER STORIES
"SHEMP"
WHO SAYS YOU CAN'T TEACH AN OLD DOG NEW TRICKS?
MAYBE YOU'LL GO TO YOUR SHELTER AND GET A MATURE DOG WHO'LL MAKE YOUR BLUES DIS-APPEAR!!!
HOW'S THAT FOR TRICKS!

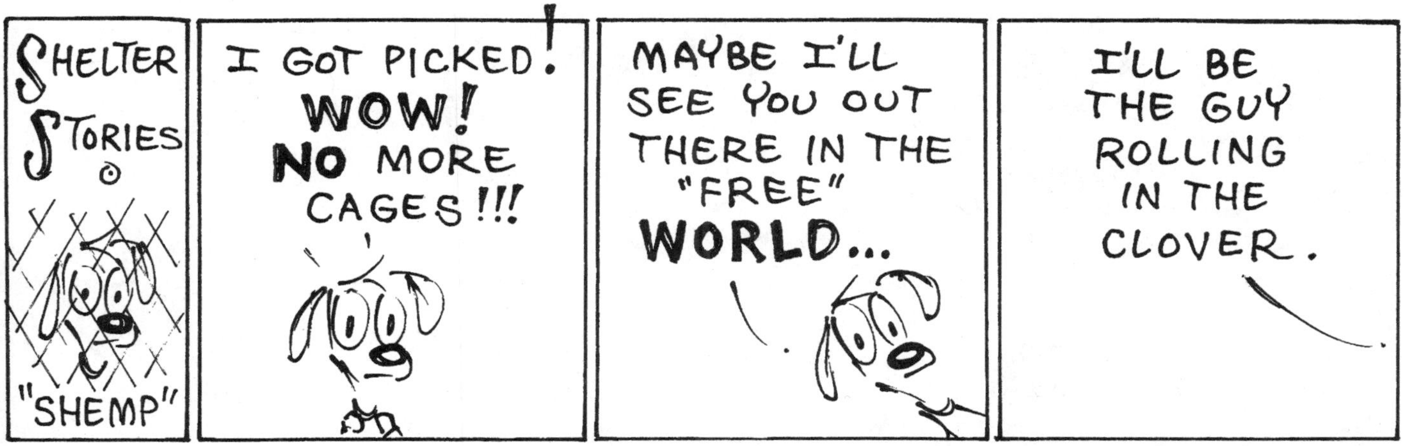
SHELTER STORIES
"SHEMP"
I GOT PICKED! WOW! NO MORE CAGES!!!
MAYBE I'LL SEE YOU OUT THERE IN THE "FREE" WORLD...
I'LL BE THE GUY ROLLING IN THE CLOVER.

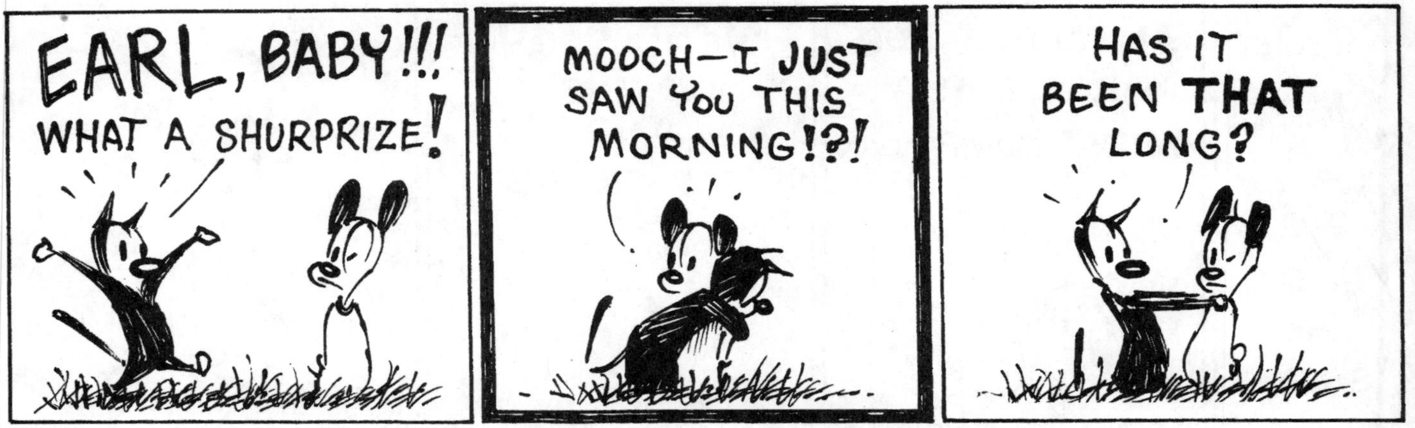
EARL, BABY!!! WHAT A SHURPRIZE!
MOOCH—I JUST SAW YOU THIS MORNING!?!
HAS IT BEEN THAT LONG?

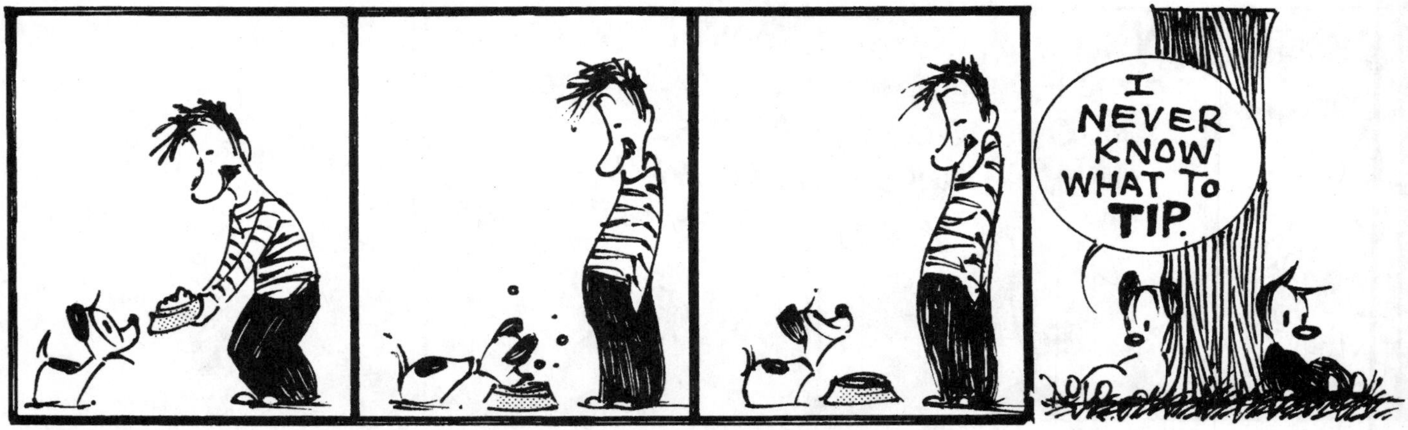
I NEVER KNOW WHAT TO TIP.

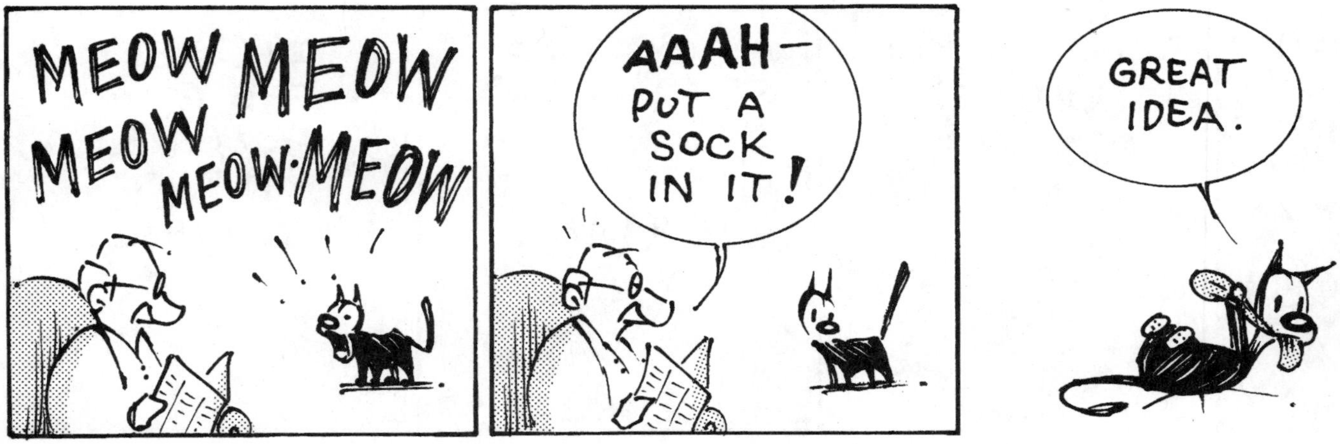
MEOW MEOW MEOW MEOW·MEOW
AAAH— PUT A SOCK IN IT!
GREAT IDEA.

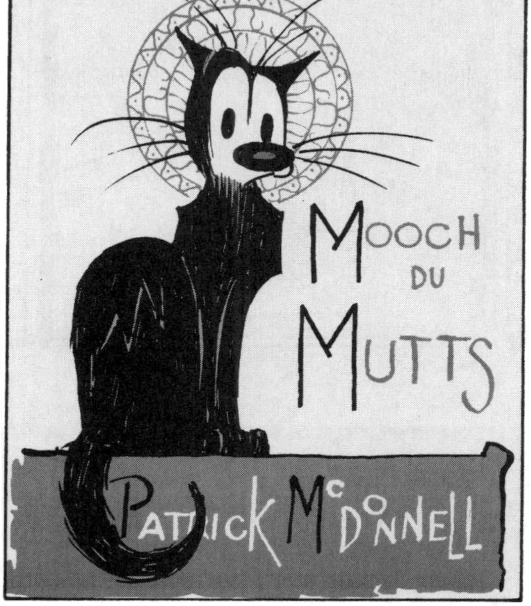
MOOCH
DU
MUTTS
PATRICK McDONNELL

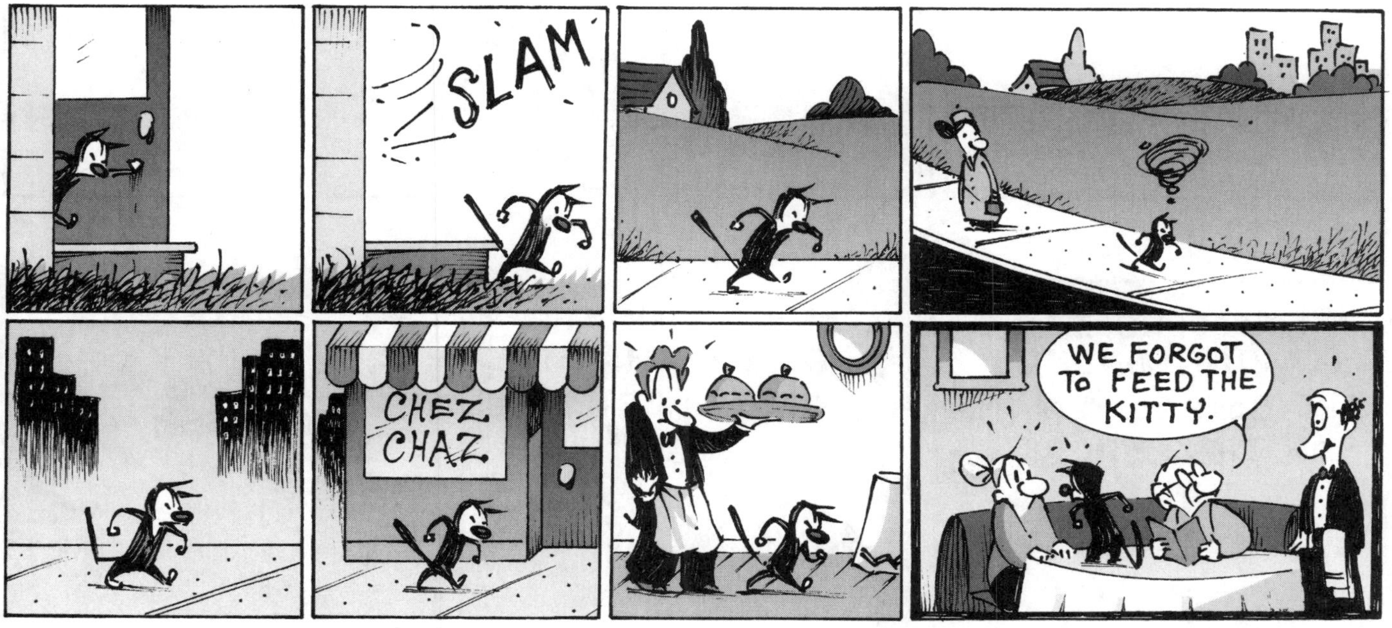
SLAM
CHEZ CHAZ
WE FORGOT TO FEED THE KITTY.

TODAY THE SEAL HUNT BEGINS...

I CAN'T LOOK.

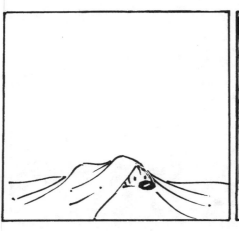

SOME DAYS ARE MEANT TO BE SPENT **UNDER** THE COVERS.

MR. NOODLES, I'M STAYING UNDER THE COVERS PRAYING FOR THE **SEALS**.

OH, SHTINKY... **WHO** COULD HARM SUCH PEACEFUL CREATURES!?!**WHO?**

I KNOW...

I'M PRAYING FOR **THEM**, TOO.

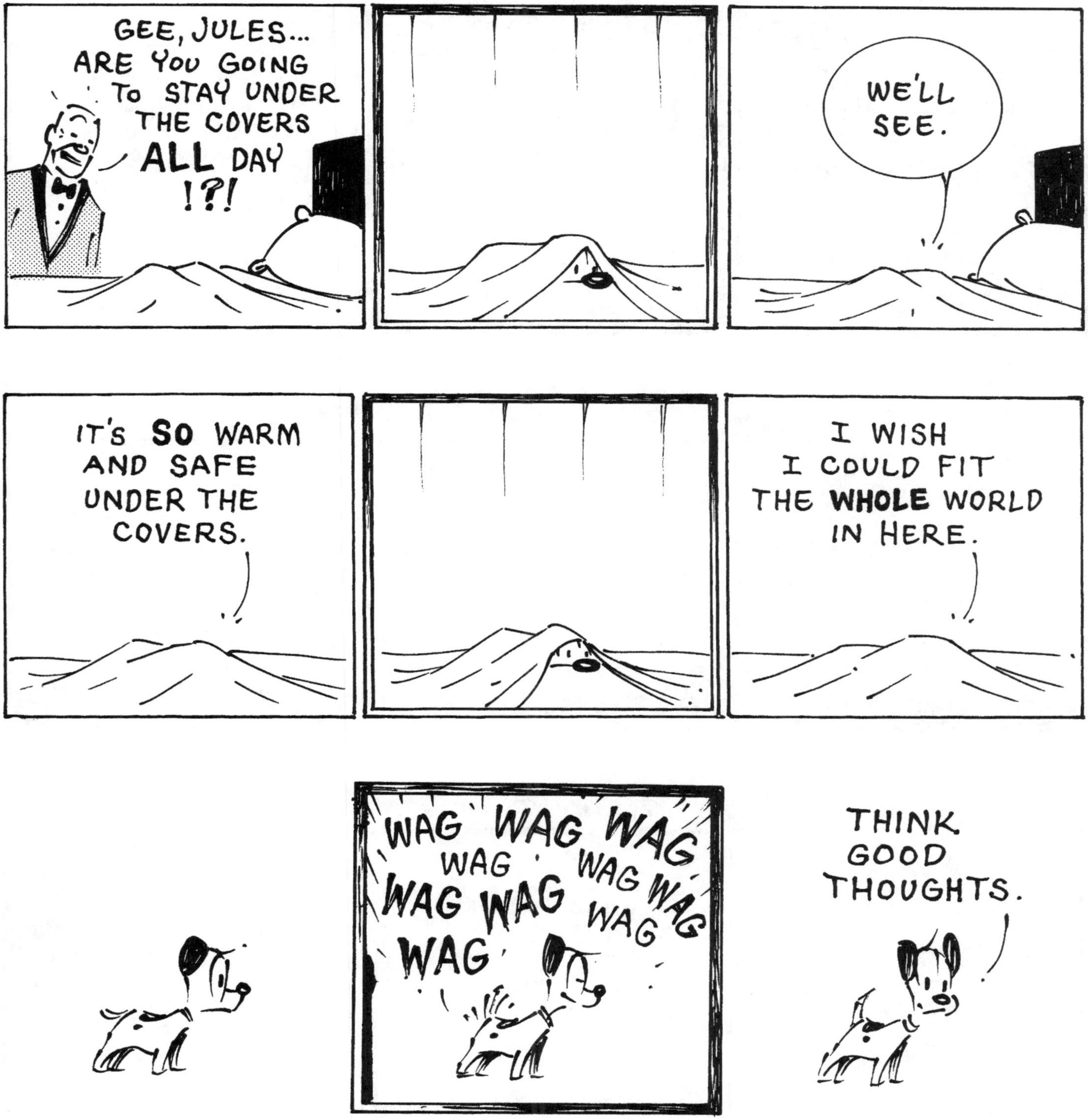
GEE, JULES... ARE YOU GOING TO STAY UNDER THE COVERS ALL DAY !?!
WE'LL SEE.
IT'S SO WARM AND SAFE UNDER THE COVERS.
I WISH I COULD FIT THE WHOLE WORLD IN HERE.
WAG WAG WAG WAG WAG WAG WAG WAG WAG WAG WAG
THINK GOOD THOUGHTS.

Giving Thanks

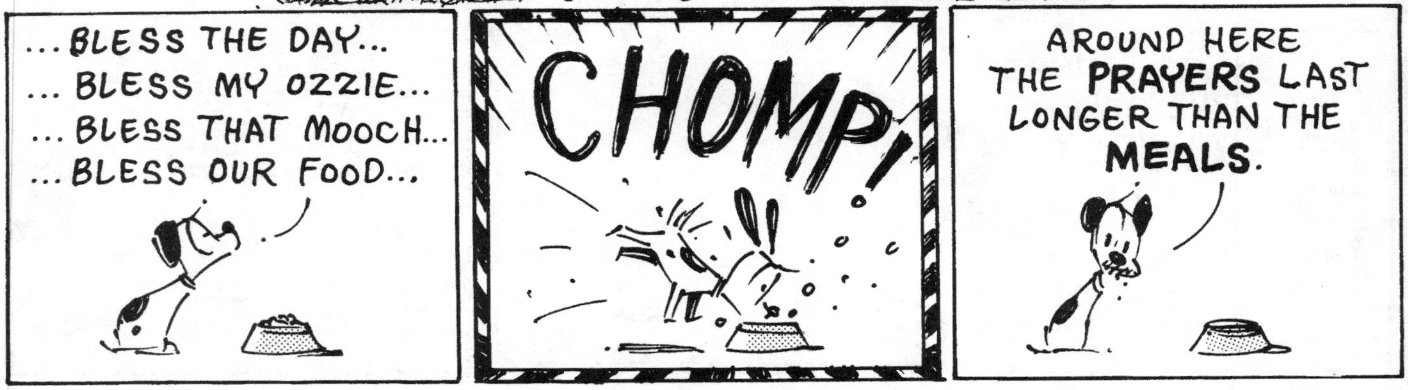
... BLESS THE DAY...
... BLESS MY OZZIE...
... BLESS THAT MOOCH...
... BLESS OUR FOOD...
CHOMP!
AROUND HERE THE PRAYERS LAST LONGER THAN THE MEALS.

Giving Thanks

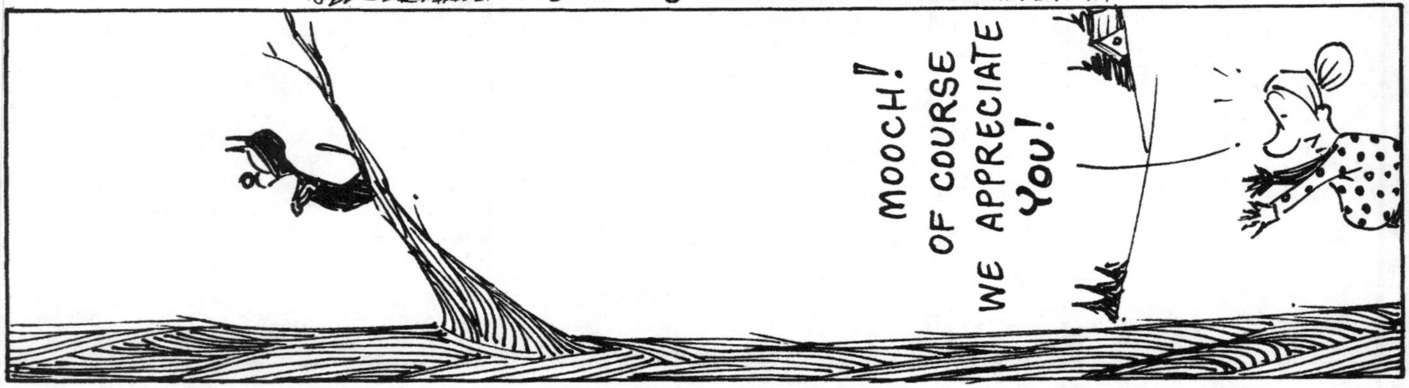
MOOCH! OF COURSE WE APPRECIATE YOU!

Giving Thanks

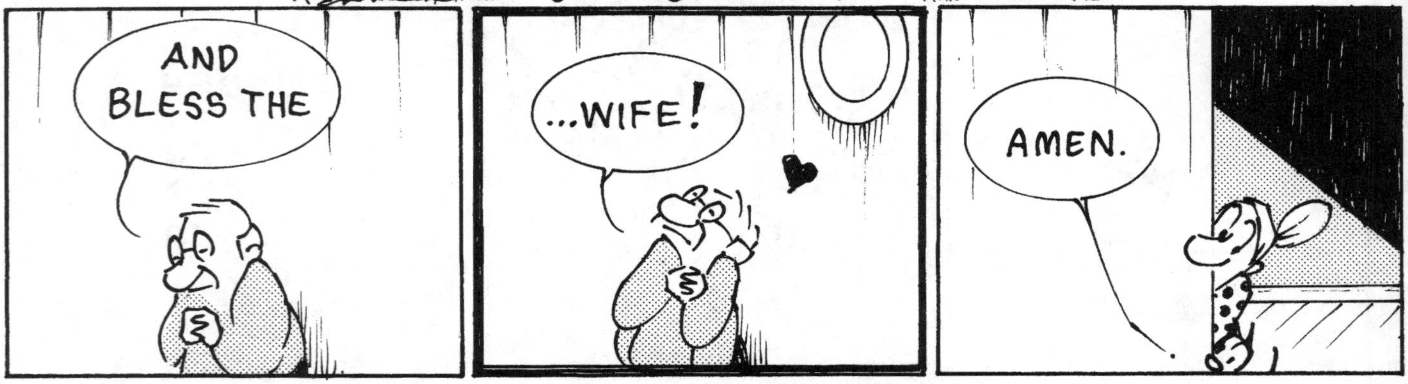
AND BLESS THE
...WIFE!
AMEN.

Giving Thanks

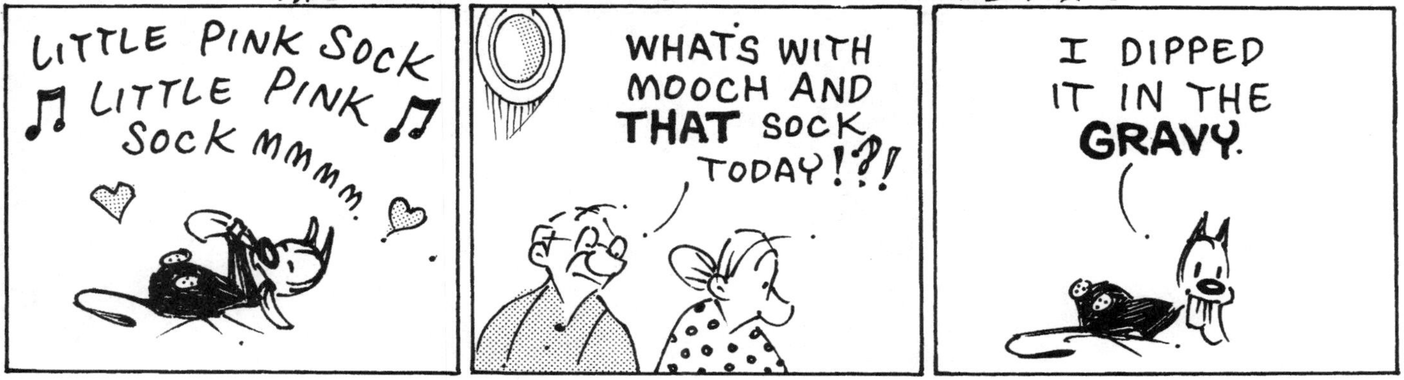
LITTLE PINK SOCK ♫ LITTLE PINK SOCK MMMMM. ♫
WHAT'S WITH MOOCH AND THAT SOCK TODAY!?!
I DIPPED IT IN THE GRAVY.

Giving Thanks

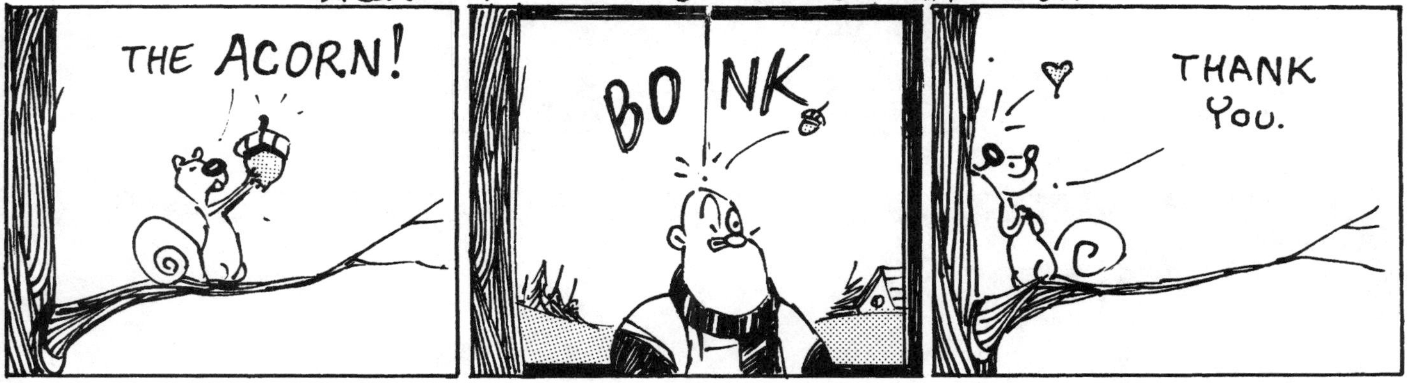
THE ACORN!
BONK
THANK YOU.

Giving Thanks

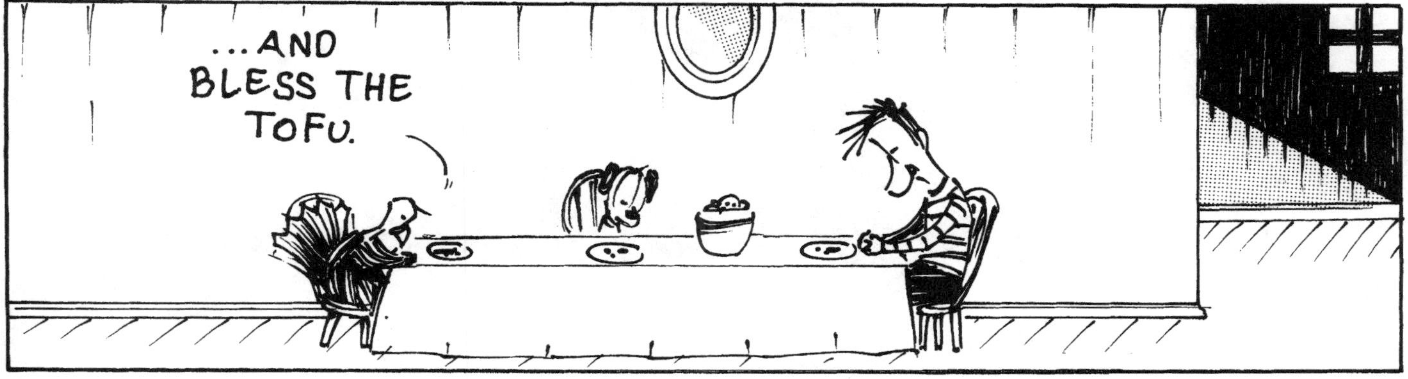
...AND BLESS THE TOFU.

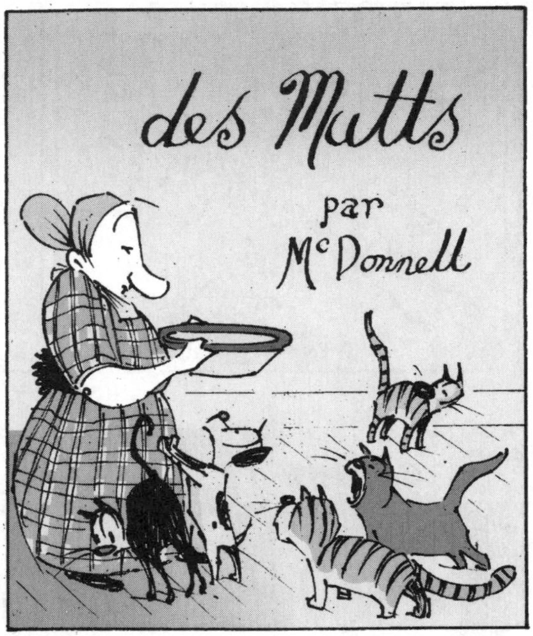
des Mutts
par
McDonnell

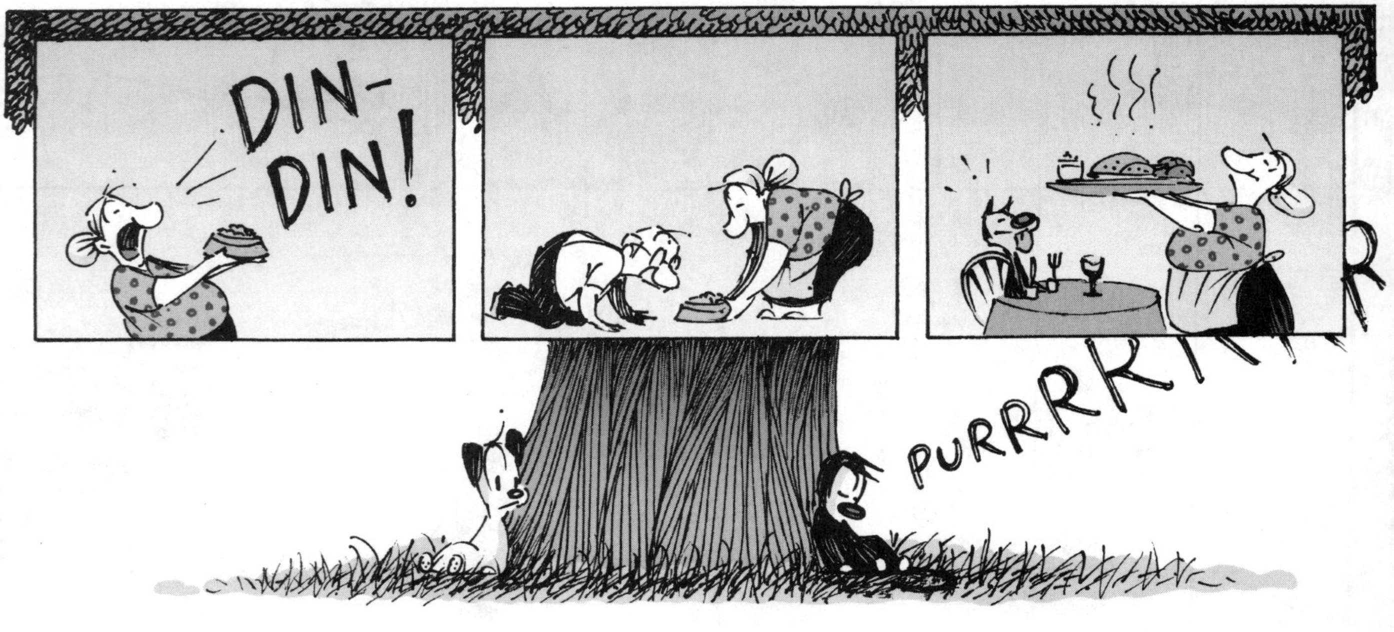
DIN-DIN!
PURRRRR

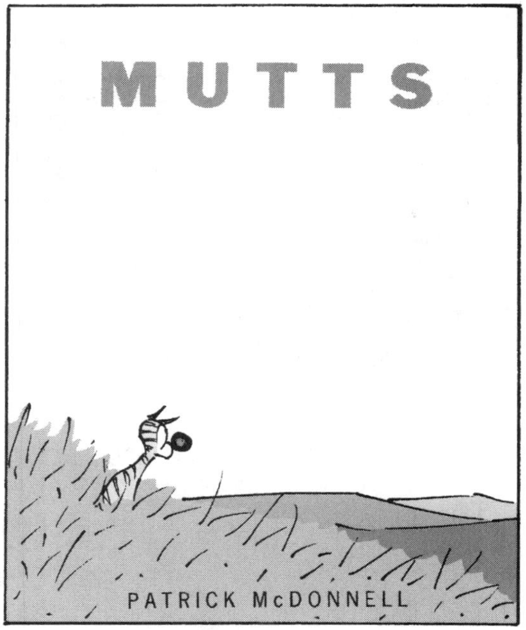
MUTTS
PATRICK McDONNELL

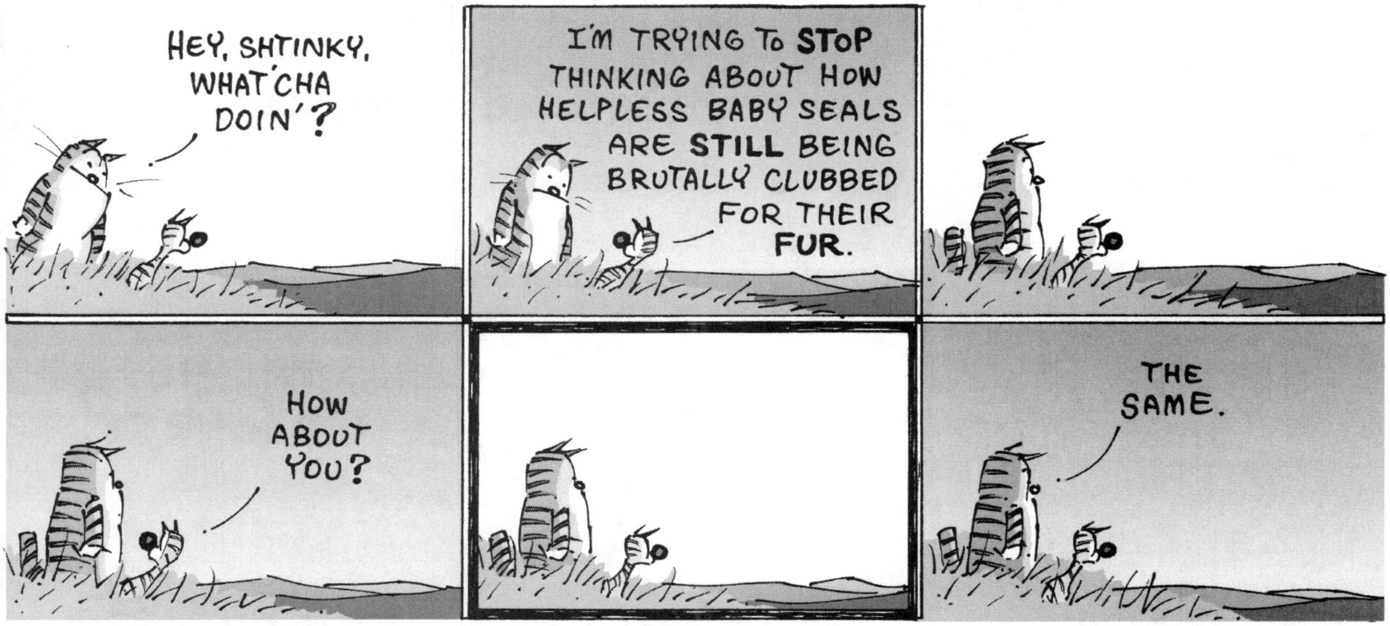
HEY, SHTINKY, WHAT'CHA DOIN'?
I'M TRYING TO **STOP** THINKING ABOUT HOW HELPLESS BABY SEALS ARE **STILL** BEING BRUTALLY CLUBBED FOR THEIR **FUR**.
HOW ABOUT YOU?
THE SAME.

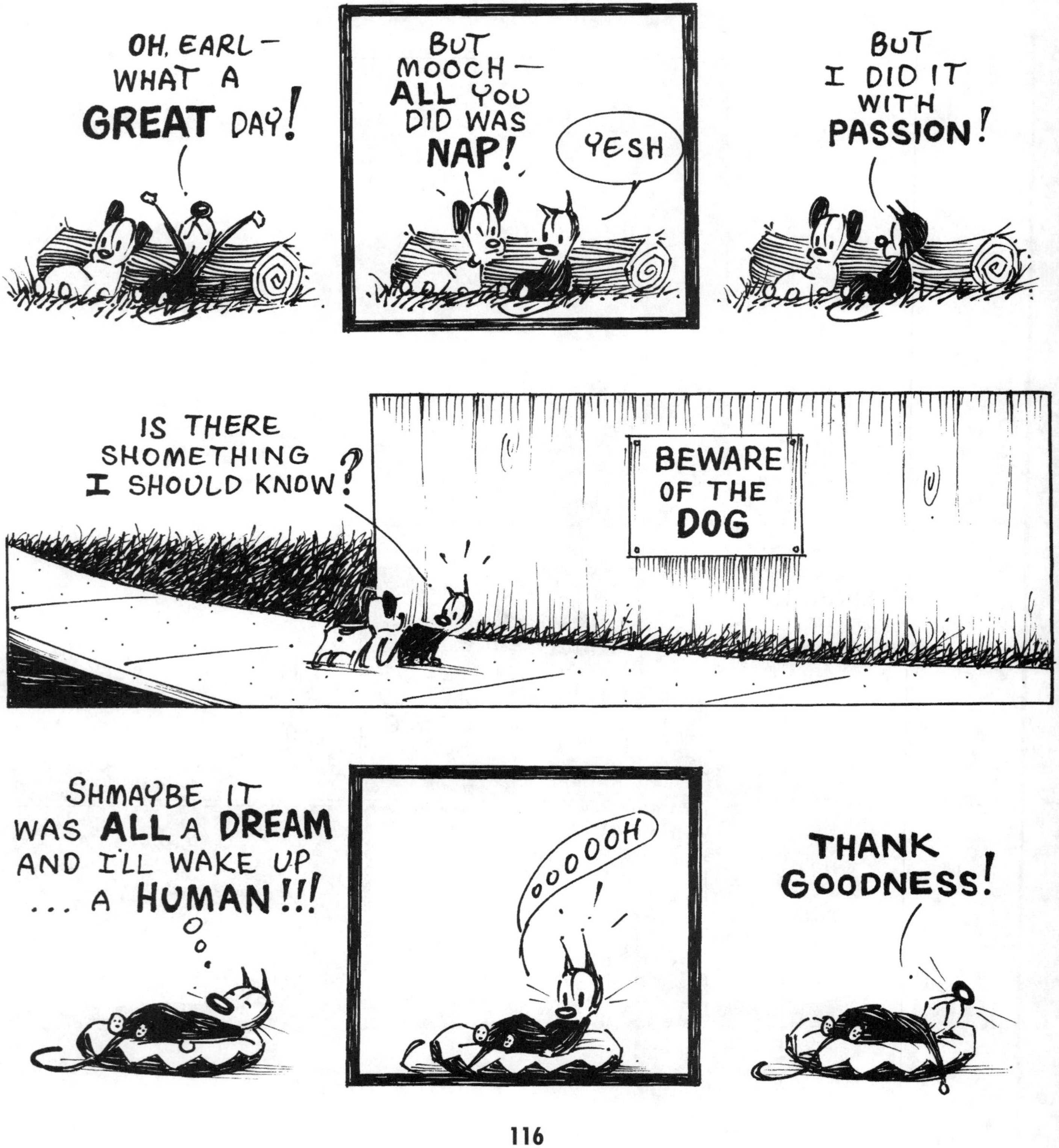
OH, EARL — WHAT A GREAT DAY!
BUT MOOCH — ALL YOU DID WAS NAP!
YESH
BUT I DID IT WITH PASSION!
IS THERE SHOMETHING I SHOULD KNOW?
BEWARE OF THE DOG
SHMAYBE IT WAS ALL A DREAM AND I'LL WAKE UP ... A HUMAN!!!
OOOOOH
THANK GOODNESS!

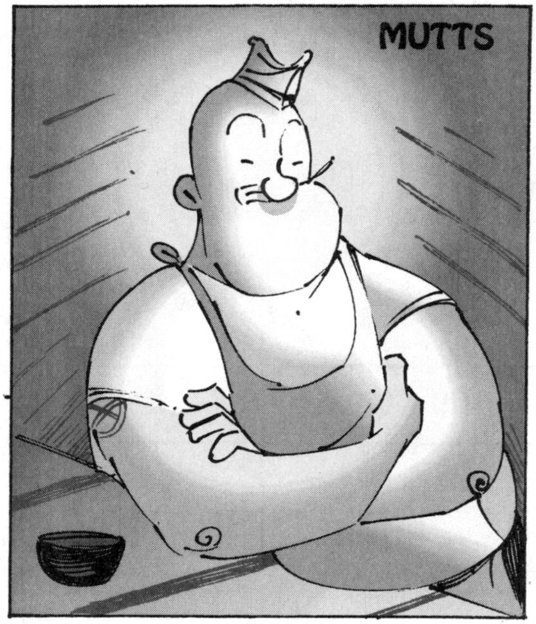
MUTTS

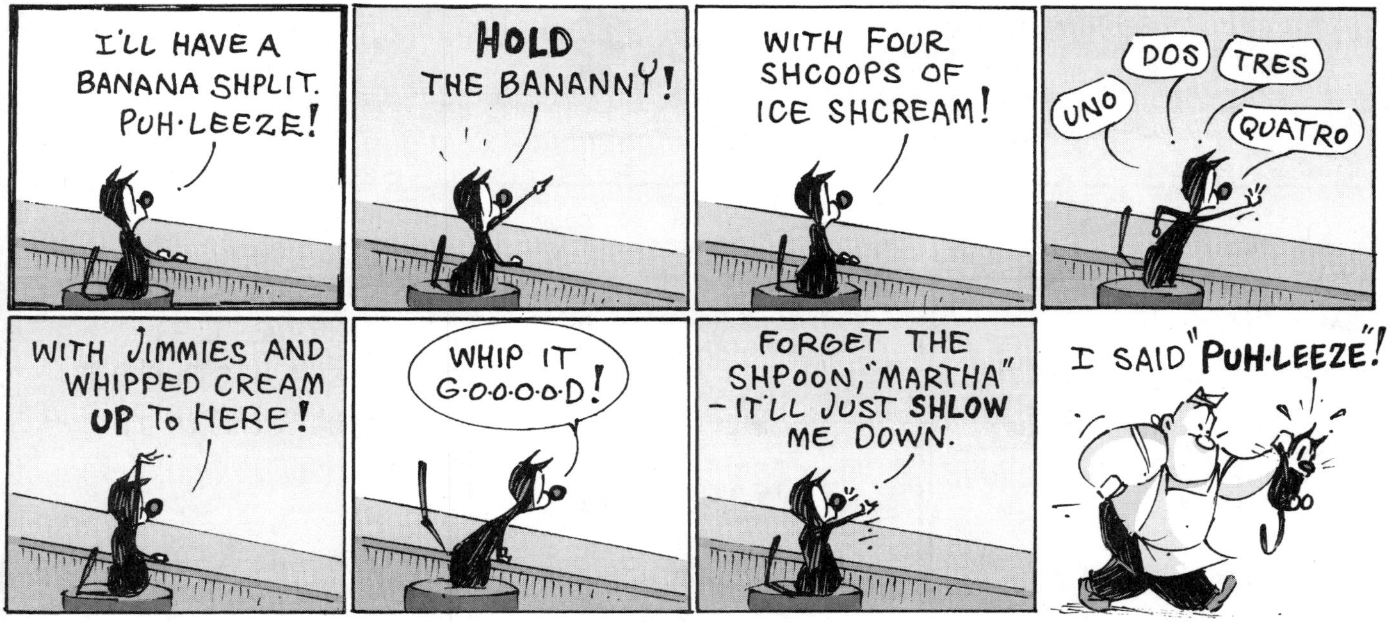
I'LL HAVE A BANANA SHPLIT. PUH·LEEZE!
HOLD THE BANANNY!
WITH FOUR SHCOOPS OF ICE SHCREAM!
UNO
DOS
TRES
QUATRO
WITH JIMMIES AND WHIPPED CREAM UP TO HERE!
WHIP IT G·O·O·O·O·D!
FORGET THE SHPOON, "MARTHA" – IT'LL JUST SHLOW ME DOWN.
I SAID "PUH·LEEZE"!

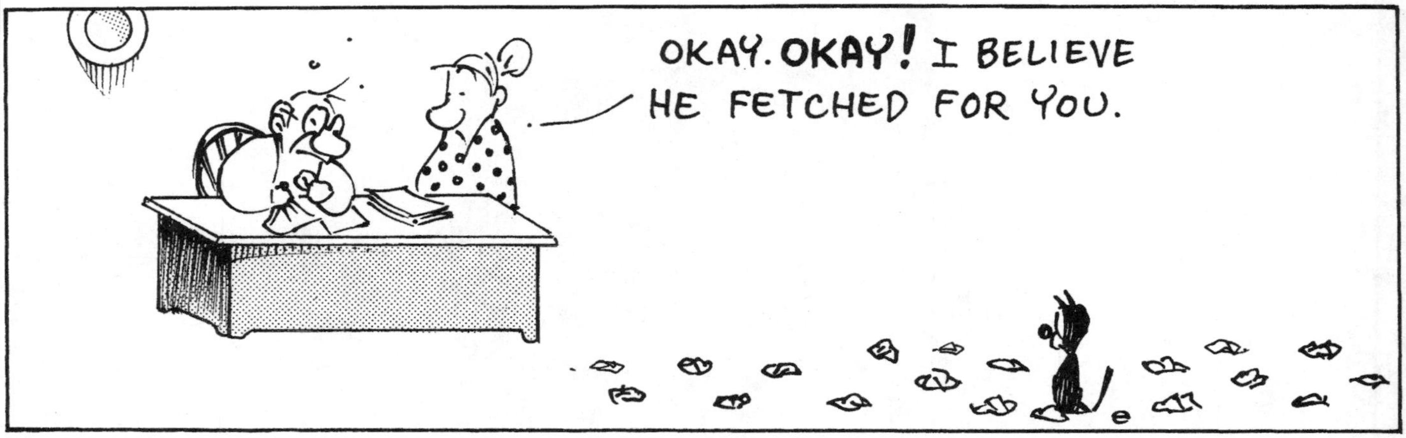
OKAY. **OKAY!** I BELIEVE HE FETCHED FOR YOU.

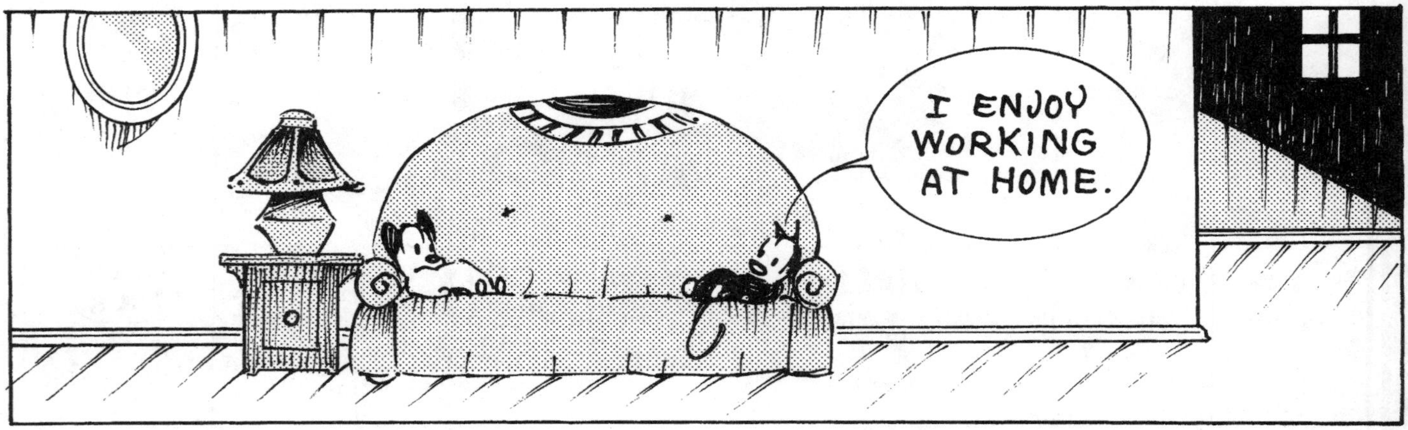
I ENJOY WORKING AT HOME.

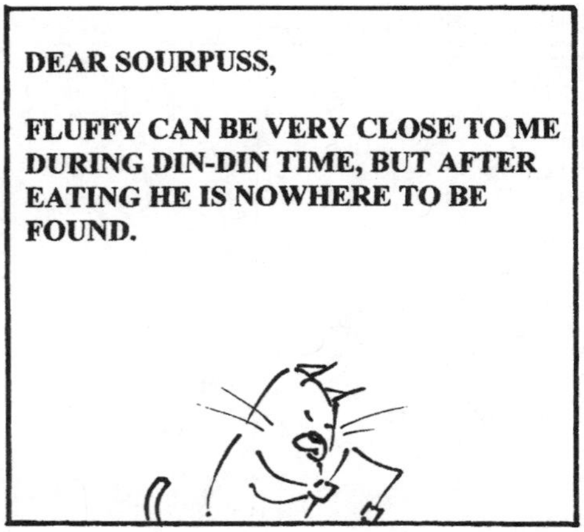
DEAR SOURPUSS,
FLUFFY CAN BE VERY CLOSE TO ME DURING DIN-DIN TIME, BUT AFTER EATING HE IS NOWHERE TO BE FOUND.

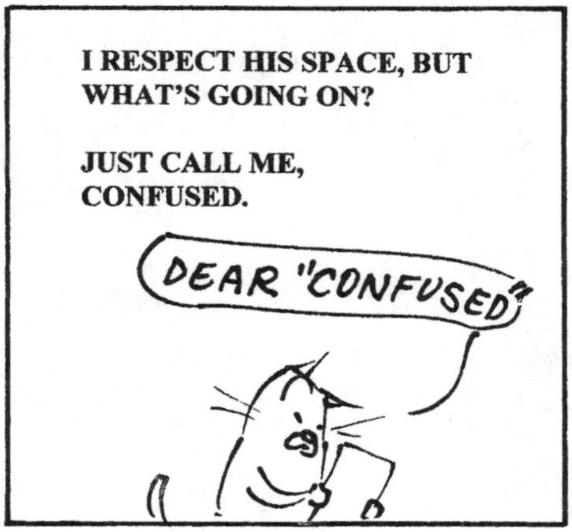
I RESPECT HIS SPACE, BUT WHAT'S GOING ON?
JUST CALL ME, CONFUSED.
DEAR "CONFUSED"

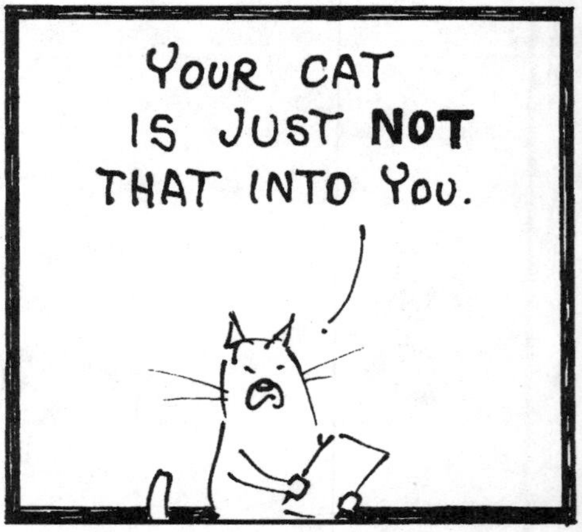
YOUR CAT IS JUST **NOT** THAT INTO YOU.

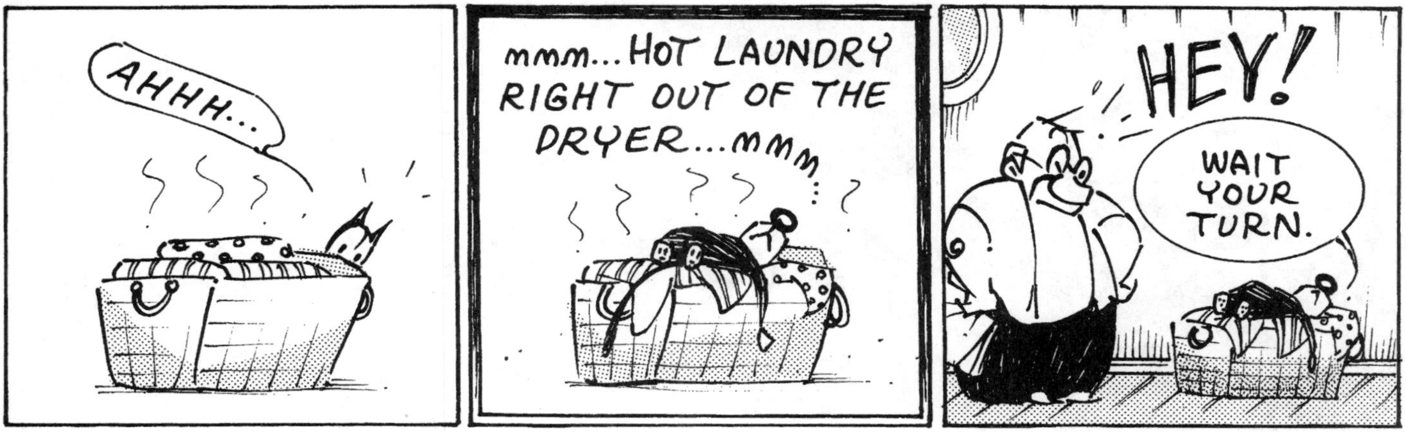
AHHH...
mmm...HOT LAUNDRY RIGHT OUT OF THE DRYER...mmm
HEY!
WAIT YOUR TURN.

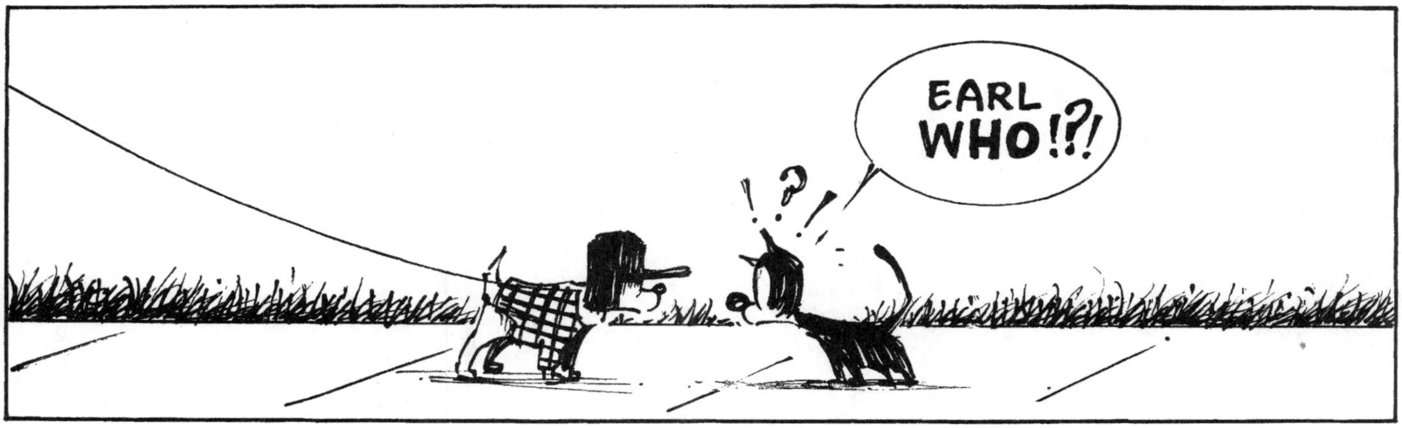
EARL WHO!?!

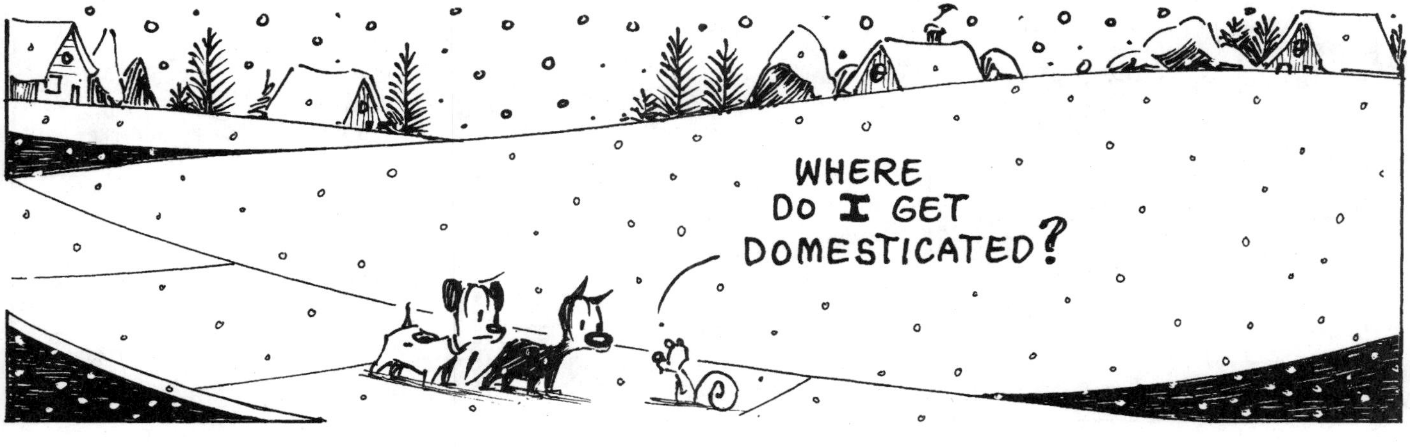
WHERE DO I GET DOMESTICATED?

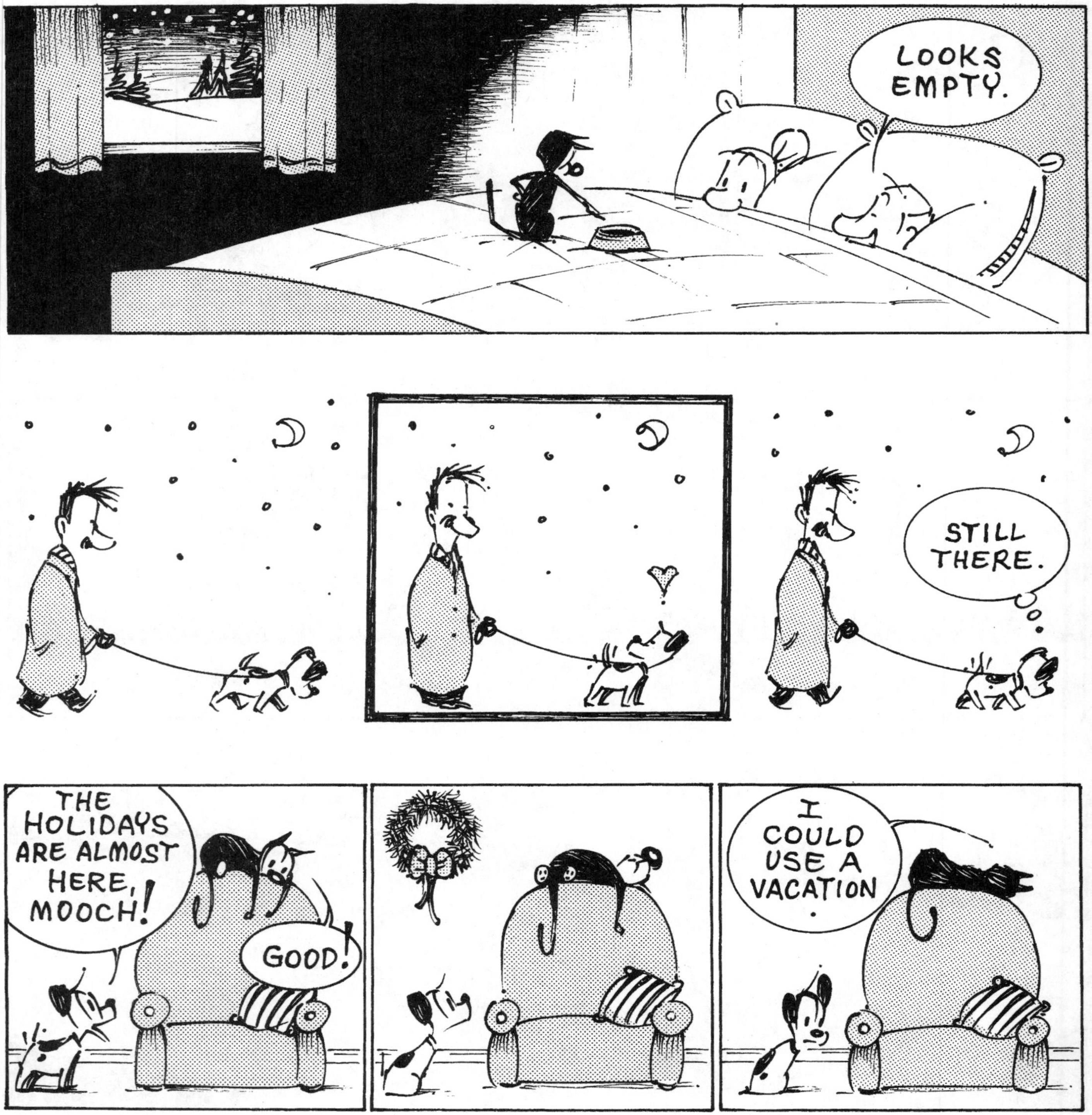
LOOKS EMPTY.
STILL THERE.
THE HOLIDAYS ARE ALMOST HERE, MOOCH!
GOOD!
I COULD USE A VACATION.

MUTTS!

Patrick McDonnell

I'M
MAKING
IT...

I'M
CHECKING
IT
TWICE...

I'M GONNA
FIND OUT
WHO'S NAUGHTY
OR NICE...

SANTA
AIN'T THE ONLY
ONE KEEPING A
LIST.

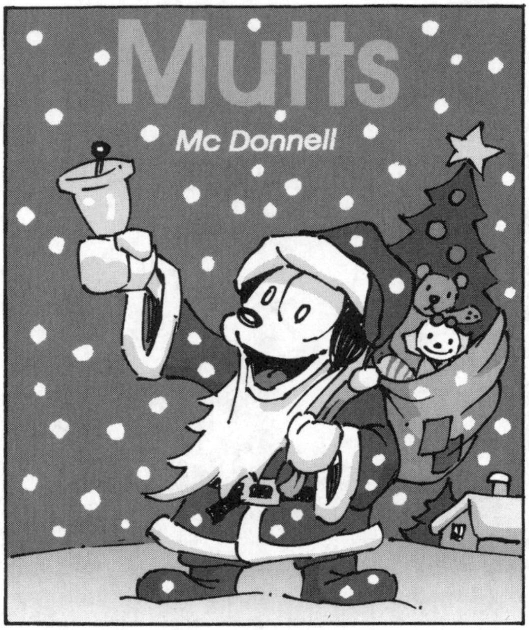
Mutts
Mc Donnell

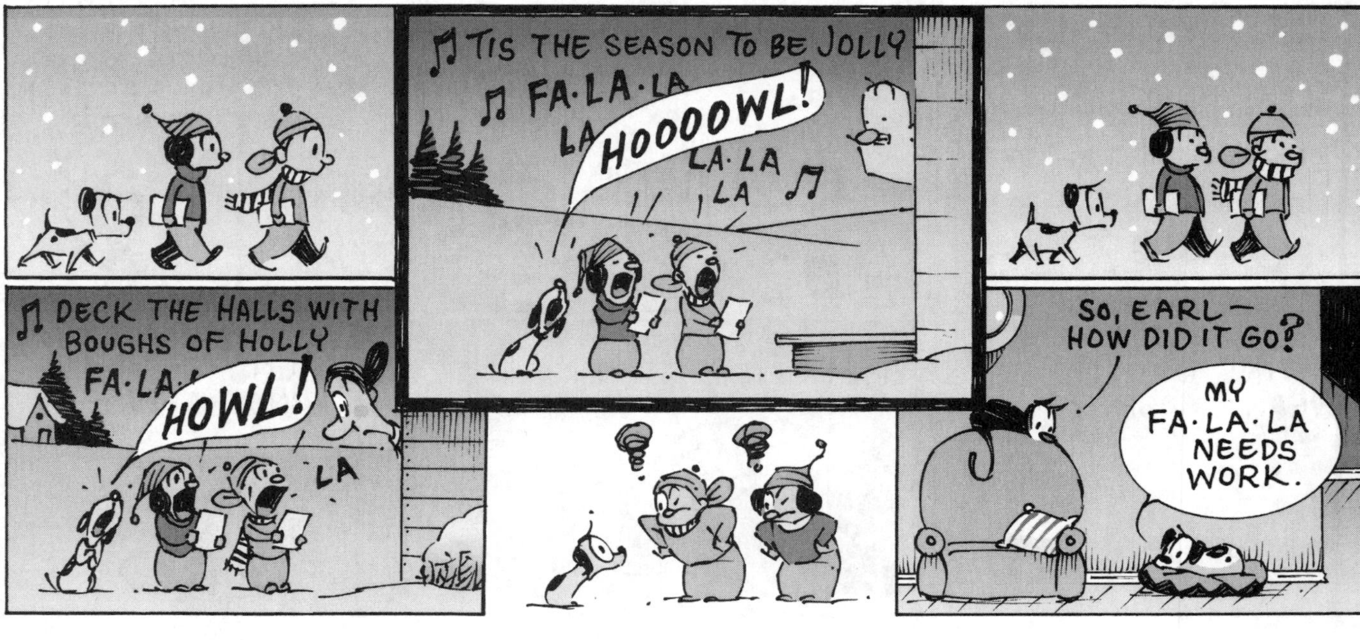
♫ DECK THE HALLS WITH BOUGHS OF HOLLY
FA·LA·L
HOWL!
LA
♫ TIS THE SEASON TO BE JOLLY
♫ FA·LA·LA
LA
HOOOOWL!
LA·LA
LA
So, EARL— HOW DID IT GO?
MY FA·LA·LA NEEDS WORK.

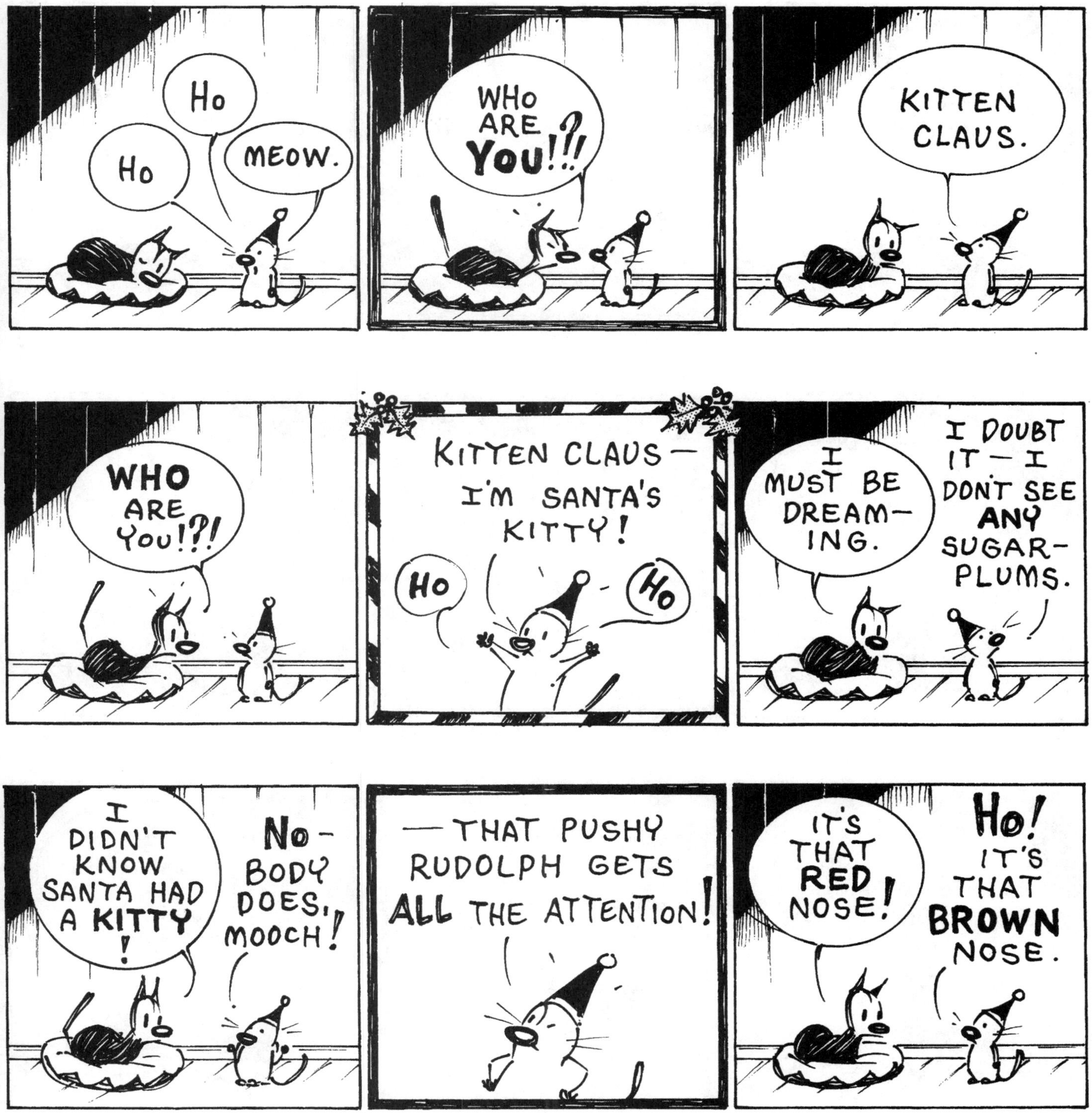
Ho
Ho
MEOW.
WHO ARE YOU!?!
KITTEN CLAUS.
WHO ARE YOU!?!
KITTEN CLAUS— I'M SANTA'S KITTY!
HO
Ho
I MUST BE DREAM-ING.
I DOUBT IT— I DON'T SEE ANY SUGAR-PLUMS.
I DIDN'T KNOW SANTA HAD A KITTY!
No-BODY DOES, MOOCH!
—THAT PUSHY RUDOLPH GETS ALL THE ATTENTION!
IT'S THAT RED NOSE!
Ho! IT'S THAT BROWN NOSE.

ON CHRISTMAS EVE **ALL** OVER THE WORLD, WHILE SANTA'S BUSY WITH LEAVING GIFTS UNDER THE TREE...

I FILL UP **ALL** THE CHRISTMAS STOCKINGS

THAT SOUNDS LIKE A **LOT** OF WORK.

Ho! Ho! I **NAP** THE REST OF THE YEAR.

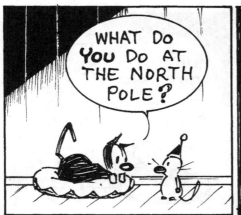

WHAT DO **YOU** DO AT THE NORTH POLE?

I CHASE **ALL** THE PESTS OUT OF MRS. CLAUS' KITCHEN!

MICE?

ELVES.

AS SANTA'S KITTY, HAVE YOU EVER SEEN THE NORTH POLE?

...**SEEN** IT !?!... Ho! Ho!

I **SCRATCH** IT.

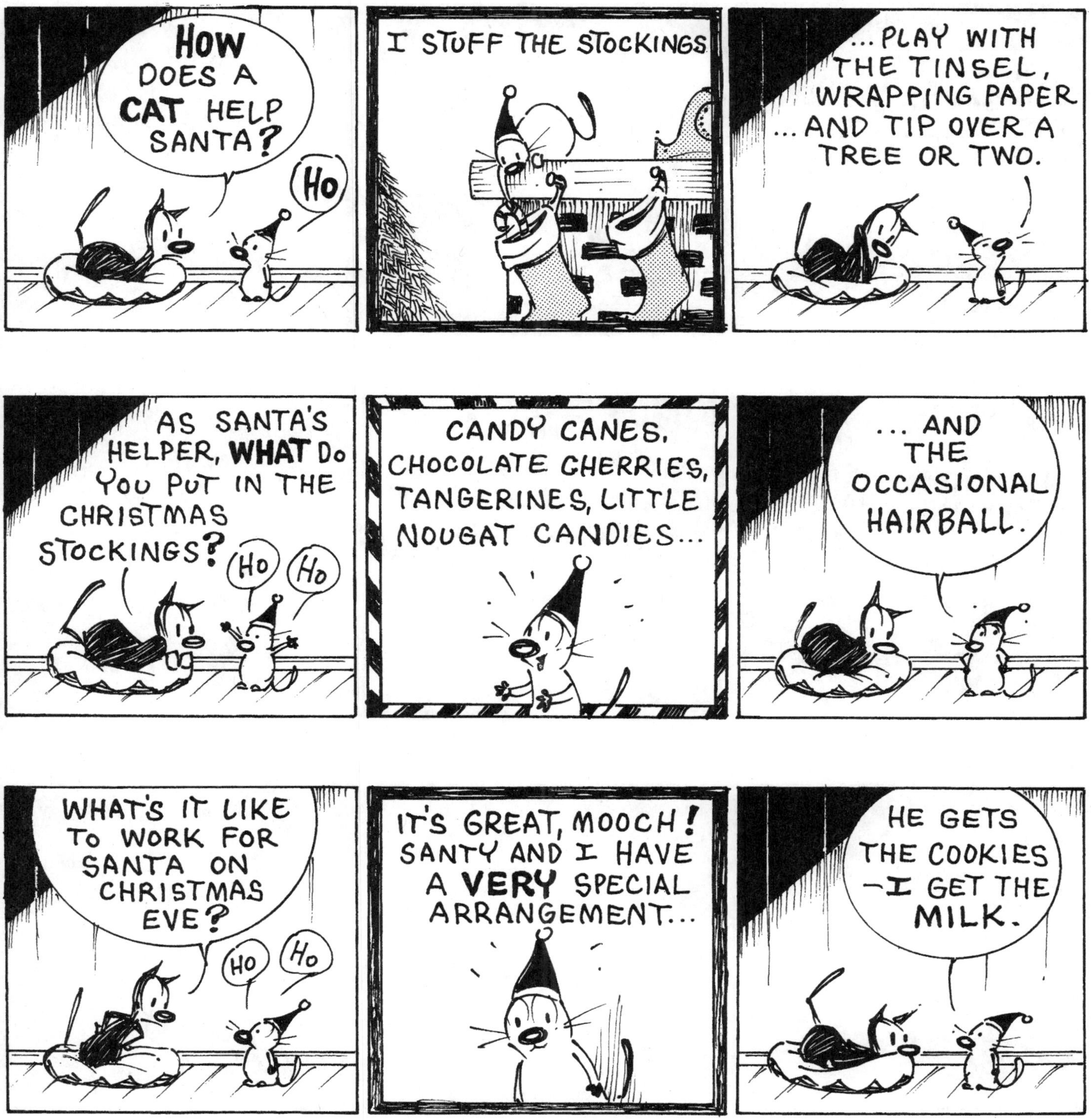
HOW DOES A CAT HELP SANTA?
Ho
I STUFF THE STOCKINGS
...PLAY WITH THE TINSEL, WRAPPING PAPER ...AND TIP OVER A TREE OR TWO.
AS SANTA'S HELPER, WHAT DO YOU PUT IN THE CHRISTMAS STOCKINGS?
Ho
Ho
CANDY CANES, CHOCOLATE CHERRIES, TANGERINES, LITTLE NOUGAT CANDIES...
... AND THE OCCASIONAL HAIRBALL.
WHAT'S IT LIKE TO WORK FOR SANTA ON CHRISTMAS EVE?
HO
Ho
IT'S GREAT, MOOCH! SANTY AND I HAVE A VERY SPECIAL ARRANGEMENT...
HE GETS THE COOKIES —I GET THE MILK.

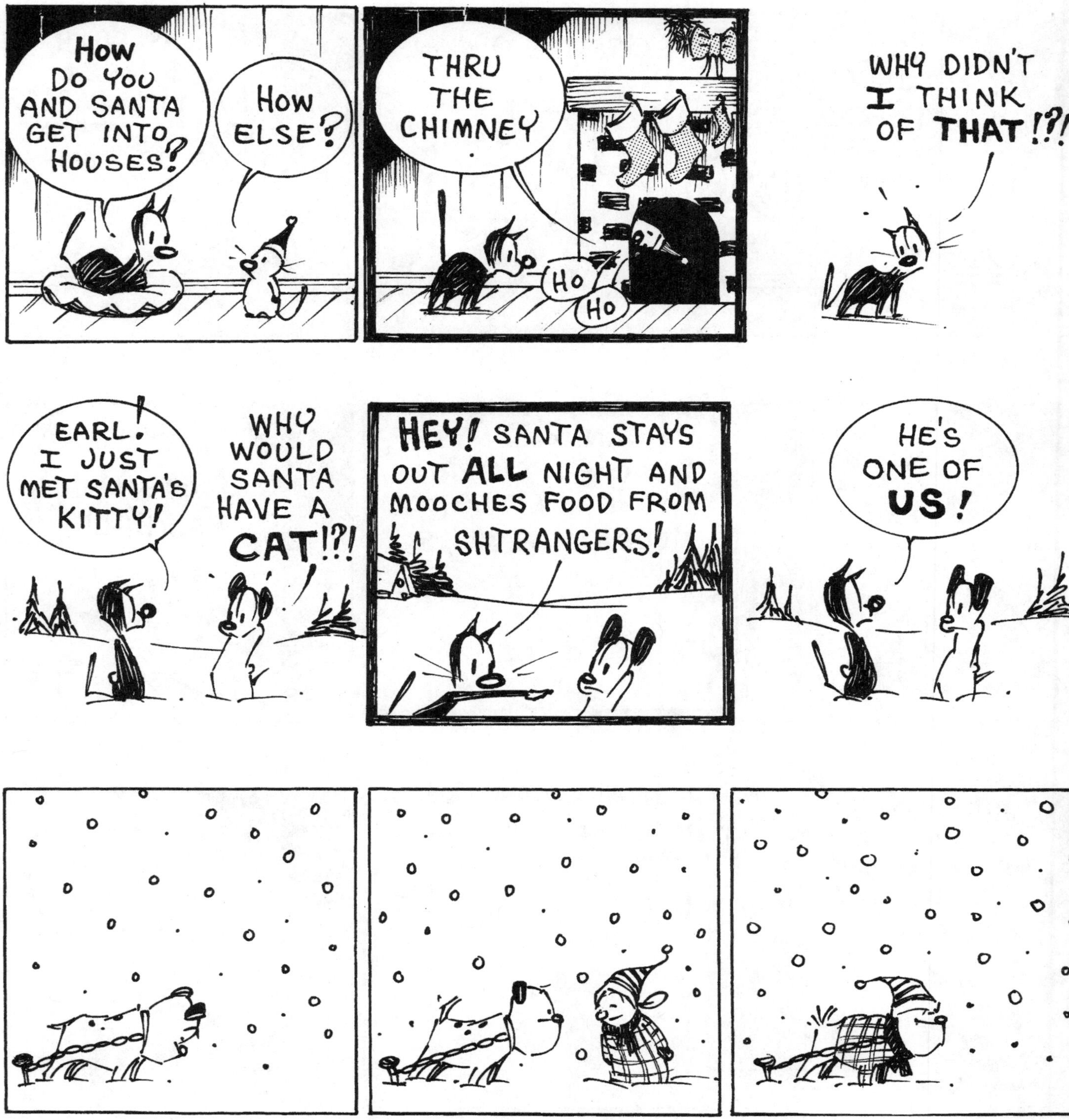
HOW DO YOU AND SANTA GET INTO HOUSES?
HOW ELSE?
THRU THE CHIMNEY
HO
HO
WHY DIDN'T I THINK OF THAT!?!
EARL! I JUST MET SANTA'S KITTY!
WHY WOULD SANTA HAVE A CAT!?!
HEY! SANTA STAYS OUT ALL NIGHT AND MOOCHES FOOD FROM SHTRANGERS!
HE'S ONE OF US!

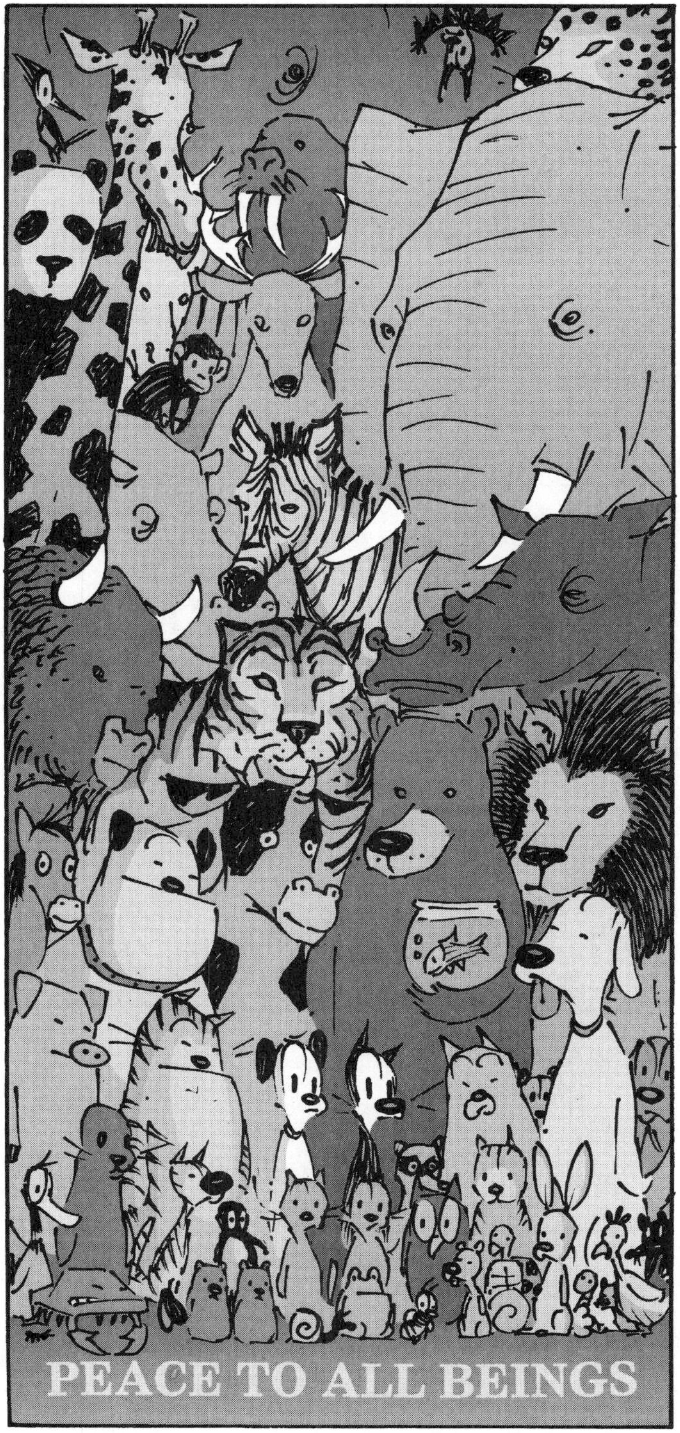
PEACE TO ALL BEINGS

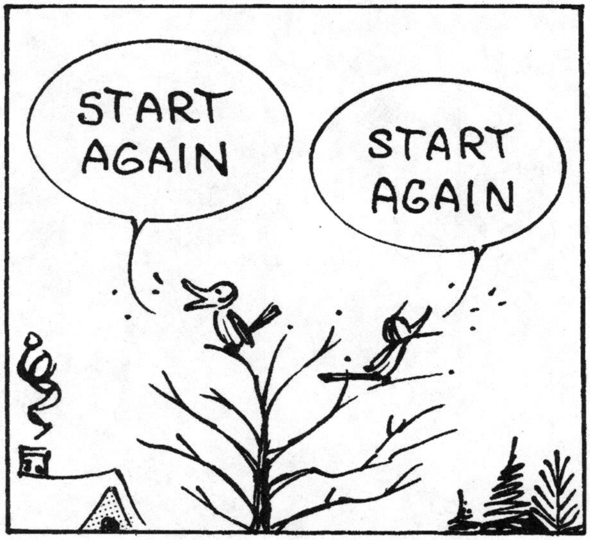
START AGAIN
START AGAIN